MEMOIRS

OF

ALEXANDER BETHUNE,

EMBRACING

SELECTIONS FROM HIS CORRESPONDENCE

AND

LITERARY REMAINS,

COMPILED AND EDITED

BY

WILLIAM M'COMBIE,

AUTHOR OF "HOURS OF THOUGHT," "MORAL AGENCY," &c.

ABERDEEN:
GEORGE AND ROBERT KING, 28, ST. NICHOLAS STREET.

1845.

PREFACE.

The occasion of my connexion with this volume, will appear from the following extract from an unfinished note in Mr. Bethune's handwriting, which I received a few days before his death :—

   *   *   *   *   'I almost wish I could have seen yourself, though it had been for never so short a time. There are many manuscripts which I should fearlessly put into your hand which otherwise I must burn indiscriminately, not choosing to leave them to the criticism of others.'

On my arrival at Mountpleasant, my friend, who was then in a very weak state, attempted to make a selection from his papers, of such as he had a wish to have preserved; but perceiving him quite unfit for the excitement and exertion attendant on this, and fearing that he might destroy not a few which might contribute, one way or other, to illustrate his mental character and history, I succeeded in persuading him to consign the whole into my hands, assuring him that it would be my earnest endeavour to fulfil, to the utmost of my power, what I might conceive to be his wishes concerning them.

Of my attempt to perform the duty thus devolving on me, this volume is the result. The materials for it have been derived chiefly from his correspondence, from unpublished pieces in verse, and from such information respecting him, as his friends could supply.

To his correspondents, who have, so far as applied to, with one or two exceptions, kindly furnished me with the use of his letters or with copies, I owe, and now beg to tender, my best thanks. Through their kindness, I have been enabled to present a considerable amount of what I am led to anticipate will be found interesting autobiography; which I have always used in preference to narration of my own, both as more intrinsically valuable, and as likely to be more acceptable to the reader.

My labour in regard to the letters imbodied in this volume, has been chiefly that connected with selection and arrangement. Correction, as to the composition, they have needed almost none. I do not know if a dozen alterations of this kind have been made in the whole series.

As to the selections from his Poetical Remains the case has been somewhat different. Few of them seem to have undergone that repeated and severe revision which this sort of composition peculiarly demands. In the want of this, however, I have resorted more to excision, than to alteration with a view to correction; and what I have attempted in this latter way, I contemplate with as little satisfaction as any part of my labours. I at first thought of printing such alterations in italics or within brackets, but a distaste for the patched and barbarous appearance it would have presented in some places deterred me from this. The parts so altered, however, are but few, and the reader accustomed to distinguish styles of writing will be very likely to detect most of them.

That the volume will be found chargeable with considerable imperfections, as to arrangement and continuity is what the editor is led to apprehend, from having been altogether unaccustomed to the sort of literary labour such compilations involve. But his hopes of its acceptableness rest chiefly on the intrinsic interest of its materials, as illustrative of the mental history, the struggles, and the literary achievements of the very remarkable man whose story it is meant to unfold.

CAIRNBALLOCH, *December*, 1844.

CONTENTS.

CHAPTER I.

Infancy and Childhood—Development of Mind and Literary Tastes, as traced by himself in Extract from ' Day Dreams'—Letter from Mr. Adamson —Autobiographical Letter from A. Bethune, to Mr. Chambers—First Contributions to ' Chambers' Journal'—Extracts from Letters to a Lady. 9

CHAPTER II.

Sets to learn the Weaving Business with his Brother —Trade fails—Accidents from Gunpowder—Extracts from ' Day Dreams' illustrative of his Feelings during Convalescence—Letters to a Young Friend, imbodying Economical and other Advice—Specimens of Poetical Attempts. 64

CHAPTER III.

Correspondence respecting the Publication of 'Tales and Sketches of The Scottish Peasantry'—Composition of ' Lectures on Practical Economy'— Submitted to Dr. Murray—His Opinion—Consequent remodelling of the work—Building of the House at Mountpleasant—Removal thither— Death of A. Bethune's Father—Verses on that Event. 93

CHAPTER IV.

Publication of 'Tales and Sketches of The Scottish Peasantry'—Favourable Notices of the Work—Correspondence with Literary Friend and Dr. Murray—Terms of publication of 'Practical Economy'—Visit of the Messrs. Bethune to Edinburgh—A. Bethune's Views and Feelings in regard to his Literary Labours—Connexion with 'Border Tales'—'The Sisters'—Dublin University Magazine—Publication of 'Practical Economy'—Neglect of that Work. ... 145

CHAPTER V.

Illness and Death of his Brother—Correspondence connected with that Event—Extracts from Journal—Letters. ... 182

CHAPTER VI.

Preparation of his Brother's Poems for the Press, with Sketch of his Life—Severe Application to the Task—Success in obtaining Subscribers—Publication and highly favourable Reception of the Work—Death of his Mother—Feelings on that Occasion—Friendly Letters of Advice, &c. 199

CHAPTER VII.

Correspondence with Mrs. Hill, embracing Opinions on General Education, Pauperism, Poor Laws, Prison Discipline, Political Economy, &c.—Visit to Glasgow—Situation of Turnkey there—Illness—Return Home. ... 221

CHAPTER VIII.

Publication of the Second Edition of the 'Life and Poems of John Bethune'—Interest excited in regard to Mr. Bethune in Two Ladies, members of the Society of Friends—Correspondence with these—Mr. Bethune's kindness to a Friend in Ill Health—Letters—Marks of Interest in Mr. Bethune on the part of Dr. Andrew Combe and Mr. George Combe. 276

CHAPTER IX.

Correspondence with the Editor—Visit to Aberdeenshire—Excursion to Deeside Highlands—Not enthusiastic in his Admiration of Romantic Scenery—Different kind of Taste, illustrated by Extract from 'Day Dreams'—'The Ruin'—Returns Home by Aberdeen—Projected Story of the Don—Visits Edinburgh—Publication of 'Scottish Peasant's Fireside'—Character of that Work—Tale of Jonathan Moudiwort—Extract from 'Things and Thoughts.' 304

CHAPTER X.

More cheerful Prospects—Is seized with Fever—Illness and Death of one of his Aunts—Partial Convalescence—Accepts, conditionally, the Situation of Editor of the 'Dumfries Standard'—Visits Kennoway for Change of Air—Disease merges into Consumption—Resigns Editorship—Correspondence with English Friends—Increased Illness—Death—Burial—Monument—Conclusion. .. 342

Appendix. 359

LIFE AND REMAINS

OF

ALEXANDER BETHUNE.

CHAPTER I.

INFANCY AND CHILDHOOD—DEVELOPMENT OF MIND AND LITERARY TASTES, AS TRACED BY HIMSELF IN EXTRACT FROM 'DAY DREAMS'—LETTER FROM MR. ADAMSON—AUTOBIOGRAPHICAL LETTER FROM A. BETHUNE, TO MR. CHAMBERS—FIRST CONTRIBUTIONS TO CHAMBERS' JOURNAL—EXTRACTS FROM LETTERS TO A LADY.

ALEXANDER BETHUNE,[*] the subject of this memoir, was born at Upper Rankeillour, in the parish of Letham, and county of Fife, towards the end of the month of July, 1804. The exact day has not been ascertained. His parents were both servants, previous to their marriage and his father appears to have wrought in that capacity for a considerable time after that event, as he is spoken of in the life

[*] In some of his earlier letters, the name is written Beaton, but Bethune is the orthography uniformly adopted after the publication of 'Tales and Sketches of the Scottish Peasantry.'

of John, as having been a servant at the time of his birth, which was in 1811. They seem to have had always to struggle with poverty, but were distinguished for their sobriety and general excellence of character. Scotland, we fear, has got more credit than she deserves, for the high character of her peasantry; but in them certainly that character was strikingly displayed. The mother of the Bethunes, in particular, was a woman of superior mind. Her maiden name was Alison Christie. She was the daughter of Annie M'Donald, so distinguished for her piety and self-culture; a memoir of whom was given to the public several years ago, by the Rev. Mr. Brodie, then parochial minister of Monimail; and another, in a cheaper form, written by her grandson, John Bethune, and accompanied with extracts from her letters, was published by Alexander, in 1842. The following sketch of the character of Alison Christie has been furnished me by a lady, in whose father's house she long served. 'She was exceedingly fond of reading, and had a good voice and ear; and I well remember sitting on her knee, many an evening, while she was spinning, listening to "Sir James the Rose," "Babes of the Wood," "Chevy Chase," and some of Hamilton's songs which I still remember. * * * She had deep religious impressions, and a great abhorrence of wickedness, particularly deceit and ingratitude, combined with great independence of character, which I think helped to give the strong bent to the minds of the youths, particularly Alexander; while her benevolence and sympathy for others, in whatever shape their sufferings appeared, led to a faulty generosity that helped to keep them poor,—listening to every tale of woe, and helping others, when her own family had more need.' My friend gives an instance of this, equally characteristic of the subject of the following memoir, as of his mother:—' A neighbour had fallen behind in the world, and the mother of the family had been making her lamentation, that if money was not forthcoming that night, their cow would be taken away next morning. Alexander had four pounds which he had meant to get clothes with, but when he heard this tale of woe, he instantly took the money, and ran through the fields with it to the woman. Aily (his mother) said to me, she looked after him with more pride and joy, than if the king had made him a lord.' When remonstrated with on her excess of liberality, and told that she should remember her frail husband, she replied, in the words of scripture, ' Whoso hath this world's good, and seeth his brother have need, and shutteth up his bowels of compassion from him, how dwelleth the love of God in him?' It is a weakness, characteristic of not a few of the finer order of minds, that they are in danger of yielding too much to sympathy for others; and such appears to have been the case with Mrs. Bethune,—in the excess of her generosity, forgetting the claims of her own household. Nor does she appear to have excelled in her domestic economy, but to have been rather defective in that neatness and promptitude which contribute so much to the comfort of a family. In the infancy of the sons, the household owed much to the provident attentions of Mrs. Bethune's sister, who yet survives, and who so sedulously watched over Alexander during his last illness. The virtues of Mrs. Bethune, however, appear to have had a striking adaptation to the circumstances of her family. They were always poor, and the education of the sons was almost entirely domestic. Alexander, if we except a short time he attended an evening class, taught by Mr. Adamson, after he was two or three-and-twenty, was never more than four or five months at school; and John, as the reader will find recorded in his life, but one day. A mother of such endowments and virtues is an inestimable blessing in any case, but more emphatically so, when, as in the present instance, almost the whole mental as well as moral training falls to her hand. A testimony to her mental and moral excellence, quite as high as that I have just adduced, the reader will find below, in a communication from a gentleman who knew her well, and was well qualified to judge. This remarkable woman adds another instance to the many already on record, that the precursors of distinguished genius and talent generally appear on the maternal side.

During Alexander's infancy and childhood, owing to his father's being a servant, the family seems to have had frequently to move from place to place. When he was about seven or eight years of age, and, shortly after the birth of his brother John, they came to Woodmill, in the parish of Abdie, and on the borders of 'that little lake,' close to which great part of his own, as well as of his brother's life was passed, and which, with its surrounding scenery he has described with so much beauty and felicity in the opening of 'The Covenanter's Grave.'* 'In the parish of Abdie, and almost immediately under the church-yard wall, lies the little loch of Lindores, which in the calm twilight of a summer's evening, appears like the eye of nature looking up to its Maker in the spirit of meek and quiet devotion.' At Martinmas, 1813, they removed to a place about a quarter of a mile further north, called Lochend, where they continued to reside till 1837. The earliest notice of the feelings and occupations of his boyhood, I have met with, is in a paragraph near the beginning of a M. S. marked 'Original Sketch of the Life of John Bethune.' Though not inserted in the published memoir, I think it will not be uninteresting to the reader.

'During the summer of 1815, my father was employed in clearing the furze, or *whins*, from a piece of ground about to be improved on a neighbour-

---

* Tales and Sketches of the Scottish Peasantry.

ing eminence, called the *Cowden-hill*. It was then my task to carry his dinner; and, as the times were hard, and he did his work at so much per acre, I always wrought along with him in the afternoon. In these daily expeditions, I sometimes persuaded my little brother to accompany me, who was then between three and four years of age. While my father was eating his dinner, I used to take him to a point of the hill, from which the river Tay and part of the village of Newburgh were to be seen; and here again, the broad expanse of water, now bright with sunshine or dark with the shadow of the clouds, according to the state of the weather, with the ships, and the rocks by which the prospect was bounded, were a perfect romance to his childish eye. He seemed never to tire in gazing at them, he had innumerable enquiries concerning them to make; and it was only by threatening to leave him alone, that I could get him to accompany me back to the place where I was to work for the remainder of the day.

'These views of the shipping on the river, together with the boat on the loch, which we were sometimes permitted to examine, gave him a sort of taste for maritime affairs. Our spare time was now devoted to constructing boats from such pieces of wood as fell in our way. But, to complete that imitation which we wished to carry to perfection, tar or pitch was a desideratum which we could never obtain.'

We see here early manifestation of what proved

to be strong tendencies in the minds of both the brothers: John's intense delight in natural scenery, and Alexander's remarkable turn for mechanics, which in after life enabled him very soon to acquire proficency in any sort of handicraft to which he had occasion to apply himself.

It cannot fail to be interesting, to have the means of tracing the rise and development of literary tastes and literary ambition in a mind so situated as that of the subject of this memoir. It has afforded me much gratification to have met with a sketch of this nature drawn by himself. It forms part of a pretty long poem, in blank verse, which seems first to have been entitled 'Day Dreams,' and afterwards 'Confessions of Convalescence,'

The occasion on which it was written is indicated by himself in the following note :—

'The "Day Dreams," are the substance of some reflections with which I endeavoured to amuse myself, while slowly recovering from an illness which confined me for three weeks, June 1834. They were written out from such notes as I could then take; notes intended to recall the same train of thoughts, and the same ideas to my mind at some future period, for I was too weak at the time of which I speak, to write them at length: it was with some difficulty that I could crawl out to a retired spot which was the scene of my musings. This it is hoped will account for the allusions to pain and weakness which are to be found here and elsewhere.'

In the earlier paragraphs, he traces with great simplicity the predominating feelings and aspirations of his boyhood; and thence, by an easy and natural transition, proceeds to record with considerable enthusiasm of spirit, and felicity of illustration, the development of those softer sentiments of the heart—to which, notwithstanding the restraints which from both principle and prudential considerations he imposed on himself, it is obvious from many parts of his works, he had been once, at any rate, no stranger.

The simplicity of the portraiture approaches sometimes to naiveté, but the reader who is interested in regard to the early dawnings of such a mind, will not relish the extracts the less on that account; nor will such fail to remark the striking manifestation of benevolence of character thus early developed, and for which Mr. Bethune was so much distinguished through life.

' AGAIN the sun is hot and high in heaven;
The rustic sweats beneath the sultry ray;
The idler seeks the shady walk; and I,
With shaken frame and slow returning strength,
Upon the sloping bank, beneath the trees,
Have sat me down to ruminate a while,
And dream away the hours till health return.
These trees which spread their branches o'er my head,
And shade me from the sultry summer sun
Were young when I was youug—we grew together:
I was a boy, and they were paltry shrubs.

Even then, this was a pleasant place to me,
And here I loitered many an hour away,
And dreamed as pertinaciously as now;
But then my dreams did differ far from those
Which now I may indulge at this dim distance.
The scene hath changed its aspect—I am changed;
Yet now I would recall the shadowy trace
Which memory holds of those departed years,
And live again a moment in their light.
  ' The mournful ballad was my earliest lore,
And long ere I could read it for myself,
'Twas music to my soul; and I would sit
With a pleased melancholy, such as steals
Over the heart when day dies in the west,
To hear it warbled. Then the strain of Burns
Touched a strange chord in my yet boyish bosom,
Which thrilled beneath the magic of his words;
And when more years had added to my stock—
My little stock of knowledge, then I learned
That Nature's poet in his early day
Was but a peasant boy, as poor as I.
Then I went on to fill the picture up,
With all the colouring fancy could devise:—
Ragged he was, perchance, as I had been,
And sauntered far by wood or lonely stream
To muse and meditate—a sun-burnt wanderer;
Or slid with desperate skill the frozen lake,
Till the big snow-flakes, drifting through the rents
Of his long worn and sorely wasted raiment,
Which opened to receive them, had transform'd
Him almost to an icicle; or plunged,
By a rash venture, as I oft had done,
Through the frail pavement over which he glided,

And almost drowned, trembled with cold and terror,
And durst not venture home for being whipped.
Yet when he grew to manhood, and had learned
To write and spell the words he wrote aright,
He made a book, and gained nine hundred pounds!
That was a monarch's treasure!—When I grew
A man, I'd learn to write and spell like him!
Then what might hinder me to make a book,
Which men would buy, and marvel how I made it.
What he had done, sure, I might learn to do!
Though rags and poverty were all my portion:
He too was poor; and I had made him ragged,
That we might be alike   *   *   *
In the beginning of life's weary journey—
It seemed not weary then, but a rich walk
Which glittered with a thousand glowing charms—
And then my book!—that was the mighty shadow
Which filled my day-dream with unnumbered schemes.
Nine hundred pounds! oh, what a mighty sum!
Had I a hundred, ay or even fifty,
I never could exhaust it—it would serve
To make a nation happy.—Then the boys
Who, clad in tatters, and with battered feet,
In winter slid like me the frozen lake,
Should all have better jackets from my store,
And clothes to keep them from the pinching cold—
New shoes too, with a hundred tackets* each
And iron heels, I would bestow upon them:
Then I would give them shillings for their mothers.
(I got a shilling once, which gave me joy,
Such as I know not that I felt before.

* Hobnails.

It was from a kind-hearted man, whose horse
I held a while; and when I brought it home,
My mother blessed him so, and said so much,
And seem'd so happy, that, to earn such blessing
From those poor mothers whom I would befriend,
Appeared the acme of all earthly good.)
Their fathers too, when sickness came upon them,
Should have for dinner wheaten bread and milk—
That was a luxury I, for once, had tasted,
And longed to do again, although it came not
Within the clutches of my ravening jaw
A second time; still I remembered well,
And deemed it daintiest of earth's dainty things.
Tea, too, should grace their boards on Sabbath-days,
And the coarse bannocks baken from the bean,
(Which last I never liked, although compelled
To take them for my dinner many a day,)
Should be exchanged for those of barley bread.
And I would buy them cows to yield them milk;
And give them meal when that was waxing scarce.
A hundred pounds would do all this and more,
Ay, twice as much, or may be twenty times.
And when my paradise was made complete
In this department, there was one old man,
Whom I had seen draining a hilly field—
That was when I was very young, but still
His picture was before me undecayed;
My memory had the scene in all its parts:—
The noonday sun was beating fierce upon him;
His coat and vest were doffed, and thrown aside,
His worn-out shirt, in rags, was black and wet
With the warm moisture which suffused his skin;
His bald head was uncovered, and his locks,
His thin gray locks, dripping and drenched with sweat;

His face was soiled, his joints were stiff, and he
Appeared to ply his weary task with pain.
I saw him once again by a road-side—
The wind was cold—it was the winter time;
And snows lay deep on hill and valley round.
Beside him lay his staff and sundry hammers;
For he was breaking stones. But it was plain
That he had seen misfortune since I saw him;
A splinter from his hammer had cut out
One eye—it was the best—and left a hollow,
Dark, rayless, tenantless, where once it shone;
And penury and sickness, blent together,
Had set their stamp upon his meagre face.
My heart bled as I paused to look upon him,
And summed up all his miseries with an eye
Which held a boyish tear although it flowed not.
  ' Oft had his shadow flitted o'er my mind,
And damped my happiness, like a dark cloud;
For it was painful to behold him thus,
And still more painful that I could do nothing
(For I was penniless) to make him better.
But brighter images now crowded on me:—
He too should be a sharer of my fortune
When it grew fine! And I would build a house—
A house for him:—I could do this myself;
For I used to repair our kail-yard* dyke,
And make it stand without or clay or mortar;
And I should then have both. Sticks I would gather
To kindle up his fire, and bring him coals
To keep him warm throughout the winter day.
My heart danced at the thought;—how happy then!

* Cottager's garden.

And for the crust of ill-baked oaten bread,
Unsavoury and unseasoned, dry, yet mouldy,
Which I had seen him labour to consume,
As he sat resting on the frozen bank,—
And the cold beverage from the way-side stream,
From which he broke the ice that he might drink,—
I would provide a comfortable meal;—
It should be new potatoes in the season,
And porridge when I could not come at these.
I never thought of slaying sheep and oxen,
To feed him with their *flesh*. That was a word
Of which I scarcely understood the meaning.
But then I should take care he had a *yard*,
With goose-berries a-plenty growing in it.
Of gooseberries I reckoned not a little,
For I had bought a pennyworth and ate them,—
And oh how sweet!—I never could forget it.
Of apples also I could tell the flavour,
For I had once ate two on the same day,
And found that they were pleasant to my taste;
And therefore he should have an apple-tree:—
O what a treasure it would be to him
To go and take an apple when he pleased!
And then if he should chance to have too many,
Why! he might sell them for a drink of *ale*,
To do him good when harvest days were hot.
Ale did not make men drunk—he might do this.
Then I would help him too to dig his yard,
And plant his kail, and hoe his cabbages;
For I was growing strong, and would be stronger
When I became a man.—My spirit drew
Nectar from these delusions, as the bee
Draws honey from the flowers on summer days.

It was a boyish weakness which the world
May laugh at and forgive, though slow to pardon
Such flagrant follies found in one so young.
  ' Thus squandered I my time, while other boys
At school were picking up some useful knowledge
Which might be for their benefit through life.
At raw fourteen I had outgrown my fellows;
Of strength too I possessed the common share
Which boys have at this early time of life,
And like a fool I was full fain to show it:
I knew not that even then my strength was destined
To a severer trial than I had recked of.
  ' My days of idleness were at an end,
My parents could no longer keep me so,
And I was sent to dig a ditch more deep,
And dirtier too, than that the old man dug;
And for my fare I ate a crust as dry,
And drank from the ice-girded stream, and rested
Upon a stone from which I swept the snow.
My dining-room had clouds for tapestry,
Mountains for walls, the boundless sky for ceiling,
And frosty winds for music whistling through it.
Thus situated and thus serenaded,
I ate my dinner with—I know not what,
If it might be content or something else.
My work was hard, my strength inadequate,—
It tired strong men, and I was but a boy.
At eventide so tired was I, I scarcely
Could keep my fellows' way in walking home;
My joints were stiffened, and became the seat
Of weariness and pain; and sleep forsook me
For many a night, or only came by fits,
From which I woke to find I was not rested.

Hard labour drives the downy god away
From bodies older and more firmly knit
Than mine could be at such an early age.
 ' This tamed me to my fate, and taught me wisdom,
And broke me to drag on the wain of life
With all the dullness of the sluggish ox
When yoked to till the field or draw the wain.
My spirits sunk; imagination strayed
No more in quest of those illusive scenes,
On which it painted happiness before;
My book-and-fortune dream was at an end;
And to obtain a little rest appeared
The greatest blessing which I could enjoy.
The sabbath then was sacred in my eye,
Not that it was a day to worship God,
But that it freed me from a galling yoke;
And I would count the intervening hours
Till slow revolving time should bring it back.
 ' Life is a drama of a few brief acts;—
The actors shift—the scene is often changed—
Pauses and revolutions intervene—
The mind is set to many a varied tune,
And jars and plays in harmony by turns;
And happiness, like heaven's blue arch, is seen
Upon the top of Expectation's mount,
And waiting for us there that we may grasp it;
But when we gain that cloud-capt elevation,
Behold! the hoped-for object is far off,
And we must start again in a new chase,
And climb another hill of greater height,
Upon whose summit gorgeously arrayed
The fair, false spirit seems to sit enshrined.
Still, still that dream runs on through every change,

And still deceives the dreamer!—Why repine?
Man's happiness is more in the hot chase,
Than the attainment of the good he seeks.
 ' My dream, though interrupted, was not ended;
Though checked, it had not reached its final close.
As I grew older, I outgrew my toil;
My limbs resumed their wonted elasticity,
My step its firmness; and I felt my arm
Was competent for that which fate assigned it;
From boyhood I was rising into man,
And trod upon the verge of growth completed.
My mind, too, had embraced a few more objects;
And I had learned some knowledge of mankind,
Their impulses, their manners, and their passions;
For they had tutored me to know their ways
By lessons which were sometimes at my cost.
My heart expanded into a new life,
Rejoicing in the skill which it had gained:—
It might be worthless, but it seemed not so;—
And I was eager to increase my stock.
But yet I must have had some petty cares
To temper happiness; for, it was said
That I at times grew thoughtful, and was seen,
Or seemed, less prone to laugh than my compeers.
It might be so, or it might not—I forget;
But be that as it may, there is the trace
Of a long cherish'd vision in my heart,
Which years and accidents have left untouched—
'Tis but the trace—the vision is no more.
When vexed by calumny, or teased by foes,
Or fretted by false friends, that vision came,
Like the full moon emerging from dark clouds,
And shed a pure, soft radiance on my soul,

Such as that maiden orb at midnight hour
Lends to the windings of the silver stream.
 ' My dream was then of some fair being, on
Whose love-warm bosom I should lay my head;
And, while I felt a fond heart beat beneath,
Forget that " as the sparks from fre fly upward,
So man is born to trouble"—whose soft voice
Should be the sweetest music to my ear,
Awakening all the chords of harmony—
Whose eye should speak a language to my soul,
More eloquent than aught which Greece or Rome
Could boast of in their best and happiest days—
Whose smile should be my rich reward for toil—
Whose pure, transparent cheek, when press'd to mine,
Should calm the fever of my troubled thoughts,
And woo my spirit to those fields Elysian,
The paradise which strong affection guards—
Whose heart with mine made one by Heaven's decree,
In mutual interchange of sentiment,
And thought, and wish—to the minutest feeling,
Should make our lives flow gently on together;
Even as two streams when poured into each other
Unite and form a broader, brighter river.
Oh! I have seen such streams, and paused and lingered
To see an emblem of that happiness
Which I was destined never to enjoy.
Where the first eddy of their meeting waters—
The deep commotion of their mingling tides
Subsided in a smooth and glassy plain,
Which, clear the placid sky above reflected—
Its fleecy vapours and its azure blue:
The banks the bushes, the surrounding hills,
They glided on in tranquil loveliness,

To mix with that eternity of waters,
The all unmeasured ocean. *   *   *
That was the spot which riveted my eye;
And there I saw—in short, I know not what—
The forms and shadows of a thousand things:—
Those eddies were the first fresh burst of feeling,
Half pleasing and half painful which love brings,
When that delicious dream, like life, is new;
Then, the subsiding point was to my eye
The calm which union brings to plighted lovers;
Then, the long mirror of its mazy windings
Might represent the deep and settled flow
Of mutual sympathy and chaste affection,
Which hearts, by nature formed to bear love's yoke,
Enjoy in journeying through the vale of life,
Till Time shall merge them in Eternity,
Again to close the link their beings wore,
And find it strengthened in another state—
Not broken by death's transitory change.
  'This was a weakness which I cherish'd long,
Even as men sometimes cherish their worst follies—
A deep delusion which was loath to part,
A dream from which but lately I awaked,
Nor waked without a pang; but it is past.
And now I bless my fate that it is thus,
Nor murmur though that pang was hard to bear.
It had been harder far, and bitterer too,
And worse to bear, to look on one beloved,
Whose destiny and hopes were ruled by mine,
And see her shrink in the November blast
Of my bleak fortune, like a northern winter,
Which broke around me and with frozen breath
Chilled those illusive fancies from my sight.'

The following sketch is also illustrative of the musings of the same early period.

'A REMINISCENCE.'

'The sun seems resting on yon western hill,
One little moment ere he disappears;
And a rich drapery of radiant clouds
Rising, and reddening in his setting ray,
Portend a day as fair as this to-morrow;
And in that smooth and softly-smiling lake,
Which lies in all the peace of infant slumber,
The hill, the corn-field, and the dusky crag,
The light tints of the sky, the living splendour
Of the rich clouds that cluster round the sun,
And the deep glory of the setting orb,
Are mirrored with a more than magic power.
    *   *   *   I, even now,
Do recollect an evening fair as this:
Oh it was in my boyhood!—with my charge,
A single cow, which grazed the daisied bank,
Whereon I lay and watched with a full heart
The scene around me:—'twas the same as now,
All loveliness and glory. The bright sun
Was setting—clouds that seemed almost too fair
For our terrene horizon clustered round him—
The hill, the corn-fields, and the cresting crag
Wore then the selfsame aspect even as now;
And that expanse of water, with its waves
Lulled by the calm which with the eventide came,
Smooth at my feet without a murmur lay.
In ecstasy of pure and holy feeling,
On all the gladness and the glow around me,

I gazed until my dazzled eye sunk down,
And my thoughts turned to dream of my own fate,
Which then to me was all a fairy-book
With happiness bright pictured on each page.
The sun of youth on destiny's dark cloud
Had painted a bright rainbow to my eye,
Whose glowing arch extended to far years,
Leaving no likeness of a thing deformed,
Or aught from which regret or grief might spring;
And many a rising vision, richly wrought,
Like rays of light shot through a shady bower,
Streamed in upon my heart, brightening it up
With that sweet light which lives alone in youth.'

In addition to the information respecting the severity of the toil to which in his early life he was subjected, it is stated in the Introductory Notice to 'Tales and Sketches of the Scottish Peasantry,' that it was in consequence of his parents being, from ill health and other causes, unable to apprentice him to any trade, that he betook himself, at the age of fourteen, to the humble occupation of a labourer. By this species of employment, so ill-suited to that early period of life, his growth was stunted, and his bodily energies impaired. The 'ditch' which, in the foregoing extracts, he describes himself as having been ' set to dig at raw fourteen,' he described to me as being of extraordinary depth, requiring the utmost stretch of muscular exertion to throw what was dug out of it from the bottom to the top.

The effects of such cruel toil on his unconsolidated frame he has himself graphically described:—'For more than a year afterwards, his joints, on first attempting to move in the morning, creaked like machinery wanting oil. Several years of his subsequent career,' he adds, 'were spent in struggles to relieve the circumstances of his parents; while those hours of leisure which he could command were employed in reading such books as he could borrow in the neighbourhood, and in otherwise endeavouring to improve his mental faculties.'

When he was about twenty-one years of age, a circumstance occurred which materially tended to quicken his taste for literature, and stimulate his ambition for literary pursuits. 'In the summer of 1825, a student from the college of St. Andrews, who was then struggling hard for his education, taught a small school in one of the houses at Lochend. He was an excellent reciter of poetry, and had stored his memory with a number of the best pieces of Scott, Byron, Moore, Campbell, and others. With these he frequently amused and delighted his acquaintances during his leisure hours, a considerable part of which were passed with us.'* This gentleman, now the Rev. John L. Adamson, late of Thornton, and now of Dundee, has, at my request, kindly favoured me with some highly interesting recollections of the subject of this memoir

* Life of John Bethune.

and his worthy parents, in a communication which I shall now introduce to the reader:—

Thornton, by Kirkaldy, 23d Nov. 1843.

'Dear Sir,—

* * * * *

'My acquaintance with the two brothers commenced in the summer of 1825. With Alexander I soon became very intimate. I had heard a good deal, from the people in the neighbourhood, of his talents and worth. I soon found, however, that their estimate of him, favourable as it was, was by far too low; and every opportunity which I had of conversing with him deepened the impression that he possessed powers, both intellectual and moral, of a very high order. One could not speak with him for many minutes without having cause to admire the sagacity and originality of his views. He had, even then, more than any man I have yet met with, an uncommon share of what Locke calls "*strong, sound, round-about sense.*" His education, as you are aware, had been almost entirely domestic. If he had ever been at school at all, it must have been only for a few weeks. I have often heard him say that to his mother (herself an extraordinary woman) he was chiefly indebted for his knowledge of letters. She, I may here remark, was extremely partial to what she called "fireside instruction," and often quoted passages from Cowper's "Tirocinium," in support of her particular views on this point. Next to the bible, Cowper's poetry was her delight. She had him almost entirely by heart, and rarely failed to " nail" her own sentiments and opinions with a line or sentence of that delightful writer. She was altogether a rare character, auld Aily!—pious, but not austere—devout, but not bigotted—beneficent without ostentation—hospitable, kind-hearted, and generous even to a fault: she deserved (if ever woman on earth deserved it) the title of a mother in Israel. What a wonderful fund of humour she had too! Had her lot been cast in a higher sphere of life, and her education been like her abilities, she would doubtless have been admired as an ornament of her sex. From her, if genius be hereditary, the poets must have derived the singular talent which they possessed. The old man too—he was a perfect specimen of all that one can imagine of Nathaniel. I see him yet, the worthy patriarch, with the snows of eighty or ninety winters on his venerable head. You could not have met him on the public road, without feeling an inclination to lift the hat to him. He was a man of few words, but they were well chosen. He had seen many changes, of course, and, I believe, had come through many in his lifetime; but he rarely spoke of himself. When he did, it was rather of necessity than of choice; and when he gave counsel, it was delivered with a sweet mixture of gravity and gentleness. If from their mother the Bethunes inherited somewhat of poetical genius, I am sure that from their excellent father's precepts and example, they derived much of that unbending integrity and noble independence, which uniformly distinguished them.

'I have perhaps dwelt too long on these matters; but I could not resist the temptation of saying this much in regard to two individuals whom I often saw with the deceased in that happy cottage where their genius first began to develop itself. Old Alexander Bethune was certainly one of the "nobles of nature."

'About the time above referred to, Alexander was engaged during the day in out-door labour. He attended, with other young men, an evening class which I had opened at Lochend. Arithmetic, I think, was the only department of learning to which his attention was directed at that time; for, while he complained much of his "far-backness" (as he then called it) in regard to English reading, he seemed to think that it was not worth while to spend much of his time in attempting to acquire what his old habits rendered it unlikely that he should ever be a great master of. If I remember rightly, too, he exercised himself a little in penmanship during those evening-school hours. This routine work being ended, we generally retired, sometimes to his friendly dwelling, sometimes to the woods of Inchrye, where he would talk over the affairs of the day, and entertain me with the " wit that fell ere well aware." Our intercourse soon ripened into friendship. Reserve, or shadow of distrust, between us there was none. He was *my* instructor in regard to all the common affairs of this everyday world, and had more advantage over me in regard to life, than I over him in point of literature. I still look back with a melancholy pleasure to those six months which I spent in his neighbourhood. They were perhaps the happiest that I have known. I had found at length one who could sympathize with all my joys, and sorrows : * * * One whose mind was a sanctuary into which every secret might be carried without distrust—whose word was as good as ten thousand oaths—whose transparency of character was a gladdening contrast to all that I had seen at school or college,—and whose high mental capacities were so meekly veiled in the modesty of a truly christian character. He had at that time read few books, but the contents of such as had fallen in his way were well digested. With him, as with his mother, Cowper was quite an oracle. Of the " Pilgrim's Progress" I have heard him speak with deep interest ;—Gray's " Elegy," Blair's " Grave," and Burns' " Cottar's Saturday Night," were great favourites with him; and he has often told me, after he became acquainted with our most admired writers, that he would rather have been the author of the Churchyard Elegy, than of all that Byron or Scott have penned. It was during the same summer that he first got a peep into the writings of the last mentioned poets. The " Lady of the Lake" was highly prized by him. I remember well the deep and delighted interest with which he perused that exquisite poem. To Byron, however, he for a long time gave a decided preference. The Astronomical Discourses of Dr. Chalmers also deeply rivetted his attention. But nothing that I recollect of pleased him so much as the neglected volume of my friend Dr. Gillespie on the *Seasons*. Of that he and his brother were passionately fond. I really believe, that at that time he thought the learned professor one of the greatest men that ever lived on the face of this blessed world; and I am strongly tempted to think that some traits of his character were brought out by his familiarity with that eloquent production. Certain it is, that the beautiful descriptions and moral loveliness of that little work, made a deep and indelible impression upon his heart. This I know from conversations that passed between us long after. I never could get him to admire Moore. The beauties of Campbell he appreciated very highly.—But I tire you with details, and shall not say more.

'The first of his poetical efforts (so far as I know) is the following:—

"How sad to see the friend we love depart
With all that's dear torn from our bleeding heart!
No pen alas! can write, no tongue can tell,
What feelings mingle with a last farewell.
While Memory traces all that's gone before,
And magic Fancy future scenes runs o'er,

Each pang we felt, each sorrow that we knew—
Again we seem to feel it all anew;
We see them now a moment and no more,
To us they're gone with those the floods before.
As waves from their deep bed heaved by the wind,
Thy sounds, farewell, convulsive heave the mind.

* * * * *

To all I'd resolutely bid adieu
With coldness, save, my honour'd friend, to you;
But in this breast thy memory still shall live,
While life one recollecting power can give.
And though my name by thee forgot should lie
In thickest shades, 'neath blank oblivion's sky,
Yet on this heart thy name shall still abide
While life rolls through my veins the purple tide;
Though Time should every other thought estrange,
To thee, my heart shall know no future change;
To me none else shall fill thy place anew,—
But now comes o'er my heart the word, adieu!"

'The above was written some time in the year 1826, and appears to have been occasioned by parting with a friend. It is valuable, only, as shewing the existing tendencies of a mind capable of greater things. So sensible was the author himself of its imperfections that he adds, "Burn this sheet as soon as you read it; if I thought you would not, it should suffer martyrdom immediately."

'I don't think it necessary to speak much of the opinions which he held in regard to a variety of topics only of passing interest. Some of these you will gather from the accompanying letters. I may mention, that from the first day that I knew him, he was impatient and intolerant of every thing like oppression—that every exhibition of selfishness, on the part either of rich or poor, was most painful to his generous nature—and that nothing so readily awakened his indignation as the heartlessness of those in the higher walks of life who must have their own luxurious desires gratified, although the widow and orphan should perish for lack of bread. He abhorred every species of affectation. The object of his deepest earthly reverence was a " *poor* but *honest* man." He was, moreover, (who would have supposed it?) a pretty successful mimic. I have known him hit off   *   *   *   *   to perfection. Take him all in all, we shall not see his like again.

'I must again apologise for this lengthened scrawl, and beg that you will believe me to be, dear sir, yours most respectfully, JOHN L. ADAMSON.'

To Mr. Adamson, Alexander Bethune was at this most important period of his mental history under the highest obligations. Not only was his attention drawn to the most beautiful and sublime passages of our modern poetry by Mr. A's recitation of them while he resided at Lochend, but after his removal to a distant part of the country, he copied and sent to him, not only innumerable short pieces, but long extracts from larger works, both in poetry and prose. Of such I have found, almost literally, volumes preserved among our author's papers, interspersed with elucidatory and critical remarks, generally evincing admirable taste and judgment. The value of such services, rendered with so generous an enthusiasm, to one who had so limited a supply of books, it is impossible to estimate.

Like many other young men whose minds have a literary tendency, Mr. Bethune's first attempts at authorship appear to have been made in the form of verse. We see from the portions of 'Day Dreams,' already inserted, that he very early felt the stirrings of literary ambition; and his early literary aspirations, like those of most other persons of similar mental tendencies, had a strong tinge of the romantic. How he first came to think seriously of attempting to write a book is thus stated by himself in one of his letters:—'As it is sometimes curious to see what a trifling incident will give an impulse to the human mind, I may here be permitted to tell you what it was that first set me seriously to the task of writing a book. A young lady, the daughter of a neighbouring laird, who farmed his own property, of about eighty acres, himself, had been in the habit of sometimes calling to inquire for my mother, who had been a servant in the family of her grandmother. From her she had learned that myself and my brother were much given to reading, and that we sometimes went a little farther, and made attempts at writing. We were accordingly favoured with the loan of a book, called, "The

Amethyst;" a sort of religious annual.　　*　　*
We were forthwith requested to furnish some verses for the succeeding number, which were to be forwarded by the said young lady to its editor. Without being greatly taken with the proposal, the verses were forwarded to our supposed patroness. About three weeks thereafter, being then employed in breaking stones upon the public road, I was saluted by the young lady, who, after enquiring after the health of my father and mother, proceeded with some embarrassment to tell me, that, after a great deal of consideration, she had come to the conclusion that it would be for my advantage to suppress the verses; but that she really felt vexed, as I might possibly feel vexed at their not being sent, &c. &c. To this I replied, that the thing had excited no expectations, and therefore, could occasion no disappointment; and that I should be truly sorry for myself, if I could be "hurt" at such trifles. But while I said this to her, I said, or rather thought, to myself,—All very right, and only what might have been expected; but, in time, we shall see if a smooth-faced girl is to have the power of determining whether I am to appear in print or not; and from that hour I never lost sight of my purpose for a moment till the M. S. of "Tales and Sketches of the Scottish Peasantry" was completed.'

Possibly the young lady may have formed as just an estimate of the merits of the piece in question as its author; at any rate young authors are generally very incompetent judges in regard to the fitness of their productions for the public eye. A boy from fifteen to eighteen is enraptured with his own mouthy rant or empty jingles, and is quite impatient for the day when the public voice shall pronounce him to have rivalled the 'Elegy in a country church-yard,' or the 'Sermon on Modern Infidelity;' when after a few years he will, probably, feel that he owes no small debt of gratitude to those who may (much to his chagrin at the time) have restrained him from very needlessly making himself ridiculous. Such repulses in the case of a person of real genius or talent, will, as in the present instance, only prove a stimulus to greater and more successful exertions.

In the month of May, 1835, Alexander Bethune addressed a letter to one of the Messrs. Chambers, Edinburgh, soliciting his advice and assistance in order to the bringing of some of his productions before the public. This letter, Mr. R. Chambers writes me, interested him and his brother much, and he expresses his regret at having been unable to lay his hands on it. In these circumstances I was much gratified at finding what appears to be a pretty accurate copy among Alexander's papers. In his statement of the views and feelings with which he entered on his early efforts at composition, the attentive reader will not fail to mark the same striking indications of benevolence of spirit which appear in the poetical extracts given above.

'*May* 15, 1835.

'Sir,—You may well be surprised at thus receiving a letter from one whom you never either saw or heard of before; and your surprise cannot be lessened if it should turn out in the end no better than a beggar's petition. And yet beggary in one way or other, at some period of their lives, seems to be entailed on by far the majority of the human race; even kings cannot always escape it. This however comes not to solicit half-crowns, as the poor poets are said to do. Its writer would be as far from asking any thing in that way—even a penny—as the greatest miser upon earth could be from granting it.

'As I am neither skilful at finesse, nor cunning to accomplish my purpose by manœuvring, it were perhaps better that I should make the matter known at once; because sooner or later it must be made known, and any attempt on my part at a long preamble would only be an unnecessary trespass on your time and patience. I have by me as many verses—which I will not call poetry, though that seems to be a common name for every thing in rhyme—as would make a small volume; I have also as many essays in prose, suppressed letters, &c. &c., as would make another; and besides these, from what I have already in imperfect manuscript, and from some floating ideas which I could easily lay hold of, I could make shift to furnish a third, composed of stories or little novels, the subjects drawn from humble life. Now, my object in thus addressing you is to ascertain if, without injuring yourself, or endangering your literary reputation, you could give any assistance in palming these upon the public, or point out the means by which this could be done; and if such were in your power, if you would be willing to lend your influence or advice, to one who has no better claim than his ignorance of these matters. Here you will no doubt think that you have enough of me * * *

'Having thus placed at the beginning what a greater tactitian would have placed at the end, I would now, if such be admissible, state a few of those causes which have produced this propensity to scribling, in one of the ignorant and unwashed many. I had in my day seen some harrowing scenes of distress, among the class to which I belong—distress for which no one seemed to care, or, if it excited any attention, it was only that sort of it which begins and ends in talk. Like Burns, I had early "some stirrings of ambition." I felt that had I been possessed of a little money, I could have oftener than once lifted a fellow creature from the gulf of misery, and made him comparatively happy. I felt also that in so doing, I should have made myself happy too; and I longed for the means of thus conferring happiness on myself, and others at the same time. But in me those risings of the heart had no outlet. What could a labourer do with 7s., or 7s. 6d. a week? My efforts I found were but a

D

mockery of benevolence, and showed rather the will than the ability to relieve. I might indeed have wriggled myself into some sort of notice, and earned higher wages,—I might have got myself promoted to be foreman over a few ditchers or dykers, and by "damning them to get on," as is customary with such officials, I might have procured a little favour with their masters, and a little money for myself. But I never considered the end, all important as it was with me, as a sufficient justification of the means which would have been indispensable for its attainment. Some tortuosity of mind, or it might be pride, prevented me from becoming, in every thing except the name, a slave-driver, and forbade me to add a link to that chain, which, when worn by myself, I felt heavy. My only other alternative would have been, to learn some more lucrative trade; but I never could discover the means by which I was to be supported during an apprenticeship. Thus shut out from every prospect of ever being able to procure more than the bare means of subsistence for myself and my parents—whose support depends solely upon an only brother and myself—it can scarcely be wondered at, that I should turn my thoughts to writing. This appeared the only open door. Others had succeeded in the same way, and why should not I? Such was the question, which in these circumstances naturally suggested itself to my mind; and, without much consideration as to its propriety, or the host of eminent authors who had gone before me, I acted upon it. My idea of the matter, it seems, had been akin to that of Chatterton; viz., that men's arms are long enough if they would only use them. I may just mention farther, that from the period at which I could read, so as to understand the sense of an author, I had been a reader, or rather a devourer, of every book which fell in my way. This served to store my mind with a few ideas upon various subjects. I had also been an observer of what was passing around me; and there is one thing which I still recollect, as having struck me forcibly at an early period; that is, the difference between the motives, which men often assign for their actions, and those from which they really proceed. This served as an inducement to closer observation. I became vain enough to suppose that I had made some discoveries, and could see a little farther into men's hearts than some others, and with this very slender preparation, and under every imaginable discouragement, I began to dabble in literature, or at least, to blacken paper.

At first, as I have already stated, I had to contend with many disadvantages. The whole of my regular education, consisted of four or five months at a subscription school, when about six years of age, where I learned the letters of the alphabet, and little more. My mother however, had in part supplied this defect of public instruction, by teaching me to read in an old-fashioned way; and my father had given me some lessons in writing, and a smattering of arithmetic. Of grammar I had heard, and knew that there was such a thing; but as a branch of education, I was perfectly ignorant of it: indeed, to a considerable extent, I am so still. When to this it is added, that I have all along lived in an obscure and thinly inhabited part of the country, where, with a few solitary exceptions, no one cared about books, or reading, or writing; it will be readily granted that my situation has not been the most congenial which could be thought of, for such attempts. Indeed others might wonder, as I have done myself, how the fool-hardy idea ever entered into my head. It did however enter, and the result has been what I have already stated. Whether I have at all succeeded, or otherwise, is not for me to determine; and this is one reason, why I should be anxious to submit a few of these unquenched snuffings of the midnight taper, to some one whose acquaintance with literature, might enable him to pass an opinion, as to the propriety of giving them to the public.

'I should ere now have mentioned, that I became a reader of " Chambers Edinburgh Journal," almost immediately after its first appearance; and the biographic sketches which I there met with, gave a new and strong stimulus to my mind. These articles gave to the world at large, and to me, a series of the lives of individuals, who like me, had been born and bred in obscurity, and who by industry and unwearied perseverance, had raised themselves to reputation, and a comfortable independence. This served to determine me. These men had succeeded, —many of them under disadvantages as great as any which I had to contend with; and, till I had made the attempt, how could I determine that success was beyond my reach?

'Though I frankly confess that I have been, and am still, ambitious, and though this ambition has paved the way for that liberty, perhaps an unwarrantable one, which I am now taking at this moment, I disclaim all ideas of "getting on in the world," as it is called. Even though successful, I should not have the most distant intention of appropriating the products of that success for the purposes of idleness and luxury. With those glorifications of folly and exhibitions of vanity, in the form of balls, dinners, feasts, assemblies, &c., to which the wealthy are so prone, I have no sympathy. After having been subjected to the most grinding species of toil in boyhood, and after having been twice blown up by gunpowder in whinstone quarries, and escaping narrowly with my life, my "right hand still is able" to provide for my few natural wants, and as I have been careful not to multiply artificial ones, comparatively speaking, I require but little for myself. And those motives which operate the most powerfully upon others should have but a small share in influencing me. I never looked upon a fine coat as the alpha and omega of man's ambition. Neither could I ever consider the ability to do nothing, and the having a horse's four feet to carry one, when his own two might serve, as the chief end of his creation—an attainment to which all others are of little importance. In accordance with these heretical opinions, I never had any idea of pushing myself into the society of the rich. I think I have discovered that in many things they are as ignorant as myself, and in most respects as selfish as one could well wish them to be; and for these reasons I do not look upon their society as an object worth straining after, or their smiles a thing greatly to be coveted.

'I am aware that these notions are sadly out of keeping with the established order of things, for it has long been a prevailing opinion, that to be either a wise or a literary man, one must be a gentleman, or, at least, that he must eat, and speak, and be on very familiar terms with those who have a right to be so called. In compliance with this dogma, I suppose, some poor authors have deemed it necessary to write whole books of flattery to rich patrons, and to treat that class to which they originally belonged with the greatest contempt. From this part of the poor author's creed, however, I am a dissenter:—I have little or nothing in common with the gentleman of the present age, nor do I wish to have more. And would the public favour me with any share of its approbation, there are some vices, and many follies, at the roots of which I could cut with as heavy a hand, and perhaps as keen a weapon, in a Galashiels coat and corduroy trowsers, as I could do in a dress of broad cloth. I cannot see how any modification of dress can produce an effect upon a man's intellect or understanding; neither can I imagine how roast beef and plum-pudding should make a man either clearer headed or better hearted, than porridge and potatoes. The last, with the addition of some milk and much water, has been exclusively the fare of the present writer; and he has no wish to change it.

'In those attempts at authorship which I have hitherto made, I have endeavoured to look upon men simply as men, and to divest my mind entirely of those invidious distinctions before which authors often bow down, sacrificing truth at the shrine of Mammon, and bartering the interests of many for the favour of a few. Had I not supposed, from the peculiarity of my situation, that I have had opportunities of taking views somewhat different from —and perhaps vanity would prompt me to add, more accurate than—those adopted by others upon some subjects, I should never have thought of making this application to you. After all, I may be mistaken; and to put the matter to a severer test than any to which it has yet been subjected,—as I have for some time past entertained a high opinion, not only of your literary abilities, but of your heart, from the many fearless, and, I would hope successful, attempts which have been made in " Chambers' Edinburgh Journal," to unmask error, prejudice, and folly, and to exhibit truth in its own broad and unequivocal light; (not but that I have seen some things in that work which I considered unworthy of both it and its conductors, for I would on no account flatter. But I am not criticising the Journal)—from the opinion which I entertain of its editors, and the hope that their written sentiments are emanations from the heart, the overflowings of their own feelings,—though my purse, from causes which I could satisfactorily explain, is all but penniless, I would undertake a journey to Edinburgh, for the purpose of reading a few extracts from my productions, and having the satisfaction of hearing your opinion of them. I would do this most readily, if you would only promise an hour of your time to a stranger who has no claim upon either your generosity or attention, unless his ignorance of these matters were to be admitted as one.

'Although, after some hesitation, and some doubt as to the propriety of the step, I have thus ventured to trouble you with my request, I am perfectly aware that you may find it expedient to reject it. You may do this without the least imputation of blame. There is however one point upon which I would wish to establish a proper understanding between us. It has been said that it is dangerous to make a poor man a dependent. Should no other weighty reason intervene, let not this deter you. In so far as any thing beyond advice and a small share of literary assistance is concerned, I have no wish to become dependent on any one. I have but a small stake in the world—one worthless life is my all; and when I cannot provide for myself, no one shall hear me murmur at my fate. I have already contemplated the worst that can befall me— I have brought it near in the nakedness of truth. It is but a few days' privation of the necessaries of life, and a few pangs such as I have suffered before —no great matter; and then I shall neither be dependent upon, nor troublesome to any. As an evidence how little I require for myself, it may be mentioned, that the coat in which I now write has actually served me since the year 1827, during the whole of which time it has been on service every day, with the exception of about eight months, for which period, between accidents, small-pox, and other diseases, I was mostly confined to bed, or at least, unable to wear it much.

'In conclusion, I may remark, that though neither conceited as to my own abilities, nor very sanguine in my hopes of success, my temperament is, I trust, equally distant from that "dreep-daily" sort of disposition which can never permit its possessor to do anything save whine out dolorous lamentations for want of ability, and hypocritical pretensions to modesty. There is nothing which I would not attempt, nor any difficulty from which I would shrink, with the prospect of being ultimately successful before me. I would not however travel the dirty road to public notice and fame which some have waddled over. I would prefer poverty and an obscure death, with an honest independence of thought and principle, to wealth and eminence procured by fawning upon the rich, and flattering lordly patrons.

'I should now proceed to unfold some plans for the future, which I have in my eye; but as this would be premature and out of place, till I am better acquainted with your sentiments on the subject, and whether you would prove friendly to the proposal which I have made, I defer it to a future opportunity. And should you, sir, deem it indispensable to decline all further correspondence upon this affair, I feel assured that it will be done civilly. But let me request that it be also done promptly, and either the real reason for doing so assigned, or no reason at all; for it would not add to my good opinion of mankind, if I had room to suspect that one of the editors of " Chambers' Edinburgh Journal," was among the little minded bodies who constantly manage every thing by deceit.

'My task is now nearly complete. I have only farther to request, as I have done my best to keep my scribbling propensities a secret, that you would keep this communication one too, and that you would answer it, should you deem it worthy of such attention, with your first convenient leisure. Some one has said, Milton I believe, that "suspense is torture." I shall neither be in suspense nor torture about it; but I feel that a certain degree of anxiety must attend me till I am apprized of your decision, from which with childish weakness I could wish to be freed as soon as possible. But do not therefore make any sacrifice either as to the time or manner of answering this letter: delay till you find convenient, and reject it in two words if you think proper. Apropos, when I speak of convenience: by writing a contracted hand I have succeeded, I believe, in cramming more matter into this sheet than you may find it convenient to read. But as I was aware that my opinions are in some respects heretical, I deemed it necessary to give you an outline of them, such as my space would admit of, that you might not be in any way deceived as to my true character. I shall only trouble you farther by adding, that I am not without some hopes of our yet becoming acquainted.—Sir, your most humble, most obedient servant, A. B.'

Among Alexander's papers, I have found another copy of a letter, shorter than this, addressed to the same quarter, and purporting to be accompanied by a tale and a sonnet. The result was, that exactly three months after the date of the letter just inserted, "The Harvest Day," a tale of humble life; and one of its author's finest and sweetest, appeared in Chamber's Edinburgh Journal, (No. 185); and "Hazelburn, a Story of Scottish Rural Life," as the leader of No. 188. These, so far as I have been able to ascertain, were the first of his productions which appeared in print. From some of his early correspondence, it appears that, a considerable time previous to this, he had through a friend transmitted some pieces to Blackwood's Magazine; but I have no reason to think that any of them were ever inserted.

The following extracts are from copies of letters addressed, or meant to have been addressed, to a lady. They are without date, but are probably referable to a period some years earlier than the date of the letter to the Messrs. Chambers; though from the bearing of the contents of that on Mr. Bethune's literary history, it seemed proper that it should precede them.

'When I saw you yesterday, I should have stated, that the verses I had transcribed, were not those which you had requested; but that if I should ever by any means discover them, they too should be sent. I should have also stated, with respect to my early scribblings, that I had only burned what I considered incorrigibly bad; and for your kind offer of protecting my worthless productions, I should have made the warmest acknowledgement, and said, that I should not only account it a favour, but that I should be most proud to be permitted to deposit them in such hands. All this I should have certainly done, had not my wits gone a wool-gathering. But my memory, and my good manners, are like Absalom's mule, they always get from under me at my need; and then, when I am afterwards caught among the briars and thorns of my own reflections, like that unhappy prince, I must suffer for this faithlessness! I suffer now, but no matter —I deserve it.

'I was heartily sorry to hear from you, ma'am, that "The ———" had been a losing concern to its publishers; yet I could have anticipated as much, from my own observations on mankind. Had Dr. ——— instead of going didactically to work, set about interesting the imagination of his readers, and then instructed them without letting them know he was doing so, he might perhaps have succeeded better. Physicians are often obliged to disguise their medicines, to make them agreeable to the taste of their patients. Why should not the moral physician follow their example? Men are scarcely to be stormed into the right way: they must be cozened, even to do their duty. And it were certainly better to write even a tale, exhibiting the sublime influence of religion on the hearts, and conduct of those who own its sway; or bringing to light, the beauty of some moral virtue, with its effects upon society; it were better to write such a tale, which haply, may be read by thousands, than to write a book full of the most valuable instruction, to lie unlooked at on the shelf of a bookseller! Wit, sentiment, satire, in skilful hands, may all be made either subservient to the cause of virtue, or brought to bear upon vice with cutting effect. I would not discourage serious and evangelical writing, for those who already *know*, and *feel the truth*. But what is to be done with the world?—Instruct it in the way in which it seems most willing to take instruction? or look upon it with the gaze of unavailing sorrow? —or, what is almost the same thing, write books for it which it will not read? These are questions which I dare not answer, though I should much wish to see a satisfactory solution of them. If the light literature of the day, instead of exhibiting absurdities about supernatural agency, which should be laughed at, and trumpeting forth the praise of human butchers, called *heroes*, who should be execrated as demons—if, instead of these, it could be turned into a better channel, and made to paint in the vivid colours of imagination and fancy, the loveliness of unassuming virtue, and the beauties of true religion, it would certainly be a powerful engine for reforming, at least, the surface of society; and even this, would be a considerable step gained in the good cause. I have often thought La-Roche, an admirable specimen of that kind of writing, which should be more cultivated than it is. I never yet knew any who had read that affecting narrative of piety and suffering, without admiring it, and, what is more, feeling their hearts for the time, bettered by the spirit which it breathes. By the bye, that well imagined story, is not altogether a fiction. David Hume was the sceptic philosopher which it represents, and he actually resided for some time in the family of a Swiss clergyman of the given name. Pardon, madam, if you can, the tediousness of these remarks, and believe me to be, with the utmost respect, &c. &c. A. B.'

'Madam,

* * * * * * *

'To show that I am not affected either by the peevishness of ill-humour or the fastidiousness of pride, I shall take the liberty of inclosing the piece, formerly sent for your inspection, with some slight alterations, and one or two trifling additions which I made to it the other night. Upon this copy, if I might presume so far, I would take it kind if you would favour me with your strictures in writing. Do not tell me, as some people of much affected modesty would do, that you cannot rely on your own judgment, and that you have no taste in these matters; but take a slip of paper and your pen, while reading it, and get on thus:—" Verse so and so, is not amiss: the third or fourth line, contains an idea with which I am pleased, because it is &c." Always assign some reason if possible. Again, "Verse such a thing, is very bad: I am quite disgusted with the second line; and the fourth, I cannot like for the life of me! it is so &c." " Verse, such another thing, is worse and worse; it has neither tune nor time, sense nor sentiment: the first line is silly, the second insipid, the third dull, and the fourth stupid! In short, the writer must have been nearly, if not wholly asleep, when he composed it." This is the sort of criticism which I should like, and the sort which you must bestow upon every one whose taste you would wish to amend: not sweeping assertions, such as, "It is too gloomy." Sentences of this kind go to cut down, not to amend—to make a ruin, not to repair an old wall; and at best, little advantage can be derived from them. Be as severe upon the piece as you think it deserves: do not sacrifice truth, or one sentiment of your own, for the sake of pleasing. If I were a-gape for flattery, I should be at no loss where to apply; but to you I look for something better—for undisguised truth! Tell me therefore candidly, if you can, what you like, and what you hate in it. If you cannot, tell me as frankly, that it is contrary to your inclination to interfere with such matters, and it shall sleep. This might indeed be some disappointment, though it would be wrong in me to take it as such; for I should be one of those to whom nothing can come wrong. Once more, though I am almost ashamed of saying so much, upon so silly a subject, I would beg to remind you, that it is *your own opinion* upon which I shall set any value. Do not show it to either ladies or gentlemen who have skill in poetry; for, for the acumen of professed critics, I can have very little respect, believing as I do, that their opinions are oftener guided by prejudice and party-feeling, than by truth; and after all they can say, either in praise or blame, experience teaches us that the unsophisticated taste of common readers must ultimately be the test of every literary production—the sentence by which it must live or die.

'As I am in the mood of writing just now, and as I have moreover a considerable portion of unoccupied paper before me, I shall here attempt to palliate if that be possible, some of the most serious objections which have been brought against the piece. To those who, from a natural cheerfulness of disposition, have been accustomed to contemplate the sunny side of every thing, and who have had ample opportunities for doing so by being nursed in the lap of an affluent or an easy fortune, my poor verses may appear gloomy indeed. But with me, situated as I have been, and am still, in the very humblest walk of life; conversant with scenes of wretchedness and poverty, of which the rich have never even dreamed, and accustomed from boyhood to read the unequivocal signs of misery, in the care-worn features and meagre countenances of individuals with whose " tales of woe" I from time to time became acquainted—thus situated, and thus trained, were my ideas of the present state materially different from what they are, I should be, what I am still loath to suppose myself,—a thing without a heart! Add to the above, a constitutional weakness of mine, the consequence of which is, that I could never look on distress without feeling its saddening influence steal over my spirit like an eclipse, and you will scarcely wonder that in those moments of solitary musing, which are in part the lot of all, my sentiments should have in them a certain tinge of gloom, which I can only conceal by silence. Perhaps too, these melancholy reflections in me, may have been nursed by the circumstance of my being often employed alone, and thus left the sole companion of my own thoughts for many days together. I deem it not altogether unnecessary to make you acquainted with these things, trifling though they may seem, in order that you may be the better able to judge of the sentiments of others, whenever you may be called upon to do so. It is only by taking a view of society in all its different phases, that an extensive knowledge of the manners, thoughts, feelings, sentiments, &c. of men can be gained; and it is only by the same means, that the art of judging accurately whether they are right or wrong can be acquired. Now, to apply all this to the difference of our tastes: we have made our observations on life, from very different points of view. You, it may be, have seen and delighted to see it, in the bright sunshine of prosperity—where Fortune was profuse of her favours, and Plenty smiled. I, on the other hand, have been accustomed to contemplate it under the cloud of adversity, where Want invaded, Poverty oppressed, and Misfortune lowered. From this cause, I am convinced, comes the difference of sentiment which I have already noticed. But,

> Hadst thou been born where I was bred,
> * * * *
> Thou would'st have felt—I know it true,
> As I have done, and aye must do."

'Among the few words we exchanged, when you passed me at Lindores, there was one remark on your part, viz. that you " wished to gather as many flowers as possible." This is a good disposition, and I neither can nor will quarrel with it. Yet, with all deference to your better judgment, I would here beg permission to arrange for your inspection, a few stray thoughts upon the subject, which have of late occupied my own head. But first, I do not make this attempt from pride, or from querulousness of temper; but merely, that you may become acquainted with the thoughts of another, worthless as they may be, upon a subject which seems already to have taken your attention.

'I do think then, that this taste may be cultivated too exclusively, and that there is some danger, that those who continually fly from the semblance of sorrow to flowery scenes, may in the end become light-hearted and unfeeling. I am also of opinion, that, as imaginary flowers cannot transform a barren heath into a cultivated garden, so neither can all the flowers of poetry which the muses ever gathered from their own Aonian mount, dispel the gloom of settled sadness, or change melancholy into mirth. So true is this, that there are times when anything of a light or cheerful nature, would be as offensive to the heart, as a puppet show placed upon the coffin of a dear departed friend would be to the eye. At such seasons, the heart will yield its sympathies to scenes of kindred gloom, and forget the pressure of its woe, in the contemplation of sorrows by which its own are outnumbered, when it would turn with disgust from all the florid descriptions of happiness which the poet or prose-writer ever produced. Here the lines of Burns are so much to my purpose, that I cannot resist the temptation I am under of quoting them:

> " The winter's howl, it soothes my soul;
>   My griefs it seems to join.
> The leafless trees, my fancy please;
>   Their fall resembles mine!"

From this it seems to follow, that there is a sort of propriety in cultivating, in poetry and works of taste which are intended for being extensively read, the mournful, the pathetic, and even the gloomy, as well as the light, flowery lay, the laughing song, and the cheerful sonnet. For my own part, I will frankly confess that I have ever been more partial to the former of these than to the latter. " The Emigrant," by Erskine, the " Elegy written in a country Church-yard," and an " Elegy," by Michael Bruce—all which I found in the tattered leaves of an old collection, were my favourites, long before my reasoning powers could be said to be developed. In these pieces there was to me, even when a mere boy, that *music of the heart*, which at this moment I want words to describe.

' It has been said, " that religion should have a tendency to make people cheerful and happy." This is certainly true, and I add my amen to it with all my heart. But let us glance for a moment on the manner in which this happiness is produced. The Christian Dispensation was not intended to change this state of suffering, which has been emphatically called "the vale of tears," into an earthly paradise; else why did our Saviour himself warn his followers, that *in the world they should have tribulation?* Here, the righteous must suffer as well as the wicked. One lot happeneth to all; and till our nature undergo some radical change, which even the most holy man on earth has no just reason to expect, men, let them talk as they will, must feel their sufferings, and grieve over them, albeit they may do it in secret. The comforts and consolations of religion, I should then humbly suppose, and that prospect of a happy futurity which it presents to those who will accept it on the offered terms, were intended to support the soldier of the cross under all the toils, sufferings, difficulties, and dangers of his present state; even as the hope of victory, and the prospect of that rest and peace which is to follow it, supports the spirit of the warrior, and cheers him on amid the mortal strife. And, to follow out the comparison, as the man who never fought, cannot enjoy the victory with half the satisfaction of him who struggled hard for it, in the midst of fallen thousands, while Death mowed down the ranks around him, and where the dead or dying body of a fellow creature received the pressure of his foot with every step he made in advance; so neither can the man who has all his life long travelled the smooth and flowery plain of prosperity—I speak comparatively—appreciate half the value of religion. It is the apparently wretched being, whose life has been one long winter; who has waded through affliction, and rested upon thorns; but who, in the midst of all his miseries, has cultivated an aquaintance with his bible, "his Saviour, and his God,"—it is he, and he alone who can with the greatest propriety, and with the most heart-felt sense of its truth, speak of the comforts and consolations of religion. Yet ask even him, and he will tell you, that he felt his sufferings bitter, that they were gall and wormwood to his spirit, and he might have sunk under their weight; but he turned from them to contemplate those happy regions whither he expected soon to go, those realms of peace from which the shed blood of a Redeemer had excluded every object which could annoy.

' From some passages in this letter, I now begin to fear that you will be ready to set me down for one of the most gloomy and unsocial beings upon earth. This however, I assure you is not the case. When in the company of those with whom I am acquainted, and indulging in tattle, my besetting sin is a proneness to what a late eminent poet has called "sarcastic levity of tongue;" and if in those hours of abstraction and loneliness, of which I have already spoken, I should sometimes indulge in a mood less light, as I ask no sympathy from the world, it should in all conscience pardon me, as I believe it does. From you I dare scarce hope for such treatment, after having inflicted on you so much melancholy stuff; yet pardon me if you can.

'I should now conclude; but there is yet one thing to which I must advert before doing so. In the course of our short interview at Lindores, you said that you "felt disappointed at my not sending something else for the A———." This you must allow me, if possible, to look upon as only a piece of good-natured civility; for I should be heartily sorry to think myself the cause of real disappointment to any one, and more particularly to you, upon whose patience I am now trespassing with a high hand. For the length of this letter I have no excuse to plead, except your own good nature; and of this, if the world would give me any credit for my skill in physiognomy, I would say, you have an abundant share. With some fears, lest the freedom I have taken may have offended where I should least wish to do so, I must now conclude in the usual way, by subscribing myself your most humble, most obedient —and I will add with confidence, for of this I am quite certain—your most worthless servant,

'A. B.'

CHAPTER II.

SETS TO LEARN THE WEAVING BUSINESS WITH HIS BROTHER—TRADE FAILS—ACCIDENTS FROM GUNPOWDER—EXTRACTS FROM 'DAY-DREAMS,' ILLUSTRATIVE OF HIS FEELINGS DURING CONVALESCENCE—LETTERS TO A YOUNG FRIEND EMBODYING ECONOMICAL AND OTHER ADVICE—SPECIMENS OF POETICAL ATTEMPTS.

THESE sketches bring down Mr. Bethune's literary history to the period of his first appearance before the public as an author. Several other matters, some of them of painful interest, which the narrative has outrun in point of time, now demand our attention.

In 1825, he set himself to learn the weaving business with his brother, who had just completed his apprenticeship, expecting to realize higher wages in that way than as a day-labourer; but, after expending all that they both had saved by 'the most desperate economy,' as he himself expresses it, in purchasing utensils, the trade almost immediately failed, owing to the general crash of 1825—6; 'and both were glad to find employment as day-labourers, the one at 1s. 2d., and the other at 1s. a day.' 'Before the trade had recovered, the house which they occupied as a workshop was required for the accomodation of a family. For a number of years afterwards it did not appear that it would have been advisable to make any great sacrifice to to obtain another; and thus the whole of the weaving utensils, which, but a short time before had cost what would have been a little fortune for them, were no better than so much useless lumber.'* This proved but the forerunner of a series of disappointments, misfortunes, and disasters, which attended both the brothers to their graves.

'From 1814,' says Alexander, in a fragment of a letter written during his last illness, and intended for a medical gentleman in the west of England, who had taken a benevolent interest in his welfare—'From 1814 to 1837, with the exception of one year, we lived in a house, which, for the greater part of that period, was in such bad repair, that when it rained, we had to place the most of the dishes that we possessed upon the top of the beds, to intercept the water that oozed through the roof; and when the rain began to fall after we were sleeping, it was no uncommon thing for us to awake in the morning with the bed-clothes partially wet about us. In winter, too, during a rapid thaw, or a protracted fall of rain, the water came in under the foundation of the back wall, and flowed in a

---

* Life of John Bethune, Second Ed. p. 29, 30.

stream through the floor, nearly the whole length of the house, till it made its escape by the door. Nor was this the worst of it; in some places it formed pools of such extent, that my brother and myself, who slept at the farther end of the house, were frequently obliged to lay stones and pieces of wood on them to enable us to reach our bed. We did not seem to suffer any thing at the time; but I am now convinced, that to the damp air with which we were so often surrounded, he owed a part of that delicacy of the chest, which at last consigned him to an early grave, while I am, perhaps, indebted to the same cause for a something of the same kind which yet remains to be noticed.

'In 1826, a severe cold caught during harvest, and with which my constitution was left to struggle unaided, produced a cough and a degree of expectoration, which lasted till next spring. Previous to this period I had never been subject to cough; but afterwards if I caught cold and did not get quit of it in two or three days, it always produced a cough which frequently lasted for three weeks or a month; and, except during the heat of summer I always expectorated more than was natural: only, when free from cold I could raise it without coughing. These circumstances impressed my mind deeply with a conviction that I was destined to fall an early victim to consumption. So deep, indeed, was this impression, that for years, at the time alluded to, on the evening of my birth-day, or of the longest or shortest day, or, in short, any other day which had any thing to distinguish it from the rest, I used to walk out and watch the setting sun with a peculiar interest, and as his parting radiance gradually disappeared behind the western hills, contemplate the strong probability of my being numbered with the things which were, before he should again set at that particular part of the horizon. Of these solemn reflections I afterwards availed myself while writing a story, which was published along with some others in a small volume last February.

'On the 11th November, 1829, (as stated in my brother's life,) while employed in a quarry, I was thrown into the air by a blast of gunpowder, which exploded prematurely; and after being carried to a distance of nine or ten yards, pitched, head foremost, upon a cairn of stones, many of them with edges almost as sharp as knives. When the people from a neighbouring hamlet arrived, the blood was flowing so fast from such a number of wounds, principally about the head and face, which appeared to them of so hopeless a character, that, for a time they did not think of calling medical assistance; believing that I must be gone long before any thing of the kind could reach me. I may mention in passing that my upper lip was cut off on two sides, so as to admit of being folded back upon the left cheek. My tongue was almost cut through on one side, and two teeth knocked out, while my nose had been crushed over upon the left cheek, with a deep cut extending the whole length of it, and then, turning outward below the left eye, terminated at its outer angle. At the inner angle of the same eye, a perforation had been made into the nostril, from which my breath issued for eight days. On my head matters were equally bad. Besides a number of smaller wounds, in one instance, the skull was laid bare to an extent of, perhaps, three or four square inches, but without being fractured. My hands and one of my legs were also sadly injured; but into these details I shall not enter.—Having been conveyed to the nearest house, after two hours of washing, stitching, and bandaging of wounds, I was put to bed; and all that the medical attendant would say, in reply to the anxious inquiries of friends and others, was, that "if fever did not come on, I might perhaps get through." Almost contrary to expectation, I soon began to recover, when the same gentleman was heard to remark that I "must have had a good constitution"—a thing, which, for reasons already stated rather surprised me. In four months from the date of the accident, I was again making some attempts to resume work.

'On the 14th November, 1832, exactly three years and three days from the time at which I met with the first misfortune, I was once more subjected to nearly the same sort of discipline. On this occasion, there were two of us employed about the blast when it exploded. The other man was dashed against a ledge of a rock, and died in less than two hours; while I, more fortunate, was thrown upon the wheel of a cart, which chanced to be loading with stones at the time, and taken up insensible from before it. I was again sadly scorched and cut about the hands, head, and face. Indeed, the one side of my face now bears no resemblance to the other. But what was worse, my right eye had been cut across both the eye and the eyelid; and in healing, a portion of the former got fast in the latter, which to the present moment keeps up a degree of chronic inflamation in it. The inflamation, however, was so acute at first, as entirely to deprive me of rest and sleep for three weeks. During this period, if I once attempted to lie down in bed, the increased flow of blood to the head, and the intolerable pain which it occasioned, made me start up again the next minute. In time the inflammation and pain began to abate; and in something less than four months I was making some attempts at labour.

'From the effects of the first of these accidents I had recovered tolerably well. Indeed, I think that for a year previous to the occurrence of the second one, I was as stout as ever I had been in my life; but from it I never fully recovered. I was able to perform an ordinary day's work without any inconvenience, and have seen a good deal of hard service since then; but when hard pushed I always suffered more from fatigue and weariness than before.'

Some of his feelings and musings during his state of convalescence after one of these disasters, probably the last of them, are disclosed to us in the following extracts from the piece in blank verse which has already enriched the autobiography of these pages:—

' AFTER seclusion sad, and sad restraint,
Again the welcome breeze comes wafted far
Across the cooling bosom of the lake,
To fan my weary limbs and feverish brow,
Where yet the pulse beats audible and quick—
And I could number every passing throb,
Without the pressure which physicians use,
As easily as I could count the chimes
By which the clock sums up the flight of time.
 ' Yet it is pleasing, from the bed of sickness,
And from the dingy cottage, to escape
For a short time to breathe the breath of heaven,
And ruminate abroad with less of pain.
Let those who never pressed the thorny pillow,
To which disease oft ties its victim down
For days and weeks of wakeful suffering—
Who never knew to turn or to be turned
From side to side, and seek, and seek, in vain,
For ease and a short season of repose—
Who never tried to circumvent a moan,
And tame the spirit with a tyrant's sway,
To bear what must be borne and not complain—
Who never strove to wring from the writhed lip
And rigid brow, the semblance of a smile,
To cheer a friend in sorrow sitting by,

Nor felt that time, in happy days so fleet,
Drags heavily along when dogged by pain.
Let those *talk* well of Nature's beauteous face,
And her sublimer scenes; her rocks and mountains;
Her clustered hills and winding valleys deep;
Her lakes, her rivers, and her oceans vast,
In all the pomp of modern sentiment;
But still they cannot *feel* with half the force,
Which the pale invalid, imprisoned long,
Experiences upon his first escape
To the green fields and the wide world abroad:
Beauty *is* beauty—freshness, freshness, then;
And feeling *is* a something to be *felt*—
Not fancied—as is frequently the case.

' These feelings lend an impulse now, and Hope
Again would soar upon the wings of health:
Yet is it early to indulge his flight,
When death, short while ago seemed hovering near;
And the next hour perhaps may bring him back,
And bring me to that " bourne " where I shall sleep—
Not like the traveller, though he sleep well,
Nor like the artizan, or humble hind,
Or the day-labourer worn out with his toil,
Who pass the night, scarce conscious of its passing,
Till morning with his balmy breath return,
And the shrill cock-crow warns them from their bed—
That sleep shall be more lasting and more dreamless,
Than aught which living men on earth may know.

' Well, be it so: methinks my life, though short,
Hath taught me that this sublunary world
Is something else than Fancy wont to paint it—
A world of many cares and anxious thoughts,
Pains, sufferings, abstinence, and endless toil,

From which it were small penance to be gone.
Yet there are feelings in the heart of youth,
Howe'er depressed by poverty or pain,
Which loathe the oblivious grave; and I would live,
If it were only but to be convinced
That " all is vanity beneath the sun.—"
Yes: while these hands can earn what nature asks,
Or lessen, by one bitter drop, the cup
Of woe, which some must drink even to its dregs,
Or have it in their power to hold a crust
To the pale lip of famished Indigence,
I would not murmur or repine though care,
The toil-worn, frame-tired arm, and heavy foot,
Should be my portion in this pilgrimage.
But when this ceases let me also cease,
If such may be thy will, O God of heaven!
Thou knowest all the weakness of my heart,
And it is such, I would not be a beggar,
Nor ask an alms from Charity's cold hand:
I would not buy existence at the price
Which the poor mendicant must stoop to pay.

  *   *   *   *   *

'—— If that change, the last on earth, might leave
Unchanged the spirit which is leaving earth,
And if that spirit might again return,
To be a witness of the ways of men,
When death hath passed, and all is earth again
Which to the earth belongs, or from it came,—
I would behold those young and happy beings
Who sport at eventide across the green
Of the brown hamlet, far among the hills,
With brows as sunny as the tropic clime,
Eyes bright as is the evening star whose ray

First greets them at their inoffensive pastime,
Cheeks fresh as the first roses of the spring,
And hearts as yet untaught one wicked thought—
Unchilled by care—untutored by deceit;
While no foreboding comes to mar their peace,
Like mildew withering the young germs of hope,—
Light as the breeze which waves their curling locks,
Sport on, nor know that " man was made to mourn !'
  * * * * *

Still I would see—if such is to be seen,
The man by adverse fortune placed below
The notice of the world and men's applause,
Who nobly tames his inclination down
To his necessities, and dares to think
Not as that world hath thought, but truth inspires,—
Who makes the headstrong passions of his youth
Yield to the effort of a powerful mind.

' If spirits for themselves their path may choose,
Then would I wander by the yet untilled
And scarcely trodden mountain, where the heath
With sterile boundary meets the upland field,
And the huge rock and giant stone defy
The feeble ploughshare and the power of man—
There would I wander in the harvest time,
To see unseen the reapers as they sit
At the shorn ridge's end upon the bank
All fragrant with the heather's purple bloom.'

  The harvest field, he informs us, was the principal, and earliest scene where he cultivated his faculty for observing human character.

F

'The many faces too which there were met,
With all the signs of feeling, passion, thought,
Which flitted o'er them   *   *   *
Formed a rich field for an observant eye—
A field where Fancy for herelf might reap,
And hold an hourly revel of her own.
Among them first I tried to read the lines
Grooved on " the human countenance divine,"
To search the eye for sentiment, and trace
Its look askance, upturned, or downward bent,
With all the attitudes—the idle hands,
Which seemed to play with trifles, or were clasped
Upon the bosom, or were firmly clenched,
Although no foe ostensible were near,
To some according impulse of the heart,
Of which these were so many outward signs.
Among them too I learned the little all
I e'er could know of human character;
And this to me was much, for I was fain
To study man, his manners, thoughts, affections;
And woman too.'

The following letters, and extracts from letters, to a young man occupying a similar rank in life with Mr. Bethune, contain suggestions and advice of the highest importance.

'LOCHEND, *Nov.* 1, 1834.

'My dear David,—Nothing could afford me greater pleasure than the simple narrative which you gave me in your last—except one—of the affair at the swallow's nest. In this I can read the workings of a mind awake to true feeling, and I am happy at it. I need scarcely add, that you must inculcate humanity by example as well as precept—the former is often the more powerful mode of the two; and without it, the latter must almost always go for nought. Forgive the freedom I am taking, for it is only to put you on your guard against those inadvertencies which the ingenuity of malice may sometimes construe into cruelty.

'The principle of cruelty in the human bosom is a mysterious one; and it were, perhaps, difficult to trace it satisfactorily to its source. Much, however, may be accounted for by bad example. No one is at pains to teach his children the evil of this abomination. Most parents are themselves often guilty of acts of wanton cruelty to animals; these their children see and imitate, and think it sport to do so, till the habit becomes confirmed, and thus the evil is perpetuated from one generation to another—from year to year, and from age to age. To be humane, it is not absolutely necessary that men should be civilized, or that they should be christians. That which can only be taught by a long course of instruction to some, is intuitive in others, and thus there have been civilized savages and barbarous christians—humane infidels and butcher-hearted believers. I am almost upon my hobby at present, but I must drop the subject else I shall have no room for a number of other particulars which I must notice.

'In answering your last, I scarcely know how to begin. Deeply have I felt, and at this moment deeply do I feel, the difficulty and danger of your situation. To a young and inexperienced mind, placed, as you are, in the midst of temptations, your circumstances must be peculiarly trying. Yet do not shrink from the path of duty: it is only he who fights, who can look for victory, and it is only to him who perseveres that the reward of virtue can be given. If there were no temptations to contend with, and no snares to be avoided, it were small praise to be virtuous; but this world has provided an ordeal by which all must be tried before they can deserve that honourable name! And here, if the voice of a friend could be of any service in strengthening your resolutions, I would raise mine, and say, Do not upon any account yield to that most debasing of all vices, Intemperance. But against this I hope you are already steeled. The man who besots himself with liquor, is worse than a beast. He reduces himself to a state, at which the veriest lunatic might laugh in perfect scorn; for what class of madmen can be so despicable—so far beneath the dignity of rational creatures—as those who court the mental malady; and with phrensied dexterity gulp down the fatal draught which destroys reason, enervates the frame, and which, if persisted in, must ultimately sink the immortal spirit to that place of horror from which the imagination appalled shrinks back. But, apart from futurity altogether, one would think that the cold, insipid, heartless drivellings of a drunken man, were enough to make drunkenness detestable in the eyes of all—a thing to be feared and hated worse than the sting of the deadliest adder! O, my dear friend, *Never suffer yourself to get drunk!* It requires only some firmness to resist the insinuations of the drunkard at the outset. He may repeat them for a time; but when he sees that he has no power over you, they must then as a matter of course cease; and he will then not only envy, but yield you the homage of secret respect, for that resolution which he knows to be wanting in himself. With respect to the other disagreeable affair with which you have intrusted me, I would only say, Be kind and affable to all, but stern and unbending in your integrity Never, even for a moment, seem to hesitate, or make the slightest compromise of your principles, for that would only open a channel for a great flood of temptations. If by this line of conduct you should happen to give offence to any, as it is most probable you will, it may be necessary in some cases to soothe them as far as possible; but in most instances you will succeed much better, by taking no notice whatever of their displeasure—by appearing cheerful, easy, and unaffected by it, in short, what you used to be, till the fit wears over; and when at last the countenance of the offender begins to brighten, speak and act to him as if no offence had ever been either given or taken. This, I am of opinion, you will find the easiest way of getting over such matters. I am glad that you have had the acuteness to discover the hollow pretences of common friends: this was what I expected of you. Self-interest is the governing principle—the great deity to which the men of this world bow the knee. What can I add: even let them adore their idol!—it is good! Yet there are many who deserve no better friends than those you have spoken of. It is flattery they are agape for—not friendship; and the sycophant who is best skilled in this sordid art, is ever sure to ingratiate himself the most deeply in their favour. I should have had more to say on the subject, but I am out for room. I should also have noticed the untoward circumstance of your leaving K—— at the term; but for the above reason, I must drop the idea of that also. All I can do now, is to state my fears that I have wearied you out, and to beg that you will believe me to be, without the least affectation, Yours, sincerely,   A. B.'

'MOUNTPLEASANT, *Dec.* 5, 1837.

'My dear David,—When you break open the seal with which I intend to secure this sheet, you will be apprised, without my telling you, of my intention to trouble you with a letter. I should not have thought of troubling you in this way, or of taking from your pocket the shillings and pence which will no doubt be demanded by that avaricious scoundrel, the *Post*, so soon, had it not been for the belief that I may be able to communicate something which in the end may counterbalance these losses. And now you will be wondering what this mighty secret can possibly be! But wait a wee lad and I'll tell ye,—only have patience, for I must not be hurried. You have, I doubt not, like most other young people, thought that those were glorious fellows—frank, free-hearted, and noble—who could part with their money in alehouses, and taverns, and in short, upon all occasions, like gentlemen,—who held shillings and half-crowns in no more estimation than so many old buttons. The predisposition to admire such characters seems to be one of the fallacies of youth, and therefore I suppose that you may have admired them too, and what is more, that you may have sometimes felt an inclination to imitate them. You have also, I presume, like me and many more, been in embarrassed circumstances; and then, in moments of mortification and disappointment, you have no doubt thought that those were happy men who had at all times the *wherewithal* to supply their wants, and never lacked a penny when a penny was really needful. Upon such occasions you have, I might almost say to a certainty, envied these men the happiness and the peace of mind which you fancied their independence must confer. You may have heard too of men who were *misers*, and you may have heard them despised as grovelling wretches—sordid, mean-spirited sinners, who never felt for the sorrows of others, and deserved no sympathy in their own. To the justness of the censure thus passed upon such characters it is reasonable to suppose you have often given your cordial assent, and deemed them worthy of unmingled reprobation. Between these conflicting sentiments it is likely your mind may have been tossed to and fro, like a ship without a rudder. It is to the unspeakable loss of most young men, that they enter life and pass through it, admiring and despising, according to the fashion of the day or the impulse of the moment, without ever having formed any fixed notion of propriety, or any definite rules by which to regulate their conduct. I have thus endeavoured to sketch the characters of those who may have been from time to time the objects of your admiration, your envy, and your reprobation. I would call your attention to what is likely to be the result of motives and pursuits so essentially different. For this purpose it is only necessary to walk on a little with the respective characters. The dashing young fellow who sports his half-crown with an air of as much indifference as if it had cost him nothing, must in time, as sure as the sun serves the world, come to have no half-crowns to sport. Want of employment, sickness, or old age, must to a certainty bring the thing to pass—and then, behold the man who was once an object of admiration among his jovial companions, tattered, torn down, and, last and worst, despised by all on account of his poverty. As to the miser, little need be said. His character throughout is a repulsive one, because, having made money the sole aim of his existence, he in general soon forgets to distinguish between the honest and dishonest means of acquiring it; and though he may be successful in the pursuit of his darling project, he loses those advantages for which the possession of money alone seems to be desirable —comfort, and the respect of his fellow creatures. Between these extremes may be found the man who, while he stoops to neither dishonest nor dishonourable means to procure a penny, knows the value of one when he has procured it, and takes care of it accordingly. Such an individual, though he may be called a hard man, and though those censures which none need expect wholly to escape, may be occasionally directed against him, yet he will ever be sure to find a certain degree of respect; and even those who pretend to despise him with their lips, will in their hearts envy him his felicity. Nor will their envy be altogether without cause; for independence of circumstances is indispensable to independence of feeling, and it is only the man who is free to think and act upon all occasions according to the dictates of conscience and reason, who can be said to enjoy either liberty or happiness. Money then, to a certain amount, provided always that it is honestly come by,—after all that has been written and said against it, and after all the bombast and nonsense about the beatitudes of poverty which has gone abroad, is as indispensable to comfort and the true enjoyment of existence, as the presence of the sun is to the making of daylight. Never suffer yourself for a moment to be deceived by those who may assert the contrary, but set them down in your own mind for either knaves or fools. Your situation and circumstances at the present time seem to be favourable for saving money; and my secret is neither more nor less than to initiate you into the mystery of doing so with all possible speed. In the first place, then, in the evening of the very day on which you read this letter, go to the nearest stationer's, and purchase a two-penny blank paper book; and when you return home with it, take your pen and write upon the top of the first page the word, *Income*, and on the second, *Expenditure*. When this is done, see what money you have in hand, and if any, place it to account as part of Income, with the date on which you received it. Let nothing deter you from entering every farthing which you receive, and every farthing which you expend, in your book, under the proper heads, and with the proper dates attached to them. This is an easy matter, and see that you attend to it:—you will find it of more importance in the end than an addition of five or even ten pounds to your yearly wages. And now, for the management of your other affairs, I must entreat you not to deceive yourself, or suffer others to deceive you, with the slang which passes so current, about " the dearness of living in England." I have been told by very sensible people who have been there, that it is quite possible to "live cheap" in England as well as in Scotland, though perhaps not so very cheap in the former as the latter. Weigh the matter well in your own mind, and fix your "living" upon as economical a scale as is consistent with comfort—which in the end will also be found most conducive to health and longevity. As to your clothes, I need hardly remind you, that to be neatly, but at the same time plainly dressed, is, in the estimation of every well regulated mind, a thousand times better, and a thousand times more becoming the station of one who has to "work for his bread," than all the trash called finery, and all the tawdry ornaments which he can possibly tie or button upon his four quarters. Let your clothes therefore be such as to unite durability of material, plainness of manufacture, and neatness of make. As it is probable by this time that you have fallen into the fashions and prejudices of the place where you live, you will, no doubt, have a struggle before you can break through them, but if you have embraced them to any extent, break you must, else, it appears to me, that your going abroad will ultimately stand you in little stead. To make this breaking as easy as possible, you may, in the first place, try to make economy fashionable, that is, you may explain to your associates the propriety of some course similar to that alluded to above, and, if the thing can be done, persuade them to adopt it. It might also be a good move to form a Savings Society—each member to contribute something weekly or monthly—the aggregate to be placed in a Savings Bank, and the whole to be again divided among the members at the end of the year, or at any other time which might be deemed convenient. I cannot find room to follow out the subject; but if you think it worth your while to take it up, perhaps I may recur to it at some future period. And now, my dear friend, I believe you will be ready to ask, "What can he be driving at with me and my money? and what has he got to do with either the one or the other?" Were you to ask these questions personally in my hearing, I might probably look stupid, and find it difficult to answer them: but with some four or five hundred miles between us, I answer with the utmost calmness, that I have been thinking, in the first place, as the sun is now shining on you in the shape of fifty-two pounds annually, it may be as well for you to be making "hay;" and in the second, as you will probably marry, and "settle in the world," as it is called, some time or other, you may not then be the worse for the "fodder" thus provided. At all events, as you owe me nothing, and as I never intend to cheat you out of any portion of your savings, you cannot accuse me of sinister motives.

'A. B.'

[*No Date.*]

'There is one sentence, toward the end of your letter, for which you must pardon me if I should reprove you—it expresses a contempt for the opinion of the world. It is not well to allow the opinion of the world to weigh too much upon our spirits: still it must not be altogether despised. You are a young man entering into the world, and, to such, an unblemished character is of inestimable value; if therefore, the good opinions of others can be made to correspond with your duty, cultivate them by all possible means. This charitable world in which we live is ever so ready to take up its testimony whenever it can find anything to lay hold of, that we would require to avoid not only evil, but even the very appearance of it. I would not however have you to banish feeling from your heart: far from it. It is our duty, both as christians and as men, to sympathise with the distress of our fellow creatures, and to do every thing in our power to alleviate their sufferings. These hints are dictated by friendship, and as such I hope you will not be offended by them, or their writer. A. B.'

Were principles such as these acted on by our working men, the nation would be in a great measure saved from those overwhelming periods of distress, which are every now and then overtaking the labouring, and more especially the manufacturing population. Whatever amount of such national calamities may be justly attributable to political causes, there cannot be a doubt, but that were our operatives to cultivate prudent habits when labour is plentiful and wages good, they would not, when employment fails, be in a few weeks reduced to absolute destitution.

From his letter to Mr. Chambers, as well as from the copious extracts given from 'Day Dreams,' the reader will have perceived that many of Mr. Bethune's earlier attempts at composition took the unpromising, and, in our day more especially, most unprofitable, form of verse. Several of these pieces are already before the public in his two volumes of tales, some of them characterized by considerable beauty. As I have no intention of introducing any formal collection of such as remain unpublished, into this volume, I shall occasionally present to the reader a few of those that appear the more worthy of preservation. I do not mean to say that many of these pieces are characterized by a high order of merit. A continuously sustained freshness and vigour of composition in verse, and more especially in rhyme, is a characteristic of the most decided forms of poetic genius, under the guidance of a taste cultivated and refined by an extensive acquaintance with the best models. To have the language flow fresh and full into the proper mould, from the living fount of feeling—to have always the requisite quantity of words and syllables, at once for the measure and the sense, along with the right words for the rhyme, has been a felicity not always attained by the highest poetic geniuses. Alexander Bethune made no pretension to such gifts or powers. He was only an occasional poet. He was little susceptible of imaginative excitement; nor did he often succeed as a versifier, unless when some real object or occurrence came vividly home to his living experience. When such however was the case, the discerning reader will already be prepared to believe that he could occasionally depict his feelings in verse, with considerable felicity and graphic power; albeit his taste never seems to have attained to that severeness and delicacy in regard to verse, which so strikingly characterize the Life of his brother, and most of his later correspondence. In these circumstances, the omission of such stanzas or portions of a piece as seem decidedly to fall below the standard which a just taste demands, is a course which I presume will approve itself to the reader.

'In the spring of 1833, [Life of John Bethune,] it was agreed that we (meaning his brother and himself) should conjointly try to produce a small volume of scriptural pieces, for which he (John) had devised "The Poetical Preacher" as a fitting name.' Owing to the repeated illness of the younger brother, and other causes, the design was abandoned. The contributions of John towards it are already before the public, and I shall now here introduce a specimen or two of Alexander's:—

SING TO THE LORD.

PSALM C.

' Sing to the Lord ye sons of earth—
   In joy and gladness sing,
And let the mountain-echoes round
   With your hosannas ring.
There comes a day when peace and love
   Shall greet your longing eyes—
When rugged rocks shall bow the head,
   Hills sink, and valleys rise.

' Sing to the Lord, ye dusky sons
   Of sun-burnt Afric's shore,
Who listen to the Niger's stream,
   And midnight-lion's roar:—
Sing! for a joyful morn shall break,
   To cheer your moral night,
And on your plains the Prince of Peace
   Shall pour celestial light.

' Sing to the Lord, ye in whose veins
   The life-blood scarcely flows,
Where frost-rocks guard the polar seas,
   Amid eternal snows:—
Sing! for a sun on you shall rise,
   Whose life-reviving ray
To light and loveliness shall wake
   Your cold and wintery day.

' Sing to the Lord, even ye, who pant
   Beneath the burning line,
Where Nature faints, and savage beasts
   To war with man combine:—

Sing! for a living stream shall flow,
   To cheer your thirsty land,
And fresher airs and cooler shades
   Along the waste expand.

'Sing to the Lord, ye isles that rise
   From the north-western wave,
Where icebergs float, and stormy winds
   In wrathful howlings rave:—
Sing! for a blissful calm shall come
   Upon the sweeping blast,
And a bright summer shall adorn
   Your frozen shores at last.

'Sing to the Lord, ye isles afar
   That stud the southern deep,
Where on the boundless ocean waves
   Your spicy odours sleep:—
Sing! for a voice of music yet
   Your lonely shores shall reach,
And o'er the fathomless abyss
   The bridge of Love shall stretch.

   *   *   *   *   *

'Sing to the Lord, ye slaves forlorn,
   On continent and isle,
For the light of Freedom's dawning morn
   On you yet soon shall smile.

'Sing to the Lord, ye prisoners
   Of Power's unhallowed sway,
Who groan beneath an iron load,
   To Tyranny a prey:—

Sing! for the walls are shaken
   Which guard your cells around,
And the lightning gathers in the cloud
   To dash them to the ground.

' Sing to the Lord in every clime
   On earth or ocean-isles,
Where endless winters freeze, and where
   Perpetual summer smiles:—
Sing! for the time is drawing nigh
   When Nature shall assume
The robe of innocence again,
   And like an Eden bloom.'

In a piece founded on Christ raising the widow's son of Nain, embedded among some very dull versifying, are two or three stanzas on A Mother's Love, which we do not think will be readily surpassed in beauty by anything that has been written on the subject—a subject which comes home to the most sacred sympathies of every rightly feeling heart.

' A MOTHER'S LOVE.'

' Unlike all other things earth knows,
   (All else may fail or change,)
The love in a Mother's heart that glows,
   Nought earthly can estrange.
Concentrated, and strong, and bright,
   A vestal flame it glows
With pure, self-sacrificing light,
   Which no cold shadow knows.
All that by mortal can be done,
A Mother ventures for her son:

If marked by worth or merit high,
Her bosom beats with ecstasy;
And though he own nor worth nor charm,
To him her faithful heart is warm.
Though wayward passions round him close,
And fame and fortune prove his foes;
Through every change of good and ill,
Unchanged, a mother loves him still.
Even love itself, than life more dear,—
Its interchange of hope and fear;
Its feeling oft a-kin to madness;
Its fevered joys, and anguish-sadness;
Its melting moods of tenderness,
And fancied wrongs, and fond redress,
Hath nought to form so strong a tie
As her deep sympathies supply.
And when those kindred cords are broken
   Which twine around the heart;
When friends their farewell word have spoken,
   And to the grave depart;
When parents, brothers, husband, die,
   And desolation only
At every step meets her dim eye,
   Inspiring visions lonely,—
Love's last and strongest root below,
Which widowed Mothers only know,
Watered by each successive grief,
Puts forth a fresher, greener leaf:
Divided streams unite in one,
And deepen round her only son;
And when her early friends are gone,
She lives and breathes in him alone.'

In a piece designated 'Consolation,' founded on the words—'He hath said, I will never leave thee nor forsake thee,' occur the following lines :—

'Hast thou on Pleasure's sunny hill
  Been lulled to sleep in rosy bowers,
And only waked to drink thy fill
  Of happy Day Dreams 'midst its flowers?
And have they vanished like the dew,
  When by the wind the grass is shaken,
Or, as the passing shadow flew,
  Leaving the heart of hope forsaken?
Seek not again the airy height,
Where gay illusions cheat the sight;
But turn thee unto Him who gave
His life th' all hopeless else to save.
Did troops of friends when wealth was thine,
  With smiles and talk thy table throng,
And eat thy bread, and drink thy wine,
  And join with thee in dance and song—
But when along thy dark green leaf,
  The mildew of misfortune fell;
Fled they with speed thy home of grief,
  All lonely leaving thee to dwell?
Mourn not their loss—a craven crew
To Mammon's worship only true:
But turn thee to that faithful Friend,
Who loves his own—loves to the end;
In want or woe forsakes them never,
Sustains them now—enthrones for ever!'

CHAPTER III

CORRESPONDENCE RESPECTING THE PUBLICATION OF 'TALES AND SKETCHES OF THE SCOTTISH PEASANTRY'—COMPOSITION OF 'LECTURES ON PRACTICAL ECONOMY'—SUBMITTED TO DR. MURRAY—HIS OPINION—CONSEQUENT REMODELLING OF THE WORK—BUILDING OF THE HOUSE AT MOUNTPLEASANT—REMOVAL THITHER—DEATH OF A. BETHUNE'S FATHER—VERSES ON THAT EVENT.

I NOW return to the history of Mr. Bethune's first publication. 'Sometime in July 1836,' he informs us,* 'the manuscript of "Tales and Sketches of the Scottish Peasantry" was finished and taken to Edinburgh; but, had it not been for its falling into the hands of one who ever after proved a steady friend, it is highly probable it might have been brought back and burned in disgust.' The individual thus referred to, was a young man then engaged in one of the printing offices in Edinburgh; but one, as the reader will soon have occasion to perceive, whose powers of mind and accomplishments would then have qualified him to fill and adorn a far higher situation. I am sorry that this gentleman's mo-

---

* Life of John Bethune p. 63, note.

desty has disallowed me the gratification of introducing his name to the reader; but justice demands that I should say, that the importance of the literary service he rendered both to Alexander Bethune and his brother, it is impossible to estimate. He procured a publisher, both for 'Tales and Sketches of the Scottish Peasantry,' and for 'Practical Economy.' Not only did he subject to a most careful and searching revision the manuscripts of these works, but also the manuscripts of all the tales contributed by both the brothers to ' Wilson's Tales of the Borders,' as well as the 'Life of John Bethune.' Indeed, there cannot be a doubt, but the general propriety of expression and purity of style, which Alexander Bethune attained, were in no small measure owing to his free and enlightened criticisms. The elements of mind necessary to constitute a classical writer were possessed by Mr. Bethune, but they needed some training and correction—as it would have been more than marvellous, considering his situation and limited advantages, if they had not. He needed a medium through which his works might reach the public with an every way graceful effect; and there could not have been a fitter than he found in the friend to whom these remarks refer. In these circumstances, I deem no apology necessary for drawing pretty largely from a correspondence which arose out of such a relation. The circumstances which led to the commencement of this correspondence and consequent friendship, are indicated in the following letters and extracts. It may be necessary to premise in explanation, that when Mr. Bethune visited Edinburgh on his literary adventure, he had been charged with some message from an aunt to a family in Leith. The first person whom he met with in delivering that message, was a brother of his future friend, from whom he experienced such kindness that he was induced to leave his manuscript with him: to him, therefore, the first of the following letters is addressed. His future friend he did not at that time see.

'LOCHEND *Jan.* 17*th* 1837.

'Dear sir,—As I have changed my place of residence since I saw you in July last, I now write to acquaint you with the circumstance. If the manuscript of which you kindly took charge, has proved, or should prove, of such a nature that no publisher will run the risk of printing it, I would beg leave to suggest, as the readiest, and perhaps the safest conveyance for its return, the "Fife Defiance" coach, which leaves Campbell's Hotel, No. 22, Prince's street, Edinburgh, three times a week, and passes this neighbourhood on its way to Perth. Instead of Inchrye (as formerly) my address must now be— To be left at Glenburnie: Alexander Bethune, Lochend, by Newburgh.

As there is at present, no great chance of our meeting soon again, and as this may be the last occasion I may have for writing you, I cannot let it pass without giving expression to that feeling of gratitude which I still retain for the kindness I experienced when I was your guest. In the words of Scripture, "I was a stranger, and ye took me in!" Be the result of my journey what it may, I do not, and never can, repent my coming to Edinburgh. The magnificent buildings, the enchanting landscape, and, above all, the hospitality, and friendly attention which I received, are things not easy to be forgotten. Give my best respects to your father, of whom my aunt's eulogiums would induce me to think well though I had never seen him; and be so kind as tell him, that I have still before me, a vivid recollection of his frank manner, and candid and truth-speaking countenance. To him my best wishes are due, for the friendly advice which he so frankly bestowed.'

'A. B.'

For a reason which will immediately appear, this communication was not answered by the person to whom it was addressed but by our author's future literary friend.

'EDINBURGH *March* 1, 1837.

'Dear Sir,—Your letter to my brother of the 17th January, would have been acknowledged ere this time, had not that duty devolved upon me, in consequence of a most serious accident which happened to him, about the middle of January. During the severe frost that then prevailed, he fell, and dislocated his ancle—a misfortune which, after a protracted period of intense suffering and imminent danger, has at length terminated (on the 1st ult.) in amputation of the limb below the knee. He has come through all, however, with the greatest fortitude, and is now fairly out of danger and doing well, although a long time must elapse ere he can be restored to a state fitted to resume his wonted occupations. This melancholy event will, I have every reason to believe, form an apology as painful to you as it is abundant for him.

'For the neglect with which, I am ashamed to confess, your manuscripts have certainly been treated, I am alone responsible, my brother having immediately after he received them, consigned them to me, as one more likely than himself, to get them advantageously disposed of. The gentleman to whom I immediately thought of offering your manuscript (viz. Mr. Shortrede, an Edinburgh printer) was so busy, that I did no more at that time than simply mention the circumstance of such manuscripts being in my possession, declining to press them on him, when his hands were full otherwise, and preferring to wait until the completion of his other engagements might permit him the more readily to come to a bargain. During this long interval, I have had ample opportunity of perusing the stories, and have thereby been enabled, heartily and conscientiously, to recommend them to Mr. Shortrede, who has agreed to print and publish the volume at his own risk, allowing the author fifty copies in boards, by way of price for the absolute copywright of the work. When published, it will in all probability sell at from three to four shillings a copy. Mr. Shortrede is still so much engaged, that I cannot state specifically when the work will be gone on with; but he wishes it to be understood as another condition of his bargain, that he be allowed to print at his leisure.

'Considering that such works are not in general a very marketable commodity, the trade being at all times inundated with myriads of a similar description, I conceive the above to be a tolerably handsome offer; particularly as I do not believe there exists another publisher in Edinburgh who would undertake even the risk of printing, &c. the sale of such books about town, being in almost all cases very meagre. They meet the readiest market in the country trade, with which Messrs. Fraser & Co. (Mr. Shortrede's publishers) have the advantage of a constant communication. The name of the printer is the best guarantee for the neatness of the typography, and that of the publishers, for general outward appearance. I shall endeavour also to procure notices of the work, in the Edinburgh, and perhaps some of the provincial newspapers. Should you feel disposed to close with the terms I have proposed, you can communicate your wishes to me at your leisure.

'The title of the work, though in itself facetious and quaint, is I think, susceptible of improvement;

for "The Watchman's Grave," is in my opinion, neither the most conspicuous, nor the best story. Long titles are agreeable to neither eye nor ear; and the one in question would be vastly improved were it more simple, concise, and explanatory of the contents. I would suggest that " Tales and Sketches of the Scottish Peasantry," be simply adopted; * * * * and your own name and occupation in life be substituted; for, besides the attraction this would be to the public, the author has no reason to be ashamed of his " brain-child." The preface is excellent. I have read over all the tales with much pleasure, deriving both amusement, and instruction from them. They throw light on many portions of the character of the Scottish peasant, which have hitherto remained in obscurity, and betray in the writer an acquaintance with human nature which could only be attained by shrewd personal observation. The story of the " Deformed," for instance, is quite original in its way. I do not recollect of ever having seen a character like that of " Hirplin Hugh" sketched before; and yet there is scarcely a village in all Scotland but can furnish a similar one. It is admirably portrayed. Indeed, all the stories are exceedingly good, being no more than copies from breathing nature, executed with fidelity, feeling, and that unaffected simplicity of language which is an essential attribute of works of far higher pretension. Should your little work meet the encouragement it certainly merits, I hope you will continue to persevere in the course you have so promisingly begun.'

'LOCHEND, *March* 11*th*, 1837.

'DEAR Sir,—I received, a few days ago, your letter of the 1st March; and I should have felt the most perfect pleasure in acknowledging it, had it not been for that—to me—painful piece of information which occupies a part of the first page. I never supposed myself remarkable for acuteness of feeling, and yet, I can scarcely tell how much your brother's misfortune has affected me. When I came to Leith last summer, I was a perfect stranger; I was acquainted with no human being, and I had not the slightest hope of meeting with any one to advise or befriend me. I was, moreover, perfectly ignorant of every thing connected with the business in which I was to be engaged; and, during the greater part of the morning, I felt a sort of depression from the circumstances in which I was placed, relieved only at intervals by an inclination to smile at the quixotic expedition I had undertaken. Upon the whole, I had no reason to congratulate myself upon my prospects; and it was only a consciousness that I had staked nothing upon the chances of success, which made the early part of that day at all tolerable. But, as Fortune would have it, I had been commissioned by my aunt to call at the shop in Leith, and made this the first part of my business, instead of the last, as had been at one time intended. Your brother was the first person I addressed; and there was a something in the unaffected frankness of his manner which gave me, almost with the first sentence he spoke, a favourable idea of his heart and general character; and after a short conversation, I could no longer resist the impulse which prompted me to communicate the occasion of my journey, and ask his advice as to the manner in which I should proceed. I did so; and I need not say how readily he interested himself in my concerns, nor need I recapitulate, though I can never forget, his kindness in afterwards conducting me through "the streets and closes, castles and palaces," of your "Modern Athens." But after what I have narrated, it can scarcely be matter of wonder if the painful question should often intrude—Is the individual who did all this, and who was then hale and healthy, now dismembered—deprived of part of one of those limbs which he used so willingly and well in pointing out the wonders of what was then to me a new world? I feel strangely inclined to dwell upon this painful subject. I too have been a sufferer from accidents, more than one of which had nearly proved fatal; and "Misfortune's sons are brothers in distress." I might say, that I rejoice at the fortitude which he has displayed under his sufferings; but, in truth, I can rejoice at nothing connected with a misfortune the consequences of which to him must be permanent. I hope, however, that it will not desert him till his health is fairly and fully re-established. Let me beg to be remembered to him, and to your worthy father.

'The business part of this communication may be soon settled. I look upon the offer which you have transmitted as every way satisfactory, and, when all the circumstances are taken into consideration, highly creditable both to Mr. Shortrede and yourself. I can therefore have no hesitation in accepting it; and I shall be most ready to enter into any agreement deemed necessary for the transfer of the absolute copyright. Concerning the fifty copies which I am to have, as, with the exception of perhaps two or three, they could be of no avail in this quarter, it would be better for me if some arrangement could be made for disposing of them, and allowing me to have the money. Perhaps this might be done without any loss to either of the parties.

'About "The Watchman's Grave" we are perfectly agreed. It was among the first written, and is by no means the most "conspicuous" of the stories: your remarks as to the propriety of excluding it from the title page are therefore perfectly just. "Dr. D———" and his fraternity may be dismissed without any ceremony. And with respect to the name, though I was decidedly averse to coming directly before the public as an author till their inclination to read what I had written could be ascertained, yet, if it were to be of any real service to the publisher in procuring a better market, I do not see any reason sufficiently strong for withholding it. My name and occupation, which is that of a labourer, might therefore be given, without mentioning anything as to my place of residence; and as there may be a number of individuals bearing the same name, of whom I, from local circumstances, am probably the most obscure, I might still escape observation. Concerning the time at which the work is to be printed, I am not, like some authors, fool enough to suppose that the stability of the world, and the salvation of its inhabitants, depend upon the printing of anything which I have written or may write; but I could wish it to be published as soon as convenient, for another reason: if the stories were to take, I might resume the same sort of writing; and time, to such a short-lived animal as man, is a thing of importance.

'I feel much indebted to you for the friendly criticism on my humble attempt at authorship with which you have favoured me; and also for the proposal which you have made of getting it noticed in the Edinburgh and provincial newspapers. Such notices, if properly managed, might produce a favourable effect, and, if I might speak my own opinion, I would say, that I know of no one so likely to succeed as yourself. My reason for saying so is simply this: if there is any merit at all in the stories, I think you have discovered where it lies; that is, in the development of some points of Scottish character in humble life, which have hitherto escaped the observation of those writers whose station in society placed them at too great a distance from the scene of action to admit of their discovering little peculiarities; and, as your own penetration has enabled you to make this discovery, I do think, that were you to take up, yourself, the office of critic, in one or two instances, you would be much more likely to draw public attention to the proper quarter, than if the task were left wholly to others. I have presumed to offer the above observations, partly from selfish motives, and partly from the idea, that by acting on them, you might render the publisher essential service, in lessening the risk which he must run in offering such a work to the public. Though I have thus been preferring my own wishes and opinions, perhaps too liberally, I am by no means insensible of the service which you have already done me, and I would not, upon any account, wish to press upon you what may perhaps be an irksome task—far from it. Pray remember me to your father and brother. With the misfortune of the latter I sincerely sympathize. And believe me to be, Dear Sir, yours truly,'

'A. B.'

While the fate of 'Tales and Sketches of the Scottish Peasantry' was in suspense, during the winter of 1836-7, the idea occured to the Messrs. Bethune of writing lectures on Popular or Practical Economy; and to this, with great zeal, they immediately applied themselves. A most interesting account of the composition of this work, and of the untoward circumstances in which it was produced, will be found in the Life of John Bethune.* The original views of the writers in undertaking it, are also indicated in the following letter, which I present to the reader, accompanied by the greater part of the answer returned by their literary friend—an answer replete with critical acumen and sound practical sense.

'LOCHEND, *July* 13, 1837.

'Dear Sir,—I am once more, as you will perceive, at my former work—that is, giving you new trouble in the old way. As the market for fictitious writing did not appear to be very ready, nor the rewards very tempting; as I had some spare time during the long evenings of last winter, which I was anxious to improve in some way or other; and wishing moreover to make myself useful, if possible, to that class to which I belong,—I was induced, in conjunction with my brother, to write Lectures on (what we have called) Popular Economy. These we had at first intended to deliver personally, as is stated somewhere in the accompanying manuscript; but somehow or other we abandoned this scheme, and resolved, after revising them, to submit them to you, as a friend, who having already performed a ser-

* Life and Poems of John Bethune, second edition, p. 63—71.

vice for one of the authors, might perhaps be prevailed on to extend his favour to both. To the last part of this resolution, as it involved no sacrifice, we have adhered; but no systematic revision has been attempted. When the winter evenings were gone, our time for such occupations was in a great measure gone also. But if revision is absolutely indispensable to their publication, by the assistance of a literary friend—one accustomed to write for the press—I think we might still accomplish it.

'With respect to the Lectures themselves, there are some parts of them which you will perhaps deem *ultra*, and others uncalled for; and yet we have adverted to nothing the tendency of which did not appear to us evidently bad. The station which we occupy however must have given us a view of some subjects rather different from that which has been presented to you; and this being the case, we cannot expect you to coincide in all our opinions, though with some of them I feel moderately certain that you will agree.

'As to the disposing of the manuscript, should it not answer the firm of Mr. Shortrede, which is highly probable, if you would show it to any other publishers in whose line of business it may more immediately lie, and try to collect their opinions as to what they would be willing to give, you would confer a very great favour on its authors. As we do not wish to dispose of the absolute copyright, we would prefer an offer for one or two editions, consisting of a limited number of copies. Offers however might be made both ways, if publishers were so inclined. And if an agreement could be made at an early period, it would be of considerable importance to us on the following account. My father and mother, through the caprice of an individual who has lately purchased the estate on which they live, must remove at the first term from the house which they have occupied for the last twenty-four years. They are now very infirm, and unable to bear the fatigue of either far or frequent removals, to save them from which, we have feued a small piece of ground near Newburgh, and are now busy making preparations for building a house for them. To accomplish this, we must perform at least one half of the mason and nearly the whole of the wright work ourselves; and even then, as materials at the cheapest are expensive, we shall hardly be able to finish it. Several circumstances have contributed to make our joint savings smaller than otherwise they would have been. Some serious accidents, by which I was incapacitated for work for a length of time—some attempts, perhaps foolish ones, to relieve the necessities of others, and the very trifling rewards for labour in this part of the country, often not more than 7s. or 7s. 6d. a-week,—these with the responsibility of providing for two aged individuals, for the last eight or ten years, have all been against us in the way of saving money. And though we have nearly enough for the outside work of our proposed erection—that is to say, though we can make it habitable—unless an additional sum can be procured, we cannot finish it within; and as this can never be done so conveniently afterwards, if anything could be made of the Lectures, it would be most acceptable at the present juncture.

'I would also be inclined to think the present a most favourable period for the publication of such a work: because, as people will not pay for medicine till they are aware of some disease; so, in other matters, they never think of seeking a remedy till they feel that they are suffering either from the effects of their own misconduct, or the misconduct of others. The distress which at present prevails in the manufacturing districts, and, in short, among the great body of the labouring population, is operating as a stimulus to enquiry. For this reason, if the work were ever to be published, I do think a publisher would find his account in pushing it forward.

'Dear Sir, I have now told you an "unvarnished tale." I have told you the plain truth, with the full conviction before me, that for a man to confess he is in want of money is, in other words, to tell the world that he is a fool, and deserves only to be treated with contempt; but as I have already experienced much kindness, and, withal, seen nothing of that policy, so frequently to be met with elsewhere, in the family to which you belong, I have done this without hesitation. I remain, Dear Sir, Your much-indebted, very humble servant, A. B.'

EDINBURGH, *July* 18, 1837.

'Dear Sir,—I hasten to acknowledge receipt of your pacquet, which reached me only last night, having been accidentally detained a day in my father's shop. Before adverting to its interesting contents, I have again to apologise for my long silence, and for the sickening delay in the publication of the Tales, which is well calculated to beget in you a suspicion of our supineness in the undertaking. This, however, is not the case—for the work would have proceeded with regularity and speed, had nothing occured to interefere with its progress. I did not think it would serve any purpose to communicate with you before the printing had begun; although now I blame myself for not having done so—as a few lines might have gone far to allay a feeling of anxiety proverbial to your tribe in like circumstances, and but too justifiable by the distressing circumstances in which I regret to learn you are placed.

'In a former communication you mentioned, and, in your last it is painfully apparent, that the price of the books would be much more acceptable to you than the books themselves. I showed Mr. Shortrede your letter. He expressed himself perfectly willing to accede to the terms you preferred, and said he would remit the price of the first fifty copies that could be disposed of. So far this was satisfactory. But as it is evident from your last, that in present exigences even a portion of the price would be of service to you, I represented the matter to Mr. Shortrede, who has directed me to enclose you five pounds to account of the price of the copyright of the Tales. I hope this will afford you some relief. You can acknowledge receipt in your next communication. By the way, I think it would be more to your advantage were you to give up the idea of making a bargain with Mr. Shortrede. I would recommend you simply to hand over to him the copyright of the Tales as a gift, leaving the price to his own liberality. As I will guarantee the value of the fifty copies, you can be no loser by such a step; and should the book succeed, the author will not be forgotten.

'The first of the Tales is now in types, a proof of which I send you herewith; not certainly for your revision, as that would create delay and expense—but as a specimen of the internal appearance of the book, and to convince you that something has been done with it. I have taken considerable liberties with your lucubrations, as you will perceive, but not to the extent I meditate, although sufficient, I doubt not, to convince you that we "trusty brothers of the trade" do not look upon you authors as immaculate any more than ourselves. The arrangement I have entirely altered—and, contrary to the usual custom, have placed the " Deformed" foot foremost. Whether I am right in this or not, is a different question; but the sketch is a good one in the main—and there is no great harm if it should be succeeded by a better. The herione I have also thought proper to re-christen, having substituted "Lilias" for "Lizzy," as infinitely more poetical and pleasing to "ears polite," and withal equally Scottish. There are some parts of your style of composition which I consider faulty, which may be apparent to any one going over your pages less critically than I have done. In many places it is redundant, expressing in a round-about, heavy manner what might have been much more clearly and effectively stated in a very few words. The introductory part of the "Deformed," for instance, appears to me to be incoherent and patched; as if the writer had not, in writing it, implicitly adhered to the rule of first knowing his own meaning, and then stating it as clearly as possible to the comprehension of his reader—eking and cobbling it occasionally as new ideas were suggested by the subject. It is mouthy, *i. e.* it is too like those concocted harangues, "full of sound and fury," which are so frequently delivered at public meetings. It is flighty and figurative to excess; and it would have been more adapted to the place it occupies, had it been clothed in the simplicity which is so becoming in a homely narrative. As it stands, it is like introducing a simple ballad with a flourish of drums and trumpets. It is an attempt beyond yourself, in which, with all deference, I think you, in common with all who have made such attempts, have failed. I cannot alter it for the life me: in the words of Ben Jonson, "a sponge dipt in ink would do the business." It is not to be compared with the description of Hugh's childhood; and why? simply because you copied the one from nature, and produced a graphic and true picture; while the other is an attempt to portray some dim and indistinct notions floating in your mind, which you yourself did not understand—producing a hypothesis made up of a compilation of trite sentences strung together in sounding language. However, if it cannot be altered and smoothed down, it may stand as it is; for there is a glitter about it that will please the multitude. This inflated style prevails in several other portions of the story, which are sufficiently pointed out by the corrections. I have also to object to the frequent use you make of long-winded words—such as "absinthiated," which is more than once introduced. It is seldom to be met with in modern literature, particularly in works of fancy; and therefore, all such obselete terms I humbly think, it would be advisable to avoid. Instead of producing the effect contemplated, they only impart stiffness to composition. Another complaint is, that frequently the same idea is twice stated in a sentence; and yet couched in such terms that you must have been quite unconscious of it yourself. One, amongst several instances, occurs at p. 42 of proof, where the very same, very simple conclusion is mystified by an unnecessary repetition of the same idea. I need not recommend you to adopt that simplicity of style which constitutes the perfection of Addison, Goldsmith, Scott, &c.; for the evidence borne by portions of your writings is sufficient to convince me that you can do it well; but it is a mistake, if you think you improve the vigour of your narrative, or the force of your argument, by couching it in high-flown or verbose language. Something must also be done with the advocate's address to the jury, which is in some respects unlawyer-like, and to which many of the above remarks are more or less applicable. The beginning of it particularly must be condensed—somewhat after the fashion of the paragraph I have written, although it is not the thing either. I have not gone over the whole of the story, but will have done so by the time of your arrival here, should you come. The introduction of more dialogue throughout the tale would have considerably relieved the heaviness which generally prevails in mere narrative.—The blemishes I have thus in a general way endeavoured to point out have, perhaps, been treated rather harshly, considering how trifling they are; but you will allow that it is much better they should be so handled before publication, than be left to the merciless cutting and maiming of small literary anatomists when the book gets into the hands of the public. It is not my province to notice any of the beauties of the story here, nor can my opinion be of any moment; and yet I may be permitted to observe, that it appears to me to be a picture from nature—from real life; containing much original observation—" a quality to which," as Sir Walter Scott has somewhere remarked, " all other qualities are as dust in the balance." I was at one time thinking to add mottoes to the Tales respectively, if it did not give them too bibliographic an air. It could be easily done. One, for instance, to the following tune, occurs in the Twelfth Night, and is somewhat appropriate to " The Deformed"—

> " In nature there's no blemish, but the mind;
> None can be called deformed, but the unkind:
> Virtue is beauty; but the beauteous-evil
> Are empty trunks, o'erflourish'd by the devil."

The lines in Gray's Elegy, beginning,

> " Let not ambition mock their humble toil,
>   Their homely joys and destiny obscure,
> Nor grandeur hear with a disdainful smile
>   The short and simple annals of the poor."

although stale enough are yet highly appropriate to the book, and might, if a better cannot be found, be inserted in the title page. I think it would not be out of place, to put some small prefatory paragraph at the beginning of the volume, alluding to the author and his position in the world, without, of course, mentioning localities. I think it would be extremely proper to do so—for many would be inclined to read and purchase a book written under so many disadvantages as you have experienced;

and I think it would be your interest,—for while people might willingly acknowledge your tales to be as good as the generality of such productions, when they knew the humble quarter from which they emanate, they would be thought extraordinary productions in the circumstances—as I think they truly are. Therefore, something brief, manly, and to the point (not after the fashion of those quacks who frequently venture before the public with poverty and want of education as their sole recommendation) might very properly be adopted. If you think favourably of this, you can furnish me with materials, and I shall try to put them together in the language of a second person. I think I shall get Robert Chambers to notice the book when it comes out, which may be of some use. I calculate the whole affair will make a volume of about 400 pages, and the price in all likelihood will not exceed four shillings. I think my father may dispose of a good many copies, and a few of my own acquaintances, who feel interested in the book, will become purchasers; and, in one way or another, I think we will contrive to annihilate the fifty copies amongst us, and then the publishers may do the rest themselves. Some delay has already taken place in correcting the proofs; and still farther delay must be incurred in going carefully over the manuscripts—which method I prefer, in order to save the very great expense of correcting in the types. I shall, however, get on with them as diligently as my scanty leisure will permit, and endeavour to keep the compositors at work.

'Into the Lectures, of course, I have as yet had no opportunity of looking farther than a slight glance here and there. I like the project well enough, and think it would do very well, provided you do not get too red-hot in your political speculations. A plain, common-sense, practical dissertation on Economy—that sure but severe nurse of present independence and future opulence—suited to the necessities of the classes for whom it is intended, would be of the highest service in promoting their comfort and happiness; and could it be brought into effective operation, and subdue the stubborn predilections of human nature which custom has rendered almost invulnerable, you would do more for the welfare of a portion of mankind, at least, than all the reform schemes that have ever been concocted. "We think too meanly of those things which habit has made common, otherwise we should correct many of them." So said Henry Mackenzie, the Man of Feeling; and he never said any thing more simply and beautifully true. I do not think it the province of such a treatise as the title of your book professes, to trench on the dangerous field of high political speculations. In these fiery times, we have too many wise-acres who " sit by the fire, and presume to know what is done in the capitol." Nor do I think that, moving in a sphere so circumscribed, you can be thoroughly qualified for such a task. But, with the talents for observation, and the power of industrious application, you possess, you are well calculated to succeed in the stern, practical topic you have chosen. I have sent the manuscripts to a professional gentleman of some eminence as a lecturer on political and other sciences; whose political opinions are somewhat akin to what I suspect your own to be, and who, consequently, will be more likely to judge favourably of the work. By his decision I would be inclined to abide in offering it to any publisher. I mentioned to Mr. Shortrede what I had done, of which he approved; and should the report of the referee be favourable, and the book be in consonance with Mr. Shortrede's views, and in unison with the tenor of the generality of the works which issue from his press—or rather, should it be such as no man of any political party or creed, whatsoever can object to reasonably—he, I think, will publish it himself. However, a short time will put it to rest. I am almost as anxious as yourself that both it and the Tales should be published as speedily as possible, and will forward their progress as far as lies in my power. Your anxiety for its publication, as far as regards yourself, is most natural, but not equally well founded, I think, in reference to those whom you expect it shall benefit; and although there is no denying the general truth of your aphorism, that few people think of a dose of salts till they have a pain in the stomach, yet there is one part of its applicability you seem to have forgotten. Be it remembered, that the present distress in the agricultural and manufacturing districts has arisen from the inclemency of last season and extensive failures at home and abroad; and although there is no denying that the operatives, who suffer most from these calamities, would have been better enabled to withstand the depressions of the time, had they beforehand acted up to the doctrines your book preaches, and laid by money to meet an exigency like the present,—yet I do not think it would be of so much use to them after the blow has fallen, when they are experiencing the truth of your doctrine—nor of any very great benefit to you, when they have not a morsel to put in their mouths, far less coin to purchase a book. However, this is no objection to publishing the book at this or any other crisis; for if its merits are such as are likely to benefit society, it will sell more or less successfully at any time.

'In the remarks I have thus ventured to make on your labours, I have adopted the recommendation contained in your last—that of delivering my thoughts freely; and if any of my strictures appear to you hyper-critical, or prove wrong, I must just take refuge under that convenient shelter—the frailty of human reason. In whatever light, however, your productions may be regarded, there can be but one opinion as to your perseverance; and, I assure you, I scarcely know whether the regret I feel for the severe trials you have had to encounter, equals a sense of wonder at the intrepid industry you have displayed among so many embarrassments. To compose a work consisting principally of facts, and requiring so much time and labour, must in any case be a heavy undertaking; but under so many disadvantages, and in so short a period, I certainly look upon it as a triumph of the mind. The benefits usually derived from such labours, and those likely to accrue to you, I am sorry to confess, are seldom or never adequate to repay the talent, and what is more valuable to you, the time and labour expended upon them. As the world wags in these our times, the value of a thing consists, not in its intrinsic merit or absolute utility, but in what it will bring; and books are no exemption from the fact. Indeed, since time began, there have no rewards been so proverbially precarious as those of literature—authors themselves even looking forward with more certainty and anxiety to the attainment of that incorporeal bubble, fame, than to more substantial benefits. I would not have you, therefore, be too sanguine as to the fruits you are likely to reap from your literary labours: at the utmost they cannot be much, and there are chances of none at all. But do not think I would discourage you in the exercise of the talents with which Nature has gifted you: "this is no world to hide virtues in," as Jack Falstaff has it; and I think you are bound to "let your light shine before men"—and women also,—provided you are contented to run the risk of a very uncertain, and at best, I fear, a very meagre remuneration. I merely mention all this to caution you against indulging in too high expectations; for bitter disappointment often follows. Yet merit often has its rewards, as Fortune her freaks; and I trust you will yet experience both. Your plan of disposing of editions instead of the copyright is good and prudent, providing a publisher can be found to agree to such terms. It is not often a publisher will undergo all the risk, and pay for an edition, unless in cases where the author has a name, or where the book is of a nature that is sure to take, or where it is one of standard popularity. However, by and bye, we shall see what Mr. Shortrede has to say to your terms. If the book turns out a lucrative source, it were a pity that the author should dispose of his hard work for little value. I will offer it to other publishers if it wont suit Mr. Shortrede.

'I am highly sensible, my dear sir, of the kindness which prompted you and your brother of the blood and the lyre to offer me the honour of a dedication; but however much reason I have to be proud of a compliment so flattering, I think there are many people on whom it would more gracefully sit, and who would do infinitely more credit to your taste and discrimination than the obscure individual on whom you have so kindly offered to confer it. My years are too few, and my standing too low, to support those "blushing honours" which best become the brows of known and respected worth. I should like to see your effusions. I hope you practice the art more as an amusement than in the expectation of gaining either riches or applause from it, however good they be. There is nothing at so low an ebb as poetry; and unless a poet could rise up, who would diverge from the beaten path, and strike boldly out into something original, he, like Macpherson, may break his fiddle and take the leap. There are some volumes of trash go down here occasionally; but it is by catering for subscriptions, and not in the legitimate way. However, something may perhaps be done with them—don't hide your candle.

'We shall be glad to see you when it shall be convenient for you to pay a visit to this quarter; and I hope you will not be in such a hurry home as you were last season. I have never had the pleasure of meeting you; although I think I have made a tolerable acquaintance with the man from his writings. There is no correspondence in which I have ever taken greater pleasure than in yours; and I hope long and frequently to enjoy it. If you have any of your neighbours who go to, or other opportunity of communicating with, Kirkaldy, I could leave proofs and such ware with my brother Charles, at the Bank of Scotland there, and you could do the same, where they might be called for, and so avoid the expense of postages and carriage. My brother comes over here once a fortnight, and will be here to-morrow; so you know how to regulate, providing this plan would suit you.

'I remitted a draft on Newburgh for £5, which I hope reached you safe. I have been unable to finish this scrawl sooner. My father and brother are well—the latter about to betake himself to the country, to practise walking on a wooden understanding. They both desire to be remembered to you and Katy.'

The first draft of the the Lectures on Practical Economy, was tinged to a considerable extent with politics of a rather violent kind. The reasons which had induced the writers to give them this complexion, are graphically stated in the following letter, in answer to the one just inserted, the earlier part of which shows the excellent spirit in which the subject of this memoir had received the criticisms of his friend. Indeed, during the whole of that literary correspondence of which the reader has just seen the commencement, one knows not well which most to admire:—the fidelity and freedom, yet respectful dignity with which strictures were offered and suggestions tendered on the one hand, or the good feeling in receiving, and the readiness to be corrected shown on the other.

'LOCHEND, *July*, 31, 1837.

'Dear Sir,—Though I acknowledged the receipt of your letter of credit in my last, I cannot forbear again recurring to the subject. Such a letter was perfectly unexpected by me; and I fear I must have given you a good deal of trouble in a quarter where I intended to give you none. I did not wish to urge Mr. Shortrede about either the publication of the Tales, or anything which he might think proper to give for them, and therefore I carefully avoided mentioning the matter in the letter which accompanied the Lectures. The money, however, is well come, and will be of considerable service, by and by. The promptness, moreover, with which you have anticipated the demand which we must necessarily have for this important article, deserves something more than a mere profession of gratitude—it deserves to be remembered. I would not however, have you to imagine, from anything which I may have said, that we are really in embarrassed circumstances. We have been too long accustomed to navigate the sea of poverty, and are too well acquainted with its coasts and currents to run aground in an ordinary gale, or to be "taken aback" by a casual shifting of the wind. Do not therefore, I entreat you, give yourself any further uneasiness on this account. With the money which we now have, we can make our new cottage at least ten degrees better than the one which we now inhabit; that is, we can erect substantial walls, and cover them with a water-tight roof, the last of which is a luxury to which we have been strangers for many years.

'With respect to the copyright of the Tales, I have no objection whatever to your proposal, of " handing it over to Mr. Shortrede." But is there not a sort of anomaly in having first taken five pounds, and then offering it as a " gift?" I merely mention this for your consideration; and if you think there would be no impropriety in such an offer, it may be made without delay.

'I send you, along with this, an attempt to amend the introduction to the " Deformed;" it is, I think somewhat less mouthy than the other, and should you approve of it, (if the work is not too far advanced,) it may perhaps serve as a substitute. For your criticisms, alterations, and corrections, I feel deeply indebted. The trouble which you are taking in this way, bespeaks no ordinary degree of interest. I have always been inclined to regard a friend who could point out an error, and at the same time lend his assistance in obviating it, as worth at least twenty thousand flatterers. Your observation about the " cutting and maiming of small literary anatomists," is a good argument for a severe scrutiny, previous to publication. Correct with the " spunge dipt in ink" where nothing else will do. Had it been winter, as it is summer, a pair of scissors and a coal fire might have been as effective. By adopting such a plan, some ink might be saved, and some additional warmth imparted to a room—perhaps about a thousandth part of a degree of Fahrenheit. This idea could hardly have occurred to any one except a Lecturer on Economy! but now that it is fairly suggested, it may be of some service in the proper season. The "re-christening" of the heroine I consider in itself as a vast improvement upon the whole story. "A commodity of good names," as Sir Walter Scott observes, "is often very difficult to be had;" and for this reason, I look upon the alteration which you have made as the more valuable. Of the other alterations which you have made, it would be mere waste of time for me to say more than that most of them are evident improvements, though in a few instances, I think I should have almost been led to prefer the old way, even if it had not been my own. For example, the new address to the jury, though considerably condensed, appears to me to be less in keeping with the style of special pleading, than the old. But this is nothing, or at most, only a matter of taste; and I conclude this part of the subject without wearying you with further remarks.

'With respect to the mottoes I think they might very appropriately be added; and from the specimens which you have sent, I believe you will have no great difficulty in selecting suitable ones. As to the "prefatory paragraph" of which you speak, "at the beginning of the volume," I could easily furnish you with the materials, if I only understood what was to be the scope of it. If you mean a sketch of my previous career, the disadvantages under which I have laboured, and the difficulties which I have encountered—the only circumstances worth noticing, at least, those which would be most likely to produce any effect, such for instance, as my having been twice blown up with gunpowder in a quarry within three years, and beginning to write stories for amusement when I was too feeble to work, and my eyes too weak, from the scorching they had received, to admit of reading—these with the name, if any copies should ever reach this quarter, (a thing which cannot be altogether provided against,) would infallibly point out the individual to whom they alluded. For this reason, and as there is a sort of general interest, even in the simplest recital of such accidents, it were I think better on the title page to put " The author of no other book," for my name; in which case, the paragraph of which you speak might commence thus, " To enable the reader to judge more correctly of the present work, the publishers have thought proper to lay before him the following brief notice of its author, &c." By these means the disagreeable circumstance of apparently soliciting for the man, what might, perhaps with justice, be denied to the author, would be avoided. Altogether, the thing would appear less indelicate, and might be rendered more effective for the purpose which it is intended to serve. I may be wrong, however, in supposing this to be your meaning; but in case it should, I will, with my first leisure, draw together a few particulars from which you may select, if you think proper, and we shall have time to consider afterwards as to the propriety of the proposed alteration on the title page.

'I must now correct a slight mistake into which you seem to have fallen, with respect to the Lectures. You over-rate my "industry," in supposing that I am the sole author. My brother performed half the work, as the hand-writing will convince you, if ever you should again look into them. We were, however, both busy enough, for it was only in last January, if I may trust my memory, that they were begun. As to the political speculations which form a part of them,—in chemical phrase, they have been subjected not only to a "red," but to a *white* heat! The blast would have been withdrawn ere the process had arrived at this point, had it not been that there was no possibility of reaching the class for which they are intended, except through the medium of *white-heat* politics. Talk to them of religion, and they will put on a long face—confess that it is a thing of the greatest importance to all—and go away and forget the whole. Talk to them of education: they will readily acknowledge that "it's a braw thing to be weel learned," and perhaps, begin a lamentation, which is only shorter than the "Lamentations of Jeremiah" because they cannot make it as long, on the ignorance of the age in which they live; but they neither stir hand nor foot farther. When you are gone, they are silent on the subject, and the acknowledgement and the lamentation, are with them the alpha and omega of the matter. But only speak to them of politics, and their excited countenances and kindling eyes testify in a moment how deeply they are interested. If, moreover, you have anything new to tell them, or even a new face to put upon an old story, the thing will serve them for a subject of conversation among their companions for weeks to come; and they will hardly fail to narrate the whole as faithfully as they can to their wives and families, should they have such, with the return of every evening. Politics are therefore an important feature, and an almost indispensable element in such a work. Had it consisted solely of exhortations to industry, and rules of economy, it would have been dismissed with an "Ou-ay, it's braw for him to crack that way; but if he were whaur we are, deed he wad just hae to do as we do." Thus, with most readers, the principles which the work was intended to teach, would be at once put aside, without so much as a trial—executed according to Cupar justice, before they could even be condemned. But by mixing up the science with politics, and giving it occasionally a political impetus, a different result may more reasonably be expected. In these days, no man can be considered a patriot or a friend of the poor, who is not also a politician. Every one who would wish to draw public attention must dabble in this science; at least, he will procure it most easily by such a course.

But to do so does not require the adoption of revolutionary principles; and the politics of the work in question, however violent they may appear, cannot without an uncommon stretch of imagination be supposed, even by the most timid, to have such a tendency, though by reading detached portions, one might be led to suspect something of the kind. The ultimate tendency of the whole was intended to be, and I think is, to convince the masses that if they will not reform themselves, as it is not the province, so neither is it in the power of others to confer any efficient reform. My brother has attacked the Corn-Laws I believe with some severity; and I have attempted to level a battery against that sort of servile homage which the poor are accustomed to bestow on the rich. The former, whatever inconveniencies their immediate abolition might create, cannot, so far as I can judge, be defended on principles of strict justice; and the bad effects of the latter upon both classes, should by this time be evident to every one who, with only common powers of observation and a common acquaintance with human nature, is willing to direct his attention to the subject. These, if I mistake not, are the most objectionable portions of the work; and, to a certainty, they would give serious offence among the higher orders. But then it should be remembered that the work is intended to strike more directly at the root of pauperism, than anything which the most zealous supporters of the above mentioned class, so far as I know, have ever ventured to put forth; and as they are deeply concerned in having this evil diminished as much as possible, when their interest comes to be balanced against its politics, perhaps even they might be induced to pardon, though they could not be expected to approve. It should also be remembered, that, if by any justifiable means, we can contrive to confer property, of whatever kind, upon a greater number of individuals than were formerly possessed of it, by the same means we provide an additional guarantee for the preservation of internal peace, and the stability of our institutions. Every sort of property to be of any use must be protected; and those who have property which can only be protected by the laws, and which they may lose the moment these are infringed, will naturally exert themselves to preserve these laws in full force,—or if they are really bad, the probability is, that they will try to change them gradually and by constitutional means. But that state of society in which the whole of the wealth and property of a country is in the hands of a few, with a very large majority of its inhabitants steeped in ignorance and poverty, may always be reckoned dangerous; and it may easily be supposed that this danger will only be increased by the masses beginning to think. When want or some other cause forces reflection upon the improvident wretch, he looks up and sees others enjoying plenty, while he can scarcely live. Forgetting that his own improvidence has been the cause of his misery, and forgetting too, the means by which the plenty of his neighbour has been acquired, his selfishness, seconded by ignorance, leads him to conclude that there is injustice in the circumstance of being its possessor, and, having nothing to lose, he is easily prepared for playing a desperate game. He needs only some demagogue to stuff his head with some popular absurdities about community of property, or equality, to make him a most devoted revolutionist, and at the same time a sanguinary villain, ready to spill blood if an opportunity should offer. In our own country there are some individuals in this state of preparation for mischief; and to prevent more from getting into the same condition, and to induce as many as possible of the labouring classes to acquire property or money by all honourable means, was one of the objects which the writers of the Lectures had in view. For this purpose, those arguments which were considered most likely to operate, were brought forward, and all sorts of reforms have been either connected with, or made to depend as far as possible upon, economy.

'I feel much obliged by your friendly caution against being too sanguine in my expectations of success. The disappointment which often follows extravagant hopes is indeed a bitter drug. But I am too old in the ways of the world now, and have been too long the step-son of Fortune, to be much elated by appearances, or much depressed if they should turn out empty.

'I have now written, what is, for me, a very long, and, I fear, also, a sadly-cobbled letter. And as you hoped that I would read yours " before going to bed," I must now hope that you will put the critic to bed before you read mine, for I am conscious that it will not bear a critical reading; but, after the critic is dismissed, I trust the man will know how to pardon such defects. I have, moreover, been too long in getting this letter ready; but, of late, I have had so much to do, and my attention has been so taken up with other things, that I could not, by any possibility, manage it sooner. Hoping that this delay in returning the proof, will not occasion any serious inconvenience, I must now subscribe myself, as before, Dear Sir, Your much indebted, and very humble servant,

'A. B.'

The gentleman our author's literary correspondent mentions having sent the manuscript of the Lectures on Practical Economy to for an opinion, was my talented and worthy friend Dr. Thomas Murray, Lecturer on Political Economy. Ever the generous friend of humble merit, he entered into the views of our authors with regard to publication, with all his characteristic ardour and disinterestedness; and while doing ample justice to the various merits of what he justly characterized as, "in the circumstances, a work perfectly wonderful," he freely pointed out some defects and excrecences which he deemed quite unworthy of men of such capabilities, and of which he was most anxious to see the pages of their work cleared. In particular, he was desirous that it might be freed from every thing that had any "tendency to place one great class of society in hateful opposition to another." The position which the Bethunes had hitherto occupied—the constant struggle they had had to maintain in the world, and which had barely enabled them to procure the means of supporting existence, combined with some very ungenerous and even unjust treatment they had experienced from persons in the possession of wealth, had tended to fret their minds, and led them to look with a rather unfavourable eye on the upper and more affluent ranks of society. The poor who only catch a passing glimpse of the rich, as well as the rich who only catch similar glimpses of the poor, must necessarily acquire but one-sided and very imperfect notions of the character of each respectively. A freer and a larger measure of intercourse among the various classes of society is much to be desired, on account of the correcting and softening influence which would thus be exercised on the views and feelings of each, in regard to the others: an effect of this kind was certainly produced on the subject of this memoir. When his intercourse with persons in the middle rank of life became more extended, and was carried on under more auspicious circumstances, he saw reason very much to modify those unfavourable views of their general character which he had been early led to entertain. He found that selfishness and contempt of the poor, were far from being such general characteristics of the rich as he had once supposed. The expostulations and advice, and not least, the silent influence of his two excellent Edinburgh friends, no doubt tended powerfully to produce this happy revolution in his views and feelings.

Dr. Murray's opinion of the Lectures was transmitted to their authors, through the medium of the friend so often referred to; on perusing which, they, in compliance with advice, wrote the Doctor the following letter.

'LOCHEND, *August* 16, 1837.

'Respected Sir,—We have been kindly favoured, by Mr. ——— with a copy of your remarks upon our little work on Popular Economy; and we beg leave to assure you, that we consider ourselves highly honoured by obtaining a report so favourable, from a gentleman so well qualified to judge of it. We regard the praise which you have bestowed upon some parts of the Lectures, and the generous manner in which you have expressed an interest in their authors, as indicative of that benevolence of disposition which is the noblest characteristic of a great philosopher. Our little work was composed under considerable disadvantages; and it must, consequently, exhibit many imperfections. We are, therefore, deeply indebted to you for the trouble which you have taken and are now taking, to point out the errors and unsound doctrines which it may contain. We are quite aware that men's minds are often insensibly influenced by the circumstances with which they are surrounded; and we believe, that a moral question, as well as a physical object, may present a very different appearance by being viewed from a different position. We are therefore prepared to acknowledge, that the circumstances in which we have been placed, may have led us into many mistakes, which your superior knowledge and better opportunities of observation, will enable you to discover. We may farther remark, that, in some parts of the work, we felt it necessary to adapt our discussions, in some measure, to the condition of those for whose use it was principally intended. We do not suppose, for instance, that the proposals contained under the head of " A New System of Combination," present any improvement upon the common arrangements of society; but we are inclined to think, that they have a tendency to attract the attention of the operatives from those ruinous schemes in which they have lately been engaged, and which they are not likely to abandon, unless some other object of pursuit be presented to their view. It occurred to us, that it would be more honourable, and less dangerous, for them to attempt their purpose by fair competition, than to continue to employ those compulsory means by which they have endeavoured to accomplish it. Similar motives have operated strongly upon our minds in various other parts of the work. It is our sincere desire to free our pages from all such matter as may be calculated to excite unfriendly feelings between the different classes of society. We would be glad to see the principle of social intercourse and brotherly kindness more extensively cultivated by all branches of the family of mankind.

'We have read over, with the greatest satisfaction, the abstract of your Lectures, which you were so kind as send for our perusal; and we were highly gratified to discover, that our ideas of a science moderately abtruse, coincide so nearly with those of a gentleman whose name must attract attention to, and confer importance upon, the doctrines which he advocates. That individuals, placed in situations so very different, and treating of the same subject without any previous knowledge of each other's opinions, should arrive so nearly at the same conclusions, is much more wonderful than that they should differ on some points. We shall only add, that we conceive it to be no small honour to know that we have, unconsciously, adopted principles so similar to your own; and, trusting that these principles may yet be more widely disseminated and more generally acted upon, We remain, Respected Sir, your much obliged, humble servants,   A. & J. BETHUNE.'

This Letter was accompanied by one to their literary friend, from which the following are extracts. It may be premised, in explanation, that Dr. Murray had promised to write more extended and specific remarks on the 'Lectures,' with a view to assist their authors in a thorough revision.

'LOCHEND, *August* 14, 1837.

'Dear Sir,—The kindness of Dr. Murray, and the promptitude with which he has interested himself in the fate of the "Lectures" and the success of their authors, is really extraordinary. That an individual in his station, reaping fame from his labours in teaching the same science, should notice such a work at all, is much; that he should have done so with the candour which his letter displays, bespeaks a mind uncommonly free from the prejudices of caste and profession; and that he should speak of any part of it in terms so flattering, is more than our most sanguine expectations could have warranted. We are fully aware of the importance of such an opinion as his, and also of the debt we owe to you for having procured it; and his written remarks which I trust will be ready by and by, with whatever objections he may have to any part or parts of the work, will be most carefully considered by us. The greatest drawback, I fear, will be the want of time to alter and rewrite, between this and the end of autumn—the period at which you hint the work should be ready for publication. At present our life, in point of labour, differs but little from that of galley-slaves. We leave home by five o'clock every morning, and it is always nearly eight in the evening before we can accomplish our return. After being thus disciplined for the day, the mind becomes inert, and unfit for following out any connected train of thinking : indeed mine is sufficently so at present, as I believe this letter will testify, from the effects of an attack of influenza, or some such complaint, which tied me hand and foot the other day; and so far from having the two hands and two feet of which I am at present possessed thus rendered useless, I should be the better for four hands, like the fabled giants, and at least as many feet, if they could enable me to walk any faster : as for more heads, unless they should be better than the thing I have just now upon my shoulders, I think they would be only a burden.—Pardon this trifling. I can write nothing at present, and therefore I am writing anything.—Harvest too is coming on, and as I am engaged for the season, and must work at least fourteen hours every day, while it lasts, with one hour more of travelling, I fear I shall be able to do little in a literary way ; but nevertheless, return the "Lectures" as soon as Dr. Murray's opinion of them can be got ready, and we will use our utmost endeavours to make them less objectionable and more suited to his views,—after which they will fall into your own hands to be ex-punged and ink-spunged as you may think proper.

'Along with this, I send you some "Lines Written in the prospect of Leaving Early Haunts." They were produced last year, when that prospect was real though the event did not then take place, and they may now serve to give you some idea of that habitation which we are about to leave. They cost some trouble and yet I think they would require to be revised. I send also, " The Voice of the Wind" and " A Poor Man's Funeral." These three would form part of the proposed " Pictures of Poverty," of which there are a number of others, if I had time to search them out. But as the Muses—good women—were never set to such work before, I will take the censure which such things may deserve upon myself, leaving them free to reap the harvest of fame elsewhere. Your deeply indebted and very humble servant, A. B.'

At Martinmas, 1835, John Bethune had obtained the situation of overseer at Inchrye, and nothing better, it appears, offering, his brother Alexander had accompanied him in the capacity of subordinate assistant. This appeared for a short time to afford a little brightening to their fortunes. John's income was more liberal than he had hitherto realized, and the labour of both would probably be less ungrateful than much they had had to submit to. Early, however, in the ensuing summer, the lands passed into the hands of a new proprietor, and almost immediately the overseer received intimation that his services would not be required beyond the year for which he was engaged. The house at Lochend, where they had resided from boyhood, was situated on this property, and in a short time they received notice from the new proprietor that it too must be quitted. The feelings of both the brothers seem to have been deeply wounded by the treatment they received from this individual; and certainly, to say the least, in the course he pursued towards them he does not seem to have shown much sympathy with humble worth, not to speak of earning for himself laurels as a patron of literature. With minds galled by this, and somewhat similar treatment received by the younger of the brothers in another quarter,[*] it was no great wonder if the first draft of 'Lectures on Practical Economy,' the production of the ensuing winter, was tinged with some asperity in regard to the wealthier classes.

Having thus, as the reader will have gathered from the preceding correspondence, to look out for a new habitation, and wishing to obtain one in the occupation of which they would not be liable to be disturbed by the caprice of a proprietor, they obtained a feu of a piece of ground (one-fourth of an acre) from D. Maitland Macgill Crichton Esq., of Rankeillour, on the Back-hill of Ormiston, better known by the name of Mountpleasant, immediately above the town of Newburgh. Here, in the summer

---

[*] See Life of John Bethune, second Edition, p. 65—67.

of 1837, by 'desperate exertion and economy,' they reared a house of two stories, thirty-six feet in length, by twenty in breadth, performing great part both of the mason and wright work with their own hands; which they were obliged to do, or involve themselves deeply in debt, having had only £30. in money and two bolls of meal to commence with. Notwithstanding the little assistance they were able to obtain from tradesmen, the building and fittings-up are substantial and workman-like; and this house, with its many interesting and many melancholy associations, will, it is to be hoped, remain for ages, not the least impressive monument of the indomitable energy, skill, and perseverance of these extraordinary brothers.

Hither the family removed on the 9th of November. The house, it is to be feared, was but in a very unfit state for being inhabited. The foundation had been laid only on the 26th of July, and it was near the end of September ere the ground-floor (an earthen one) was laid, and the walls plastered. So short a time intervening, and in the fall of the year too, the house must have been in a damp state when they came to occupy it—a circumstance which could not but operate very unfavourably on the health of the inmates. Of this there is a strong impression on the mind of Mr. Bethune's surviving aunt; and either she, or their kind neighbour, Mrs. Ferguson, remarked to the writer, that the family had never been all in the enjoyment of health after coming to occupy their new dwelling.

Early in December, the 'Lectures on Practical Economy' were returned to their authors, accompanied by the extended and very valuable criticisms of Dr. Murray, in which he recommended the omission of whatever bore on party politics, or indicated asperity of feeling. Along with his remarks he kindly sent them the printed abstract of his own Lectures, accompanied by a letter, in which he spoke of their 'ideas of Economy and Capital as being equally original and useful,' and stated that 'they were, so far as known to him, the first writers who had treated these subjects in a proper light.'

Our authors now set to work in earnest in re-modelling the Lectures agreeably to the suggestions they had received. For this the severe and protracted snow storm which began in the early part of January 1838, afforded them much leisure.

In the midst of their labours, however, the writers were interrupted by the demise of their father, who, after a few days' illness, died on the 8th February. He had long been in a very weakly state, and unable to perform any other than the lightest sort of out-door labour; and his sons, through all their misfortunes, had struggled hard to provide for his sustenance and comfort during his declining years, and, in particular, under their extraordinary exertions in rearing the house they now occupied, had been greatly sustained by the thought that they were preparing an asylum which he and their other beloved parent might enjoy in undisturbed possession during the remainder of their days. They little thought, probably, that the remaining days of one of these were to be so few.

Alexander's feelings on this occasion are recorded in some verses, among which the following occur:—

* * * * *

Shall I, Alas!

* * * * *

'No longer hear the friendly tone,
  Which welcomed me of yore
From many a wet and stormy day,
  At the paternal door?

'No longer see the evening fire,
  By thee replenished well,
As from the cold and biting frost
  I came, when evening fell?

'No longer see thy aged form
  Pass to the cottage door,
Or move, with gentle step, and slow
  Across the dusky floor,

'As from its place beyond the fire,
  Thou brought'st some ancient book;
Thy hand still firm, although thy head
  With a slight tremor shook?

' And can those hands, which busy still
    Some lighter task would ply,
Nor shrink from labour to the last,
    All cold and stiffened lie ?

' And can that eye, which still was bright
    Beneath its time-bleached brow,
Cold, lustreless, and lifeless, lie
    In the lone churchyard now ?

' Now in my ear a voice proclaims
    At morn, and noon, and night—
No more thy word, or look, or smile
    Shall make my heart feel light.

' No more for me thy task shall be,
    Dry clothing to prepare,
When Winter's drenching rain had made
    Such needful task thy care.'

*   *   *   *   *

CHAPTER IV.

PUBLICATION OF 'TALES AND SKETCHES OF THE SCOTTISH PEASANTRY'—FAVOURABLE NOTICES OF THE WORK—CORRESPONDENCE WITH LITERARY FRIEND AND DR. MURRAY—TERMS OF PUBLICATION OF 'PRACTICAL ECONOMY'—VISIT OF THE MESSRS. BETHUNE TO EDINBURGH—A. BETHUNE'S VIEWS AND FEELINGS IN REGARD TO HIS LITERARY LABOURS—CONNEXION WITH 'BORDER TALES'—'THE SISTERS'—DUBLIN UNIVERSITY MAGAZINE—PUBLICATION OF 'PRACTICAL ECONOMY'—NEGLECT OF THAT WORK.

THE following Letter from Mr. Bethune's literary friend, of date the 6th February, 1838, announced the publication of 'Tales and Sketches of the Scottish Peasantry'; as also the appearance of some highly favourable reviews and notices of the work:—

'*February* 6, 1838.

'My dear Sir,—The Tales are "just published," and I am proud to say, what I think you, with all who have seen it, will acknowledge—that the book is a handsome one. For one opinion—one valuable opinion, in which many with myself most sincerely and cordially concur—I refer you to Dr. Murray's Notice in the accompanying Newspaper, which does high credit alike to his discrimination, good taste, and generous, kindly feelings. In addition to this, my ears have, unobserved, drank the applause bestowed on your work by those whose opinions were worth having and unprejudiced. Its faults too have been commented on, you need not doubt; but these are few in number, and far more than counterbalanced by its beauties. I have already said too much on that score. Mr. ——— has willingly entered into the proposal that you should become a contributor to his Border Tales—and he has promised to send me a parcel for you ere this departs—and to it I refer you for particulars.—I have this moment been most agreeably interrupted by the entrance of a friend bearing the enclosed copy of the Athenæum, containing a review of the Tales. I cannot tell you whether I am most surprised or delighted at this most desirable circumstance. The paper is of very high literary standing in the metropolis; and as the review comes, unsolicited, from the pen of a stranger, you have great reason to be proud of it. But you can judge for yourself—and I will not take up your time with my chaff when you have so much good corn before you. This however, I may say—that since matters have turned out so favourably, or rather begun so auspiciously, I would not advise you rashly to close with Mr. ——— in any engagement which might in the smallest degree fetter your exertions in other literary undertakings. This may pave the way to a future volume of Tales; and I would not—at all events till it is seen how your volume succeeds—throw away your good things upon any ephemeral periodical of the time. If, however, you think your resources sufficient, which I doubt not, to supply them and keep something good in reserve, you by no means should hesitate to become a contributor. It is always a marrow bone to pick, and " ae' bird i' hand is worth twa in bush." I have this moment received ———'s parcel, which appears to contain a copy of the Border Tales. Work is pouring in upon you—I hope you will be able to accomplish it all. I beg you will let me see any manuscript you may send for their work, which I shall read and despatch to them with all expedition. Your compunctious visitings about getting all the credit of the book, you ought to send to the right about. I regret that your brother's three poems should not bring him all the credit they merit—I think, however, you will not cast out about it.'

The following extract from the Life of John Bethune, will explain the allusions, in the foregoing letter, to his contributions to the volume just published. 'In the composition of this work, it was at first intended that he, (John,) should have taken a larger share, but circumstances prevented him from doing so; and "The Dedication," "The Decline and Fall of the Ghost," " A Wish," " A Vision of Death," and " An Infant's Death-bed," were his only contributions. * * * * Literary fame being no part of the object of its obscure authors when they undertook it,' they meant the work to be published anonymously. 'The publisher, however, wished to have the name of the principal author; but on the latter representing at some length his motives for wishing to elude notice, it was given up, and nothing more was heard of the matter, till a letter announcing "the completion of the printing of the work," stated that "the name had been given after all." It was then too late to remedy the error of having given only one name; and thus the subject of the present notice was never known as the author of the pieces already mentioned, beyond his own neighbourhood.' *

The following are extracts from two replies of Mr. Bethune's to the letter given above.

'MOUNTPLEASANT, *February* 10, 1838.

'Dear Sir,—I hasten to acknowledge the receipt of your letter, which came by post; and also that of the parcel which it announced. The first I received one day after date, and the last this afternoon; and if they do not "rejoice my heart" it is because at present it cannot rejoice. Eight days ago, and they would have made me happier than any other earthly thing; but within this short period I have seen my father sicken; I have watched

* Life of John Bethune, second edition, P. 63—64.

his bed, I may say, night and day; I have seen every remedy which medical skill could devise prove fruitless; I have seen his lifeless clay; and I am but now returned from consigning his remains to the dust. Thus the deepest sorrows of men, and, what would otherwise be, their greatest pleasures are sometimes strangely blended. The scenes which I have thus so recently seen, the part I have acted in them, and the impression which they have left on my spirits will, I hope, be some excuse if at present I cannot thank you as I would wish to do, for all your kindness, and all your exertions in my behalf. Do not suppose however that I am insensible to the extent of my obligation—I feel it; and after having read your most friendly letter, the reviews &c. I had for a moment half forgotten my late bereavement, but a sad recollection was at hand—namely, that one parent for whom I had toiled, and thought, and written, could never more be benefited by toil, or thought, or writing of mine.

'The copies of the "Tales and Sketches" which I have received are, in all respects, elegant beyond any thing which I had ventured to conceive of them. With respect to the success which the work has met, or may yet meet with, I cannot err in attributing it chiefly to your own efforts.—The "Lectures" would have been on their way to Edinburgh before this time, had it not been for the event previously noticed. I was so anxious to get on with them that on the second day of my father's illness I had dragged myself to make an attempt, but felt altogether unequal to the task. There is not however much to do now, and as soon as we can resume writing, we will endeavour to finish them. We have adopted a new arrangement of the subjects, and introduced some new ones—treating them in the best manner we could, with only our own understandings to trust to; but in what remains we shall have plenty of prompters, for which our thanks are due to yourself and Dr. Murray. I may just mention farther, that by the time the manuscript reaches you again, you will find it divested of all sorts of politics and politcal feeling.

'Mr.———'s terms are "three guineas for the manuscript and copyright of eight printed pages." If you think it advisable, I will try to furnish him with a tale or two as soon as possible after having completed my present engagement. I will also endeavour to answer his communication, in an open letter, which, after having read you can close and forward, whenI return the "Lectures." In the mean time pray be so good as make some acknowledgement to him for his present, (a volume of "The Tales of the Borders,") and state the circumstances in which I now stand. I think I could still write two or three volumes of tales as large as that just published; though I dare not venture to specify the time in which it could be done—for my head will not always work when I want it.   A. B.'

'Mountpleasant, *February* 20, 1838.

'Dear Sir,—I once more beg to trouble you with the "Lectures on Popular Economy;" and, to you, this is almost all I need say on the subject. I know you will find a publisher for them, if the thing is at all possible. It has struck me, just now, that it might be of some advantage to have every Lecture divided into Sections, with a short and appropriate name. That on Marriage, for instance, might be divided thus:—Section I., Introductory Remarks; Section II., Errors of the Young with respect to Marriage; Section III., Hardships which early Marriages commonly produce to the parties, &c., &c. Were the whole thus divided, with "Contents" at the beginning, the reader, after having read the work once, would be enabled at any future period to find those portions of it to which he might wish to refer, with comparative ease. Not being skilful in these matters, I merely mention the subject for your consideration; and if you deem such an arrangement proper—should Mr. Shortrede be willing to run the risk of publishing—I think we may draw on your friendship for the making of it. Even if you should be obliged to seek elsewhere for a publisher, perhaps you could still favour us with your assistance in this respect; or, if that is incompatible with your other engagements, let us have your advice, and with this we will endeavour to do the best we can. I hope, however, Mr. Shortrede may be induced to undertake the work; in which case, farther care on our part will be unnecessary.

'It might be of the last importance to have Dr. Murray's opinion still; but, after what he has already done, and when the laborious life which he leads is considered, it would be, in us, presumption grown intolerably presuming, to trouble him again. Indeed, I fear that I, in particular, have availed myself of his kindness to an unjustifiable extent already, by quoting too largely from his "Summary," in the concluding part of the Lecture on Marriage. But his views and sentiments seemed to be of so much importance in the path I was pursuing, that I could not prevail upon myself to do otherwise. I have quoted as from the "Edinburgh Chronicle"—not venturing to state the manner in which we came by the "Summary," lest it should look like arrogance. I much doubt, however, some apology would be necessary for these quotations; and, to say truth, I do not know well how to make it. You will also see other quotations, but as these are from books which have been fairly given to the public, I suppose there is no great matter—the thing seems rather fashionable. You will now find the Lectures entirely free from politics. Economy is uniformly spoken of either as a science or a virtue; and whatever errors they may contain, I scarcely think any individual, or any portion of the public press, could possibly find fault with them on that score. Having said this much, I would only request, farther, the favour of a few lines, with your first leisure, to satisfy us as to the safe arrival of the manuscripts.

'I regret, exceedingly, not having seen the books with which you have kindly favoured us, before commencing the work at first. With such assistance, the task would have been rendered easy; and, it is probable, too it might have been performed in better style, though I am not certain that it would have been more original; and with this thought we must endeavour to comfort ourselves for the little information we could procure on a subject of which we presumed to treat. But, if the present attempt should meet with any share of public approbation, as there is a number of subjects connected with Economy left untouched, these stores of knowledge may be made available at some future period. We have not yet found time to master Adam Smith; he will, however, be read with great care, and returned when this is accomplished.

'I can now tell you an anecdote of your foster-child, which I think will not displease you. Some copies of the "Edinburgh Chronicle," it seems, come to Newburgh. By accident, some one had discovered the review of the "Tales and Sketches" which that paper contained, and the story ran. The paper was handed from house to house, and from man to man, till the whole was made public. On the following day, the door of a quiet stationer, a Mr. Wood, who, hitherto, has dealt almost exclusively in school-books, cheap periodicals, and writing paper, was besieged by a number of persons enquiring after the book. In this emergency, he despatched a letter to Perth, for what was deemed an adequate supply; but there, only one copy could be obtained; and, on the day after its arrival, my brother saw a letter lying in his shop addressed to "Fraser and Co. Edinburgh," which he intended to send off with the guard of one of the Perth coaches. He, at this time, regretted his not having been able to procure a supply of the books, to throw in upon the good people of Newburgh, when the mania was at its height. How the matter terminated I know not, but so far all was highly pleasing to me, and I trust it will not be displeasing to you. Really I cannot forbear expressing a wish that you would be so kind as to acquaint Dr. Murray with this circumstance. To a mind like his, I am sure it would be pleasing to know that his benevolent exertions have not been made in vain. Up to this time, I had never supposed that any review, however powerfully written, could have produced half the effect.

'As the Lectures are now arranged, the 1st, 2d, and 4th, are my brother's; the Preface, the 3d, 5th, 6th, and 7th, are mine. This will enable you, wherever you find a "saddle" to put it "on the back of the right horse." My brother wishes me to send his compliments to you; but not having seen them, I know not what space they might occupy, and as I have little room left, I suppose they must remain where they are. A. B.'

From among the many favourable notices of the 'Tales and Sketches' which appeared shortly after their publication, I shall select one or two extracts, which, while they embody the feelings that would naturally be excited by the appearance of such a work, from such a quarter, seem at the same time the most discriminately characteristic of the merits of the book. The first is from the 'Fifeshire Journal :'—

'Did we know nothing whatever of the author of this little volume, we should not hesitate to pronounce him a person of no ordinary genius. His delineations are so truthful—his sense of the beauties of inanimate nature so lively—his perception of character so acute—and, above all, his book, from beginning to end, indicates, what in these utilitarian times is so rarely to be met with, such a large measure of high moral feeling, that one could scarce have failed to characterize him as possessed at once of singular talent and great moral worth. But, as matters actually are, the work is quite a literary phenomenon. The author is—it may be said without a figure—self-educated. Born in a very humble condition of life, nursed in poverty, and having had to struggle with adversities under which persons of inferior energy would have sunk in weakness to the grave, he has at length succeeded in elevating himself to an honourable station in the literary world, and is on the eve, we doubt not, of acquiring an honest and extensive fame through the country which gave him birth. But lately the admirers of native genius mourned that with the Ettrick Shepherd the Scottish muse seemed to have departed. But it is pleasing to know that the genius of Scotland never dies. Hers are a noble-hearted peasantry; and where there is noble-heartedness there is also intellectual vigour. The heart, if it do not form, at least fires, the genius; and in the case of the individual now before us, this maxim unquestionably holds. His natural abilities are undoubtedly great, but a high sense of the excellent and honourable has, as it were, stimulated them into action. The moral has vivified the intellectual, and the consequence of all is, that the peasant of Abdie has produced a work of which many an approved master of literature might well be proud.'

Our next extract shall be from the generous and effective notice in the 'Edinburgh Chronicle:'—

'The perusal of this book, just published, has affected us more than any thing we have read for many years past, and has revived in our bosom recollections of youth and rural manners, which, though they may be dormant for a time amid the engrossing cares of the world, can never be obliterated, and can never die. The author has taken the best way to rivet the attention, and to interest the heart, of his readers. He has unvarnished tales unfolded of the Scottish peasantry; tales drawn from his own observation and from truth, devoid of all improbability, of mawkish sentimentalism, and over-wrought character or incident. * * Mr. Bethune, who is literally, as he himself tells us, a labourer, lives near Newburgh in Fife, of which county, we believe, he is a native. He would certainly do honour to any rank of life; and we believe, after all, the nobility of talent, when emblazoned by virtue, as in this instance, is the proudest species of nobility. We never had the gratification of seeing the author, nor do we know more of his history than he has thought it proper to unfold; but his work is enough to recommend him, and should secure him the notice both of the rich and learned. He never hitherto, he says, has had a patron, nor does he seem to wish one; but assuredly he deserves notice and preferment: and we think that if there are persons of influence in Fife who have any sympathy with men of genius, they cannot overlook the great literary, not to say personal, claims of such a gifted individual, and thus do justice to him and honour to themselves. Such a man in such circumstances is seldom to be found, and ought not to be lost. We feel confident, that the present volume will be so well received, as, whether the author continue a labourer or not, to elicit some other, perhaps even better, work from his pen.'

In the following extract from 'Chambers' Journal,' the writer indicates, what I am inclined to regard as Alexander Bethune's greatest forte as a delineator of human life—delicacy in painting the gentler emotions of the female mind.

'While it is impossible to avoid being favourably affected towards a poor but honest man under the circumstances above described, we believe ourselves to be quite independent of all such feelings when we recommend Mr. Bethune's productions to notice on account of their literary merits. Of the excellence of his verses, our readers are already enabled to judge :* the above tale, *(The Deformed,)* though necessarily abridged to suit our pages, will also serve to impress a respectful opinion of his prose. It does not, however, afford any idea of a certain power of describing external nature, which the author possesses in an extraordinary degree, nor the almost unrivalled delicacy, as we cannot help calling it, with which he paints all the gentler emotions of the female mind, and of which many

* Two Sonnets of his, had been introduced into a previous number of the Journal.

examples occur throughout the volume. In general, his pictures of rural life and character appear to us remarkably true, as well as pleasing.'

The success of this, his first publication, gave a momentary brightening to the fortunes of Alexander Bethune. While his engagement with the publisher of the 'Border Tales,' and the prospect of the publication of a small volume of poems selected from the compositions of both the brothers, which was then in contemplation by the publisher of the Tales, opened up, what was to their circumscribed ambition somewhat flattering prospects of literary employment and remuneration.

The following letter embodies a rapid, but graphic sketch of himself, in answer to anxious enquiries of readers of the 'Tales and Sketches,' transmitted to him by his literary friend :—

'MOUNTPLEASANT, *March* 3, 1838.

'Dear Sir,—As I did not receive yours of the 21st ult., till the day after despatching the last pacquet, I felt vexed at having lost that opportunity of acknowledging it; but, though that was the case, I must now be permitted to offer you my best thanks for its contents. Your friendly condolence and friendly counsels I can appreciate; and I hope to be benefited by both. Though, as a consequence of my father's death, I believe we have of late done less in the way of scribbling than would have otherwise been the case, you will see we have not been altogether idle, but endeavouring to do the best we could. From that father I learned to be busy—to do whatever might be done; and, where Providence interposed to thwart our schemes, to submit. By his lessons and his example I have been endeavouring to profit, now, when he is no more; and I believe the necessity which I have been under of keeping my mind in some measure engaged with literary matters, has not been without its use.

'There is no reason for either your eyes or mine being "dazzled;" the whole of the "sunshine" proceeds from those inky luminaries which glimmer in every corner of the country, though nowhere so thickly as in your own metropolis—of these you have kindly directed the rays upon a certain obscure quarter, and, for the time, they have made it bright. This is all, and I can see it well. About two years ago I read a work which had reached the second edition: with the exception of a few splendid passages, it was a chaos throughout; bombast and obscurity appeared to be its prevailing characteristics,—and yet in, "the opinions of the press," which were carefully added at the end of the book, it was spoken of as an "original production of genius," a "first-rate performance of its kind," and, "a standard work." Time, however, has, I fear, or, at least, shortly will try its "originality" and "standardability." I could, then, easily guess that the whole of the fame which had accrued to the author was the work of the inky luminaries, or rather, of the invisible spirits who direct their spheres, and, as my sight has not suffered since that time, I can still see these matters in the same light.

'For a man to deal largely in his own biography is, I fear, a sad way of fishing for fame—little better than fishing with a cable; and ten to one, but the fish sees the line and flies from the bait. There is, besides, but little in my history worth noticing. Of privations I have had my share; but who cares for these things? Nevertheless I must give you such notices of my life as will satisfy yourself and friends. I owe you this and a thousand times more, but must defer it for the present. And, in the meantime, though I can perceive that you are only jesting when you put certain questions concerning the author of the "Tales and Sketches" in the mouths of certain individuals; you may tell the romantic damoselle, if ever she should call again—or rather, I may tell you in case she should not—that so far as I know, he is in his thirty-first or thirty-second year—too old by at least a dozen years to be at all interesting. You may also tell the maiden of a certain age, that, though unmarried, he lately wore a coat that was out at the elbows!—tell her this, and she will ask no more. For other inquirers, you may tell them that he is about five feet ten inches high, and, so far as I can judge, of such proportions as other men; that the hair on his forehead, from that part of his upper story having been partially unroofed, is thin; that though both his eyes are still in their sockets, only one is serviceable; that his dinner in winter, year after year, was wont to be a little bannock of barley-meal with such a quantity of snow as would serve to moisten it, that is, when the last mentioned article of diet could be found, and when it could not, it frequently cost him a journey to the nearest burn to supply its place with water. I might tell you a good deal more about the habits, appearance &c., of my acquaintance, but must desist; and if these notices, notwithstanding their length, should still seem unsatisfactory, I will try to pack him up, some time or other, and send him over to Edinburgh for your inspection, A. B.'

The lively interest Dr. Murray continued to take in the literary success of the Messrs. Bethune is evinced in the following extracts from a Letter of his to their literary friend. While expressing his high sense of the honour of the proposed dedication of the 'Lectures' to him, he shows a generous anxiety that they should, if possible, be made the means of bringing the merits of their authors under the notice of some one who might have it in his power effectually to advance their fortunes.

'HOPE PARK, EDINBURGH, 19*th March*, 1838.

'Dear Sir,—I was duly favoured with your Letter of the 16th inst., and take the earliest moment I can command to acknowledge receipt of it. There is nothing that I can do that I would not willingly undertake for the Messrs. Bethune; and shall, accordingly, be most happy to see the proof-sheets as they issue from the press.

'I humbly think, that the " Lectures on Popular Economy" will be a most successful speculation, and will do great honour to the authors. Indeed, the work is full of original views, and cannot but prove signally useful. We must take care that justice is done it on its appearance, and bring forward its peculiar and original views before the notice of the public. You may rest assured, that, in my humble way, I will do all that I can, both in Edinburgh and in Glasgow. * * * *
I regard the industrious classes there, [in Glasgow,] called upon to take a peculiar interest in the work. Every one of the cotton-spinners there should have a copy of it. It is calculated to give them a new view of human life, and of the mechanism of society. I shall also get my friend Mr. M'Culloch to give it a lift—in short, all that I can do (which, however, is very little,) I shall most cordially perform.

'There is another most important subject alluded to in your kind letter—namely, that the authors have expressed a wish to dedicate the work to me. I humbly think they are wrong in this; and that the wish proceeds rather from the kindness of their heart, than from sober reflection.

* * * * * * * *

I feel mortified to see the authors—men of genius and of noble thought—condemned to live in so humble a sphere of life, and to earn their bread by the sweat of their brow. I would delight to see them in a more elevated situation—a situation more congenial to their tastes, and that would afford them more ample means of intellectual culture and study. Now, could they not contrive to dedicate their book to some one who might possess both the wish and the power to withdraw them from their present laborious employment, and secure for them employment more remunerating, and more suitable to their taste and their literary character? I beg to say, that, in dedicating their work, they should have some such object in view; though I am aware how little literature and how little sympathy with literary men, exist in certain quarters. Perhaps, you will yourself reflect on the propriety of these hints, and suggest this view of the matter to the Messrs. Bethune. I need not say how proud I should feel, if the Lectures were dedicated to me. I should feel that I had been too highly honoured. Only I do beg, that you and they will consider the propriety of sending the book forth into the world under higher auspices, and making the dedication an instrument, if possible, of direct benefit to the authors.

'Perhaps I may be allowed to state, that in inculcating the nature and value of Capital and Independence, in my public Lectures, I have already taken the opportunity of referring to the forthcoming volume of the Messrs. Bethune. I have done so in Dunfermline, in the presence of a thousand auditors; and I mean to do so in Kirkcaldy, where my class is equally numerous. I have also done so elsewhere. And, when the work is published, I shall quote from it, and never miss an opportunity of recommending the "Lectures on Popular Economy." In this way I may be enabled to do some good, as well as add to the fame of the authors. The truth is, I feel a deep interest in these excellent men; and I do hope their publications, particularly the "Lectures," will be so well received as to realize some little capital to them, however small: and that thus they will have the satisfaction of being the architects of their own independence—a circumstance that will confer on them equal honour and happiness. I have another plan in my mind for improving their condition, if none more influential step forward; but of this I shall write you again.

'I beg to return their very interesting letter, which you were so kind as enclose to me. It is exceedingly interesting; indeed, peculiarly so. I am, dear Sir, yours, very faithfully,

THOMAS MURRAY.'

The success of the Tales naturally led the authors of the 'Lectures' to expect that they might be able to turn them to some little account, in a pecuniary point of view. The 'trade,' however, were by no means so sanguine as to the success of the work as Dr. Murray, and the best offer their literary friend could obtain for the copyright was from the publisher of the former volume, to the following effect: "That the authors consign over to him the entire copyright, on condition of his paying them forty pounds when a thousand copies are sold." The specified number of copies, however, never were sold during the lifetime of either of the authors, and consequently, they did not receive a farthing for all their labour; a fact which furnishes rather a melancholy illustration of the state of public taste and feeling, in regard to a subject of so much importance to the individual and social well-being of the community.

The authors' acceptance of the above offer was conveyed in a letter from Alexander, the following extracts from which imbody some interesting facts respecting the pecuniary difficulties of the Bethunes, connected with the building of their house, and highly characteristic of their independence of spirit:—

'Mountpleasant, *March 27th*, 1838.

'Dear Sir,—Lest our avarice, as expressed in some former letters, should appear unaccountable, though nearly half asleep, I shall here endeavour to give you some account of its cause. Last summer we commenced building a house, with only £30. The additional £5. which you were so kind as send us, led us to deviate from our first intention, and make the house two stories instead of one. Our motive for doing so was a wish to make the outlay productive, if possible. As the roofing would have been the same, it was only a little more expense on the walls, and then, if ever we should be able to finish the upper part, it would bring a rent. After this determination was come to, we prosecuted our scheme with a perseverance which almost amounted to desperation, and completed it without debt. But, to make the lower part as comfortable as possible for those for whose accommodation it was principally intended, every farthing which could be rendered available was expended, and we came to our new habitation literally with empty pockets. During the first months of winter, when the weather was favourable for out-door work, we had saved something; but a period of nine weeks in which no work could be performed, and my father's illness and death, with the expenses consequent thereon, left us again empty-handed. So that, while finishing the Lectures, which was previous to the melting of the snow, the authors were living upon oaten meal and potatoes, with scarcely any addition whatever, except water and salt. Money we might have had to borrow, but it was our object and our interest to keep free from debt as far as possible.

The crisis, however, is now over: we have both more work at present than we can manage; and though our financial embarrassments were carefully concealed while they lasted, now that they are told, they may perhaps serve to account in some measure for that avarice which otherwise might have seemed unaccountable; and, as there is no great chance of such embarrassments occurring soon again, perhaps the cause, and its effects may serve as the subject for a jest at some future period.

'Though I do not think my coming to Edinburgh can be of any importance, I will try to come some time next week, perhaps on Monday. There is nothing in my personal appearance or conversation which can have the slightest tendency to interest any one: the former is the worse for wear, and the latter considerably below mediocrity; and if you figure to yourself one of those labourers, about forty years of age, which you have been accustomed to see on the highways, (though I am little more than thirty,) you will, in all respects, have a pretty accurate idea of me. I should, however, like to see you; and, when the exertions which you have made to bring my very humble attempts at authorship before the public in the most favourable point of view, are considered, this liking is easily accounted for. If I could reach Dysart by half-past seven in the morning, I might spend a good part of the day in Edinburgh, cross the water again in the afternoon, and prosecute a part of my homeward journey before bed-time. From Mr. D———'s exertions in my behalf I do not anticipate much, though it was certainly very kind in him so to exert himself. For this, worst of all the ill-written letters I ever wrote, I must request you, if possible, to pardon—Yours faithfully, though now more than three-fourths asleep, A. B.'

Early in April, the Messrs. Bethune paid their visit to Edinburgh mentioned as in contemplation in the preceding letter. After their return home they set about the formation of a Savings Society in Newburgh. 'I have also been labouring,' says Alexander, 'to get a branch of the Government Savings Bank established in the same place. These were great undertakings,' continues he, 'for little men; and to accomplish them, people had to be canvassed, meetings called, prejudices combated; but as the things promised to be practically, I wish I could add with certainty permanently, useful, they were worth the labour.'

The occupations of our author during great part of the summer of 1838, with his views and feelings in regard to his literary labours, as well as some of the results of these, are indicated in the following letter:—

MOUNTPLEASANT, *August* 9, 1838.

'Dear Sir,—I am most happy in being able to tell you that this is a rainy day! The people here are all mourning over "the state of the weather," and beginning to terrify themselves with apprehensions that the promise of "summer and winter, seed-time and harvest," is about to fail. "If these rains continue there will be no shearing this season," say they; but, at present, I have no inclination to join in the general lamentation as the cause thereof gives me an opportunity of answering your last letter.

'You might, perhaps, blame me for abandoning writing, as I hinted I was about to do in my last very hurried communication; but I scarcely think you will deem such an abandonment wrong when you are made acquainted with the circumstances which led to it. Within the last four or five months, I had written nearly as much of one sort and another as would have made a volume of the ordinary size, which, according to Godwin's account of himself, was no bad work even for a professional writer. To accomplish this, manual labour had been to a considerable extent neglected. Of the labour which I did perform, the greater part was devoted to making improvements about our own premises, which, though the whole were necessary, and some indispensable, brought no return. The only thing in the shape of money which I had received for a long time, was the three guineas for the copyright of "The Young Laird;" shillings and pence were fast disappearing from my purse, and what was worse some trifling debts had been contracted. With things in this state, I had become rather anxious to learn how affairs stood, that I might thereby form some resolution as to my future conduct; and when your letter with the useless manuscripts arrived, I had only to choose between two courses, namely, whether I should go about, as the poor poets are said to have done, and " solicit half-crowns as the reward of genius!" or entitle myself to demand whole crowns as the reward of labour. The soliciting concern I did not at all like. I could not, moreover, recollect having done or suffered any thing so meritorious as to make me a fitting object of charity; and therefore, I resolved to try the last of these alternatives: as Mahomet went to the mountain when the mountain would not come to Mahomet; so when the wind would not sail with me, I resolved to sail with the wind. I was to have moved somewhere in quest of employment, but most fortunately I received an offer of work on the same evening, which I most readily accepted. Before going to bed, I revised our financial concerns, made out accounts for some small sums of money which were owing, and, without so much as "cursing the rhyming" (in my case only, the writing) "trade," which would have been sheer loss of time, the following day saw me in a ditch nearly knee-deep in mud, from which I dug treasure to the amount of eighteen-pence before I quitted it. My next step was to collect the money for my accounts, and to satisfy the demands of creditors as far as it would go, giving them at the same time a promise of payment of what remained as soon as I could dig a sufficiency of treasnre from the said ditch; after which, I returned home to a night's rest, which labour and a consciousness of havving done what I conceived to be my duty rendered sweet. This, then, is a full, true, and faithful account of me and my doings, since I had the pleasure of seeing you last. Hogg has somewhere spoken of the pleasure which it gave him to write and talk about himself, and though I am not aware of any particular fondness for this species of writing, you see I have supplied from it a pretty long paragraph—which paragraph I cannot conclude without telling you that I have got something like clothes on my back, and something like flesh on my bones since I gave up scribbling. A. B.'

The printing of 'Practical Economy,' somehow or other, was not commenced till about the beginning of October. Dr. Murray looked over the work once more, and, while expressing his high approbation of the matter, as well as of the temper which now characterized it, offered some suggestions as to improvements in the arrangement of the different parts, which were promptly acted on by the authors. Some of his remarks on the importance of a severe logical arrangement in works partaking of a scientific character appear so just and forcible, that I cannot refrain from quoting a sentence or two:—

'A treatise on Practical Economy, or any other scientific subject, should be treated mathematically, each head or proposition being proved as the work proceeds, and afterwards, if referred to, assumed as having been previously established, and as undeniable. Thus the reader will peruse the book with greater ease and interest, every step of the reasoning taking effect on his mind and commanding his assent, as he proceeds. The sentiments of an author may be perfectly just and his principles irrefragable, and yet the composition in which they are enforced may be so disjointed, so loose in the arrangement, and so broken down, instead of forming a consecutive and harmonious train of thought, that, though they cannot but be assented to, they fall on the mind as a thrice-told tale falls on the ear, without making any definite or lasting impression.'

To the exemplary spirit in which our authors received his criticisms and suggestions, Dr. Murray bears the highest testimony, in a letter to the editor of this volume.

EDINBURGH, 26*th Aug.*, 1843.

'My dear Sir,—All that I did for the Messrs. Bethune consisted in giving certain hints, and offering certain critical remarks, which they valued above their deserts. These remarks and hints referred both to principles inculcated in their work, and to the logical arrangement of their various Lectures. I had the greatest pleasure in doing this; and candour compels me to say, that the Messrs. Bethune received these, (poor as they undoubtedly were, though I submitted them candidly,) with a degree of ingenuousness perhaps never equalled. Their object was truth, and they were willing to listen to truth, though it might be contrary to, or subversive of, their own preconceived opinions. They had no literary pride: their character was essentially humble, though based on a noble spirit of independence; and I shall ever regard them as honourable equally for their talents and moral worth.'

Finding our authors still intended to dedicate the work to him, Dr. Murray suggested that it should rather be inscribed to a gentleman, whom he named, holding an official situation connected with the government, in the hope that it might facilitate an effort for obtaining his influence in order to procure some public situation for the authors. In reference to this, Dr. Murray remarks in the letter just quoted,—

'Mr. Alexander Bethune, in the Life of his brother, refers to an offer being made to them to procure them an office in the excise, or some other public employment. By referring to the biography, you will find the subject there treated in a way which cannot be regarded but as extremely interesting and high-minded. Mr. A. Bethune declined the offer in the most modest yet manly terms,—in terms that excited my admiration. Perhaps no such instance of real self-denial ever existed. But I deeply regret that the letter to me containing the declinature on their part has been by me mislaid. I have spent many hours searching for it, but I cannot find it. If I can yet lay my hands on it, I shall send it to you forthwith; but I fear it is lost. I fear also other letters of theirs have shared the same unworthy fate.'

This letter has not been recovered. In accordance with the long cherished desire of their authors, the Lectures were dedicated to Dr. Murray: their publication, however, did not take place till May, 1839. Meantime, both the brothers continued to write for 'Wilson's Tales of the Borders,' and this connexion, though the remuneration was far from high, I believe brought them as much money as all their other literary labours put together. Both brothers contributed some very graphic and delightful tales to this publication; indeed, in the opinion of a highly competent judge, theirs were far above the average merit of the series. 'The Sisters,' perhaps the finest of all Alexander's stories, constitutes No. 251. In regard to this beautifully touching tale, I entirely concur in the opinion expressed by our author's literary friend, when it passed through his hands in manuscript:—

'Of this delightful little tale, I must say, that of all the good ones you have written, it is decidedly my favourite. I believe it to be perfectly true—if not, the more credit is yours. It contains numerous beautiful pictures, and is full of manly, simple tenderness, which, I confess, awakened chords within, that have long, long slept. I admire your nice and tasteful appreciation of the female character, which few possess to an equal degree. In these respects, it much resembles some of the best productions of Miss Edgeworth and Washington Irvine, neither of whom would be ashamed of such a story. But there are other points which even they cannot excel. You say, you are not "what poets call a lover of nature." What sort of a thing you or they mean by such a distinction, I know not; but certes it appears to me that nothing but the most intense love of nature, constant familiarity with her, and keen appreciation of all her scenes and moods, could have dictated or inspired those vivid, simple, and graphic delineations, which here, more than any where else in your productions, have flowed from your pen.'*

Sometime in 1838, several poems of the Bethunes were admitted into the Dublin University Magazine; and, encouraged by what appeared a favourable opening for their productions in such a quarter, Alexander and John prepared each a story, which

---

* The reader will find an abstract of this tale in the Appendix.

were duly transmitted to the editor. But years elapsed, and no notice whatever was taken of them; and it was not without great difficulty that they were at last recovered from the conductors of that periodical by Alexander, in 1842. The story sent by him was that entitled 'The Drunkard,' the first in 'The Scottish Peasant's Fireside.' It might be quite as worthy of a place as many tales that have appeared in that periodical, but influence and friendship, fully as much as merit, rule the decision in such cases. Much preposterous sympathy for the hardships, privations, and disappointments of authors who have had to struggle with poverty, defective education, and uncongenial circumstances, is often expressed when they are gone; but how few who have it in their power effectively to show such sympathy, care to do so while they are living. By the exercise of a little of that discrimination and perspicacity which their position certainly demands of them, the editors of periodicals, (constituting as they do the medium through which so many who aspire to the distinction of authorship must endeavour to gain the public ear,) might lift from the heart of humble merit the load of despondency, cheer it on in its exertions in spite of conspiring difficulties, and stimulate to higher and more successful efforts. In these remarks no particular reflection is meant on the conductors of the periodical in question. The Bethunes experienced treatment of a similar kind from individuals connected with other departments of the popular periodical press, as the reader acquainted with the life of John will be aware.

At length, in the beginning of May, 1839, the 'Lectures on Practical Economy' were published; but their reception by the trade and the public was very different from what the generous literary friends of the authors had anticipated. The booksellers in Edinburgh did not subscribe for a single copy! And until the sympathies of the public were somewhat roused by the death of one of the authors, and the appearance of the affecting memoir of him by the other, the work might have been considered as little better than dead. That this neglect was not deserved, any reader may convince himself by procuring and perusing the work, which would not have been so treated had a healthier feeling either in regard to economy or literature, possessed the public mind. But it is not works of instruction that the multitude run after, but of amusement or party abuse; and as there are too many who make no study of practising economy, the number of those is small who care to be told how much on doing so depends individual comfort and independence, as well as national prosperity. The feelings with which its authors consigned their work to the public, are indicated in the concluding sentences addressed to their fellows, the working-men of Britain. 'Its authors can have no object in deceiving you: they have suffered from all those hardships and privations which you can possibly suffer; they have been as poor as you can possibly be; and they have the advantage of economical and systematic management; they expect neither place nor pension from any political party; and they look for no favour from any great man whatever. It is your interest and the interest of your class which they wish to promote; and if this attempt to serve you is forgotten they can suffer nothing. If these ideas of the authors are correct, the public may perhaps recognise the same principles at some future period, and your children, or your children's children, may reap the harvest which you might have gathered in; but to you it can be of no avail. The whole is now in your hands. You may not be inclined to go so far, in some respects, as we have gone; but only make a beginning, and with perseverance you will not be disappointed in the end. Trusting to your growing understanding, and trusting too that every fabric of error, whoever may have reared it, will one day fall before the omnipotence of truth,—we bid you an affectionate farewell!'

The very cold reception the 'Lectures' met with, had, as may be readily conceived, a depressing effect on the minds of their authors.* Shortly after their

* Repeated literary disappointments occurred to them about this time. 'At any other employment,' says Alexander, 'after you have performed a quantity of work, you may calculate with some certainty on receiving your reward, trifling though it may be; but in literary pursuits the mischief of the matter is, that after you have performed never so much work, and bestowed never so much pains upon it, you cannot say you have earned a single penny.

publication, we find Alexander thus writing to his Edinburgh friend:—'At present I believe everything is against us in a literary way. Had the Lectures been selling rapidly, it might have produced a favourable impression on the minds of editors, &c. But the work I suppose is not selling; and what is worse, I fear it is not likely to sell. So little noise indeed does it make, that scarcely a tenth part of the people hereabouts seem to be aware of its existence. Why is it that men will purchase and read everything with avidity, but what is intended to benefit them? Perhaps the answer may be found in the abilities of the authors not answering their intention. We took the wrong road, however. In these days, if a man would make his way to fame, he should, in the first place, persuade people that they are not at all to blame for their own poverty and misfortunes—these having been wholly brought upon them by others; and, in the second place, he should arraign the government as the prime mover and the great first cause of all the misery in the country. Or he should bespatter either the Tories or the Radicals with all his might; it matters little which, provided he do it consistently, because in any way he identifies himself with a party, and is thus almost certain of success.'

In a letter to Dr. Murray, in reference to the same subject, he says—'I am convinced, however, that until the people begin to look upon themselves as their own regenerators, and to take the matter fairly into their own hands, no government will ever be able to make them either comfortable or independent, and if they could only be persuaded to do this, I feel confident that no government would be able long to oppress them. In this view of the matter, I am glad to find that we agree; and though the "small craft" for which you have already done so much, should absolutely founder before it gets out of the harbour, I hope your own labours will be more successful, and that you will one day succeed in convincing the industrious classes, that it is to themselves they must look, in the first place, for every permanent improvement in their condition. This were indeed to confer a boon on the country; and if such a boon is conferred, we shall rejoice, though our own humble attempt should be entirely forgotten.'

CHAPTER V.

ILLNESS AND DEATH OF HIS BROTHER—CORRESPONDENCE CONNECTED WITH THAT EVENT—EXTRACTS FROM JOURNAL—LETTERS.

ALEXANDER BETHUNE was now about to suffer a bereavement which was destined to cast a gloom over the remaining portion of his existence, and which, not improbably, hastened his own descent to the grave. Early in 1839, his brother caught a severe cold which gradually settled on his lungs and passed ultimately into confirmed phthisis. Sick of that severe, and, to such a spirit, distasteful drudgery to which he had hitherto been compelled to submit in order to obtain the bare necessaries of life, and encouraged by the prospect of remuneration (small though it was) which their connexion with the 'Border Tales' led him to indulge,—he had in the latter part of 1838 resolved on giving up manual labour, and devoting his time wholly to writing. This change in his mode of living, no doubt, made him much more susceptible of injury from changes of temperature. 'On the evening of the 28th of January, 1839, he had sat for two or three hours in a room thoroughly heated with a stove, attending to the business of the Newburgh Temperance Society, of which he was secretary; the night was one of intense cold; in his eagerness to succeed as a writer, for months previous he had scarcely passed the threshold of his own dwelling; and he was thus prepared in more ways than one to suffer from the severity of the weather. On coming out to the open air, he immediately felt a tendency to shivering, and before he reached home he had caught that fatal cold which paved the way for his dismission from this world!"* During his illness, his brother attended and watched over him with a tenderness, a care, and a self-denial hardly ever paralleled,—forgetting the demands of his own health, in his anxiety regarding one in whose life his own seemed bound up. In order to attend to his wants, he gave up all labour—he conducted him to such places for change of air as their limited means would admit of—he attended him in his walks, and supported him when too weak to support himself—he put on his clothes in the morning to warm them for him ere he got out of bed, a proceeding, which, however much we may admire it as indicative of fraternal affection and care, cannot but be regarded as one of great indiscretion as respected his own health. All was, however, unavailing: the disease made rapid progress; and on Sunday the 1st September, 1839, John Bethune breathed his last.

* Life of John Bethune, p. 83.

Alexander was inconsolable. One with his brother in tastes, in pursuits, in labours, in aspirations, his death was to him like the rending asunder of existence. But the state of his mind on this melancholy occasion will be best indicated by the following extracts from a letter to his friend, Mr. Adamson, and from a record of his feelings in the form of an irregular diary which he appears for some time afterwards to have kept.

'Mountpleasant, *October* 1, 1839.

' My very Dear Friend,—Being, as you are aware, engaged with harvest work, and having but little command of my own time, I now take advantage of what shearers call " a rimy morning," and what promises to be a wet day, for the purpose of scrawling a few lines to you. It is now exactly a month since the occurrence of that never-to-be-forgotten event, which cast a shadow on all my future prospects—I mean the death of my only brother; and how it is I know not, but to-day I feel even more melancholy than I have done for some time past. I have no need of any thing to keep me in mind of him, for he is never absent from my thoughts; and yet it seems as if every thing recalled the memory of the past, and brought it before me in a fresher colouring. We had lived so long under the same roof, and nestled at night on the same couch of repose—buffeted so many stormy and dark days in company—been so often engaged in the same pursuits—and encountered so many hardships and struggles together, that we had become almost a part of each other's existence; and now when I am left unaided and unfriended, and, as it were, alone in the world, I feel as if the better part of myself, and all my hopes and prospects of future enjoyment were buried with him in the grave. In short, it seems to me that we were not made for separation, and that we should have either lived or died together. But this was not decreed for us; and now when he is gone, I can only mourn his untimely fate, and endeavour to say, The will of Heaven be done. These are vain regrets, you will say. But I cannot banish them, nor would I wish to do so, even if I could. After leaving you on Monday forenoon, I reached home without any inconvenience; and, to deceive the time and shorten the road, I fell in with a poor boy from Glasgow, who was going to Dundee in quest of employment; and as he was too late for the boat, and had, besides, no money to pay his passage, I brought him along with me, and gave him a bed for the night. I did this the more readily, from the recollection of what I had myself suffered from storm and darkness before I could procure shelter in Path-head. The little incident which I have just mentioned, supplied a fund of pleasing, and, at the same time, melancholy reflection for a season; and the afternoon passed away in fancying the feelings, the words, and the look of benevolence with which my departed brother would have welcomed such a poor and unprotected stranger to a share of our humble meal, and the shelter of our humble dwelling. When these fancies began to lose their force, I felt myself growing ill; and for the next two days I experienced a sort of gloomy pleasure, from the idea that I had caught the infection of that fatal disorder of which my brother died, and that, perhaps, we might soon sleep side by side in the same churchyard, as we were wont to do in the same bed. Why I should trouble you with an account of my own melancholy musings, I know not; save that the thoughts which are uppermost in the heart, are ever readiest to flow from the lip or the pen. In this instance, however, I was deceived; and I am at present enjoying tolerable health.

'The following Lines of my much-lamented brother's, I found this morning, written in pencil upon a brown paper bag. The Lines, as it would appear, had been dashed off in a moment of poetical feeling, after it had become evident that he must leave that habitation which, in his mind, was associated with all he could know of the hopes or the fears, the joys or the sorrows of life—he having been but a mere infant when we came to reside there :—

" HAUNTS of my boyhood, and home of my youth,
Ere the sunshine of Fancy was shaded by Truth—

Ye woodlands and moorlands, and valleys and streams,
Ye scenes of my earliest affections and dreams;
Long loved as ye have been, and lovely,—to you,
And the friends which endeared you, I now bid adieu!
I leave you, but not in the pursuit of wealth;
I leave you, but not in the prospect of health.
May the God who decrees my departure, prepare
Me with poverty, sickness, and sorrow to bear."

'A. B.'

But the fullest revelation of his habitual feelings and musings is to be found in the journal above referred to, and from which the following are extracts:—

'*February* 10, *Monday*—11 *forenoon,*—A shower has driven me to the house. I have just been engaged in removing some young gooseberry bushes raised from slips or cuttings which, sometime in the month of March, nearly two years ago, my dear departed brother and myself placed in the earth—each assisting the other, as we always did. These bushes I should not have removed at all, had it not been to get a favourable situation for the last apple tree which he grafted; the operation being performed after he was under that fatal illness which carried him hence. The tree I should therefore like to thrive as a last memorial of his ingenuity. To-day, too, I used the garden line for the first time since he was no more, and the circumstance brought a strange feeling of deep melancholy over my heart. About the 1st February, 1839, we had commenced our operations in the garden; but alas! what a change one short year has produced. It brought fresh to my mind the time when I was twenty-two and he was seventeen, when we began to toil late and early to improve and make perfect our little garden at Lochend, which formerly had been little better than a gravel hillock surrounded by a bank overgrown with nettles instead of a fence. From that time forward, every spring we laboured at it assiduously to bring it to something like perfection. This formed a part of our enjoyment; and though often thrown back into the gulf from which we had been struggling to extricate ourselves, in the midst of contempt, poverty, and misfortune,—hope still gilded the prospect before us with a cheering beam and pointed to some fair future day of peace, and rest, and prosperity, which was to be the reward of long years of bodily and mental toil which we had chalked out for ourselves. We regarded no undertaking as too arduous, and no task too hard; and these delusions continued to haunt us till the spoiler came; but now all is gone, and I am left alone in a world divested of its latest charm.'

'*March*, 8, 1840,—To-day the air is calm and still with a slight haze hanging on the distant hills. Not a breath of wind is stirring. The sun shines bright and warm, and it seems as if he would round the highest summit of the rocks to the southward without sinking beneath it;* thus giving us, for the first time this season, his cheering influence throughout the day.'

'*March* 29, 1840,—To-day the crocuses, after having been in bloom for a fortnight, are withering. Last Sabbath the whole tuft was fully expanded; and now, there is only one flower whose bosom meets the sun, while the rest are drooping in decay. The auricula and narcissus are both opening; and the whole lilies are green above the ground, having been pressing through for the last eight days. Time speeds on his rapid and never ceasing flight. Only one year ago, and nearly about the same season, these flowers were planted by my only brother and myself,—after the rock had been cut away with much labour, and its place supplied by earth to form a border for them; and now they put forth their leaves and blossoms as green and as gay as if they were still only in the infancy of their existence. The voice of spring has found them out "in their dark and dormant cells," and again called them forth to bask in the sun;—but where is he who planted them, and whose heart might have now

* Mr. Bethune's house occupies part of a terrace, upon that steep acclivity on which the town of Newburgh is built; while right in front of it the rocky top of the hill springs up almost perpendicularly to the height of several hundred feet. This eminence, called the hill of Ormiston, entirely intercepts the sun's rays from the late dwelling of the Bethunes for several months during winter.

been cheered and gladdened by their reviving bloom? Alas! it lacks but five days of seven months since he was laid to sleep in the dust, never again to be awakened by spring, or summer, or any returning season, till the mighty angel shall come forth and swear that time shall be no longer. The recollection of him, and of what he did and suffered has already passed away, and to all, save a very few friends, his name is a forgotten thing; but 'though all forget him, I will ne'er forget.' Every morning when I awake, every night when I lie down, every solitary meal which I swallow, the house, the garden, his vacant chair and empty clothes, and, in short, every thing with which I am surrounded, and every moment which passes, brings him freshly to my remembrance. To me the rising sun shines on loneliness, and his setting beam writes in shadows the deep and sad conviction that my most valued and almost my last friend is gone. I never feel more deserted than on Sabbath—that day of rest, which, though frequently separated throughout the week by our different employments, we always calculated on being able to spend together. When the morning till eight o'clock, or till breakfast time which with us was at that same hour, had been passed in reading some pious book, we in general went forth to take a short walk, and to contemplate the face of Nature in that repose which belonged to the sacred day. These walks and the directions we took—threading the shady and sheltered foot-path among the trees, or moving along the sunny bank, according to the season of the year and character of the weather—are still fresh in my remembrance. We never began to dress ourselves till it was nearly time to go to church; matters were in general so managed that we were ready to a minute; and then, if it chanced to be summer, while I moved slowly onward, he hastened to the garden for a flower and came running after me. We always sat together; from being near the door, we were almost always first out of the church and first home; and when we returned, our clothes were, in general thrown off, folded with care, and laid in our chest before we sat down to dinner. Our Sunday clothes were of the same colour and the same cloth; if one got a new article of dress, the other got its counterpart; one chest served us both, and consequently they were there mixed together, as they are still. But now I must dress and undress, and fold and unfold my part of them in utter loneliness, while his remains untouched; except when I move them from side to side to get at my own, or open them out to look at them and idly ponder over the days when it was otherwise—the days when I had a brother who has now gone down to the dust and left me friendless and alone in a world which, since he was no more, has scarcely a single charm to draw my attention for a moment. On Friday last, I went to Perth to settle with a printer, for the printing of his posthumous works—it was a sad and melancholy journey.'

As was to be supposed, Mr. Bethune's grief on account of his brother's death found vent in several pieces of verse, from which I select the following :—

> ' When evening's lengthened shadows fall
> On tower, and tree, and castle wall,
> Then homeward bends the toil-worn hind,
> The bliss of mutual smiles to find,
> The comforts of his home to share—
> The blazing fire, the ready chair :
> But home, alas ! no more can be
> With such enjoyments blessed to me.
>
> ' No friendly hand remains to greet,
> No eye with welcome bright to meet :
> But shadowy walls and fire extinct,
> As evening bids the day-beam sink,
> Give solemn welcome, still as death,
> To him who yet must draw life's breath,
> And stumble on, devoid of cheer,
> A sad and lonely pilgrim here.
>
> ' When evening's lengthened shadows fall
> On cottage roof and princely hall,
> Then brothers with their brothers meet,
> And kindred hearts each other greet,
> And children wildly, gladly press,
> To share a father's fond caress :
> But home to me no more can bring
> Those scenes which are life's sweetening.
>
> ' No friendly heart remains for me,
> Like star to gild life's stormy sea,

> No brother, whose affection warm
> The gloomy passing hours might charm.
> Bereft of all who once were dear,
> Whose words or looks were wont to cheer;
> Parent, and friend, and brother gone,
> I stand upon the earth alone.'

To Mr. Bethune's friends it was matter of regret, that the affliction produced by his brother's death should have settled into such a depth of melancholy as to overcloud the sources of solace and comfort to which the occasion warranted recourse. John Bethune's last days were cheered by a realizing faith and a humble but stedfast hope—as his life had been eminently distinguished by those graces and virtues which are the only sure indications of vital christian principle. In reference to such a one, the survivor had no reason to doubt but he had received the gracious approval of his Master, and had 'entered into the joy of his Lord.' And it is matter of regret, that he did not oftener rejoicingly realize, even under the sorrow of bereavement, the fulness of that unassailable felicity which the scriptures reveal to us as the enjoyment of the spirits of the just.

The following letter to one who had been a companion of his youth, but had several years previously removed to England, shows that he knew and could point out to others, the only unfailing source of strength either for duty or suffering; though such happier sentiments were too much overborne in his own case by a morbid state of feeling.

'Mountpleasant, near Newburgh,
'Fifeshire, *February* 29, 1840.

'My Dear Friend,—If any advice, or opinion, or praise of mine could tend to make you press steadily forward both in your temporal and eternal concerns, it would not be a-wanting. Your ideas of "the purposes of existence," as expressed in your last letter to me, are sound and practical, and do honour both to your head and heart. Without industry and a becoming care for our worldly concerns, we can neither perform those duties which we owe to others, nor get honourably through life ourselves; and without a better and a more abiding portion, the fairest earthly prospects and the greatest earthly possessions will, in the end, be but vanity. It seems therefore—nay it certainly is—our duty, while here, to improve all those advantages which Providence may place within our reach, and to lose no honourable opportunity of bettering either our own condition or that of others; but at the same time neither to trust in our own strength nor our own righteousness; for daily experience teaches us that the one is but weakness, and a little self-examination would convince the most self-conceited that the other is rotten at the core. I, at least, must confess that I am very, very far from being able to do anything to deserve the approbation of

Him whose eyes are purer than to behold iniquity; and, with respect to earthly trust, I have seen the object to which I was most warmly attached—that one object which was the whole world to me—withering away before my eyes and becoming a heap of senseless dust, when my own wants appeared to be the greatest. I pray God that you may never experience such a fate, and I hope you never will. Yet trust not too much to earth: rather let your hope and your trust be directed to that everlasting inheritance which is laid up for those, who, through the imputed righteousness of the Saviour, shall be heirs of the kingdom of heaven.

' As to the management of your income and your other worldly concerns, pardon me for reminding you that steadiness is an indispensable requisite. Some people may by a sort of trick, or what is sometimes called cleverness, succeed for a time; but of all who have ever been successful in any extensive undertaking, a slight acquaintance with their character, would, I am convinced, show that steadiness of purpose, and a patient perseverance in the use of means, were the principal causes which contributed to their success. In this world, Fortune, or, more properly speaking, Providence, does not always reward those who, to our view, have toiled the hardest and done the most, with a successful termination to their labours; but still it is only on the diligent use of means for the accomplishment of an honourable purpose, that we have any reason to expect the blessing of Providence. Miracles have long since ceased, and therefore we must steadily and perseveringly use our own endeavours for every object which we would wish to obtain—leaving it with the Supreme Disposer of events to determine whether we are or are not to be successful: He knows best whether success or disappointment is best for us. In all this, I do not suppose that I am telling you anything but what you knew before. I hope, however, you will pardon me for simply reminding you of these things. Yours sincerely, A. B.'

The following extract from another letter to the same friend, imbodies some very interesting and characteristic traits:—

'MOUNTPLEASANT, *Feb.* 16*th*, 1840.

'My Dear Friend,—In your own case, you say that "works of fiction" have lost much of their charm. With me it is exactly the same. Before my brother's illness and death, I was never idle: if I had but two minutes to spare, I had a book of one sort or other in my hand; I devoured eagerly every thing which came in the way; and rather than allow a book to leave the house unread, I would have sat a whole night to read it. But, since the occurrence of this mournful event, my very nature seems to have undergone a change. During those moments which I can spare from that drudgery of mind and body to which, for the last five months, I have been subjected, I never think of lifting a book; I feel no inclination to do so; for me it is quite enough to dose away the short interval in melancholy musing by the fire. You kindly invite me to come and see you; and gladly would I have embraced the invitation, had it been in my power; but, though I had the wish and the will to do so a thousand times, I lack the means of doing it once. I have now lived nearly thirty-four years,* and, from the time at which I was fourteen, I cannot recollect of more than two whole days which were devoted to pleasure. On these I attended Auchtermuchty Midsummer market two successive seasons, when in my fifteenth and sixteenth years. Since then I have rarely been an hour idle, except during my brother's last illness, when I attended him, and perhaps when some friend or acquaintance whose company I valued was in the house. I should also except those seasons when deprived of the ability to work, of which, as you know, an abundance has fallen to my share. But, with these exceptions, I have rarely been an hour idle, as said above, since I was fourteen; and, if we leave the unfinished house, which you saw when here, out of the account, I am still almost as poor as when I was commencing

* In several parts of Mr. Bethune's correspondence, I have observed that he reckoned his age two or three years below what, by the statement I received from his aunt, would be the case, and which I have every reason to depend on as correct.

my career—with this difference, that when I was young, however disastrous the present might be, Hope was always busy with the future; but now, she too seems to have lost the power of deceiving, and I must keep to my task and plod on as before, without any of her pleasing flatteries. I had almost begun to give you a history of the oft-repeated efforts which my brother, now no more, and myself, had made to save a little money from our miserable earnings, which rarely exceeded eight shillings a-week; of our partial success; and the manner in which some accident or other always came to blast our hopes in the first moments of prosperity, and throw us back upon our primitive poverty: but I spare you the cheerless recital of such events. I have already given you a gloomy picture of my own state and prospects; but it is a true one, and I hope it will account for my declining at present to make any attempt at complying with either your wishes or my own, by coming to England.   A. B.'

CHAPTER VI.

PREPARATION OF HIS BROTHER'S POEMS FOR THE PRESS, WITH SKETCH OF HIS LIFE—SEVERE APPLICATION TO THE TASK—SUCCESS IN OBTAINING SUBSCRIBERS—PUBLICATION AND HIGHLY FAVOURABLE RECEPTION OF THE WORK—DEATH OF HIS MOTHER—FEELINGS ON THAT OCCASION—FRIENDLY LETTERS OF ADVICE, &c.

At the request of a number of the friends of his deceased brother, Mr. Bethune resolved on publishing by subscription, a selection from his poems, with a sketch of his life. The views and feelings by which he was actuated in coming to this resolution, will be best learned from the following extracts of a letter to Mr. Dalgliesh, a gentleman who took a warm interest in his literary schemes, and procured upwards of a hundred subscribers for the Life and Poems.

'Respected Sir,—I herewith venture to trouble you with a quantity of manuscript, which I have copied from my much lamented brother's papers. I need hardly say, that my object in doing so, is to get your opinion as to their fitness for being offered to the public. When you were so kind as to call here, before the funeral, you will recollect I mentioned the subject to you. I was then sanguine in my expectations of being able to publish a small volume of his poetry, with the profits of which I had intended to place a stone over his grave. A little reflection, however, convinced me that I was by no means qualified for going through with all the canvassing necessary to get up a list of subscribers, sufficiently numerous to defray the expense of publishing; and, while I had determined to put the papers in printing condition as fast as possible, and to watch every opportunity of making them public, I had almost entirely abandoned the idea of making any attempt by subscription. Matters stood thus when, some time ago, I called upon Mr. Brodie. In the course of a short conversation, he mentioned the subject, and said, he thought there might be a possibility of disposing of a small edition by subscription and private distribution. Since then, I have seen a number of people in this neighbourhood who appeared anxious for a volume of his posthumous papers, along with a sketch of his life; and to show that it does not lie at my door, I am now ready to make the attempt. I must say, however, that I have no very sanguine expectations of success. A number of people will talk of anything, and everything, which takes nothing from them, with the greatest apparent pleasure, but whenever they must put their hands in their pockets, they are silent; and it is highly probable, that of those who have advised me to publish a part of my brother's papers, by far the greater number may belong to this class. Indeed, I almost expect that such will be the case. I have, however, been too long accustomed to see my own hopes, as well as the hopes of that friend who is now no more, terminate in nothing, to be at all disappointed if the present attempt should prove an entire failure.

'If I might beg so great a favour of you as the reading of the manuscript implies, I would have you to judge of it exactly as you would judge of any other production of which the author was entirely unknown; and if, after having done so, you thought that you could conscientiously recommend such a work to your friends, in the same manner as you would recommend the purchase of a printed book which you had read and they had not, I would certainly feel it as a very great obligation—otherwise, I would not wish to have a single word spoken upon the subject; nor would I wish to have a single unwilling subscriber. I have already said that my principal object in making the present attempt, is to raise a few pounds wherewith to place a stone over my brother's grave.

'Begging your pardon for having troubled you with these wearisome details, I must now be permitted to thank you for your very generous offer of assistance, at the time of my only brother's death. While I feel as much indebted to your kindness as if I had availed myself of that offer to the fullest

o

extent, I am glad to be able to inform you, that I am still able to meet my little engagements, though I have not a single halfpenny to spare.

'Begging your pardon once more for thus obtruding myself at such length upon your notice, I am, with the greatest respect, Sir, Your very humble servant,
A. B.

The sketch of his brother's life, as he states in a letter to a friend, he had set himself to compile immediately after his death, without any view to publication; though, afterwards, he could not but be gratified when such an interest was manifested in the subject as seemed to call for, and warrant this. Few of his brother's poems had received a final correction—many of them were in the first rude sketch; but never did an editor enter on his task with greater zeal, or with more reverence for the materials falling into his hands. Every scrap was numbered and registered, and described if it had not a distinct title. Care like this was necessary, as the manuscripts were in a very chaotic state—many of them having been written on whatever fragment bearing the name of paper might come to hand. The ardour with which he applied himself to this labour of fraternal affection, furnished some antidote to his melancholy, still the state of feeling often indicated in his letters, is gloomy enough, as, for example:—'There breathes not upon earth a more solitary thing than I am now. Though there is little to laugh at in the matter, it might, perhaps, make you smile, to hear my present mode of life. I rise, if I can make it out, about an hour before day-break;* kindle the fire; bring in coals and water to serve for the day; prepare my breakfast; and, if the morning is favourable, go to work as soon as I have a sufficiency of light; if it threatens rain, I remain at home—and of this there has been but too much of late. At night-fall, I return—write till within a little of midnight—go to bed; perhaps lie awake for nearly half of the time I should spend there, and then sleep too long next morning, which occasions me a sad hurry before I can get ready to go about. Thus one day follows another, in the same monotonous round, with nothing to checker or to change the prospect or the scene. In all my former struggles I had hope, however distant, to cheer me on.'

In addition to the time thus stolen from the night, and those days on which he was precluded from labouring out of doors by the state of the weather, we have reason to believe he devoted to his editorial labours as much more as he could possibly spare, consistently with obtaining the necessaries of life for himself and his aged mother; for we find him writing thus, in November :—' If

* The Letter from which this is extracted bears date, December 23rd.

S—— accepts of the present story—the money for which will free me from pressing necessity—I shall once more drop labour, and devote the whole of my attention to copying, correcting, and arranging his [John's,] papers, and writing a sketch of his life.' The story here referred to, was that entitled, 'The Unexpected Meeting'; in addition to which, we find him stating, in May, 1840, that, 'Since November last, he had contributed to the " Border Tales," " Wreckers and Smugglers," (No. ——;) " Julia Edwards," (No. 293;) " Caroline and her Cousin," (No. 298;) and " A Legend of the Coast," (No. 308).' These Tales alone would have involved no inconsiderable amount of literary labour; but when we think that he had, in addition to this, to transcribe and correct his brother's Poems, and write his Life; and at the same time reflect, that all this labour was undergone by a poor, solitary, disconsolate day-labourer, who had often to submit during the live-long day, to the severest drudgery, in order to procure the necessaries of life—conflicting emotions crowd on our minds. In proportion as we admire such exertions, and such strugglings, we feel a rising resentment at that state of public feeling which could allow such a man to remain in such a situation; and we ask, Could nothing have been done to raise him above such anxiety, and such toil, without wounding even his morbid sense of independence? Were our nobles and gentry but one-tenth part as alive to the claims of struggling merit, as to what they deem dangers to their peculiar interests, from some contested election, or some popular agitation, we will venture to say, that Mr. Bethune needed neither have remained under the necessity of submitting to the severest drudgery for bread, nor have felt himself degraded by being treated as an object of charity.

The Life and Poems enjoyed the advantage of passing under the revision of the literary friend so often referred to, as well as the other productions of the authors. Subscribers were obtained for between 500 and 600 copies; and the impression amounting to but 700, the remainder were almost immediately disposed of. The work was most favourably reviewed at length in the "Athenæum;" the "Witness," &c.; while highly favourable notices appeared in many of the Newspapers. The reception the book met with, was far more favourable, indeed, than its editor had ventured to anticipate; and, had the impression been larger, he might have derived considerable pecuniary benefit from it; but, from the limited number of copies printed, the delay which, owing to various circumstances, occurred ere a second edition was issued, and another cause which will bye and bye be adverted to, comparatively little profit was realized.

The gratification afforded him by the favourable reception of his publication, was marred by another melancholy bereavement. His mother was seized with paralysis towards the end of July, and after repeated shocks, which ultimately deprived her almost entirely of the power of speech and motion, she expired on the 21st December. During the whole of her illness, her son attended and watched over her with the most affectionate and self-denying care. In a letter to the writer of this, he states, that 'for nearly five months his clothes had never been off, except to shift his shirt.' After repeatedly taxing the powers of nature to such an unwarrantable extreme, can we wonder at his own early demise?*

His feelings on this occasion are well expressed in the following letter to a friend, then engaged in tuition in England.

'MOUNTPLEASANT, *December* 24, 1840.

'My Dear Friend,—After a period of the deepest anxiety, suspense, and alarm, I now take up a pen to inform you that my last remaining parent—she who was at least one of your warmest earthly friends—is now no more. The few words which I have already written, will make you acquainted with the annihilation of the last shred of that little world of domestic affection, in the midst of which

---

* Of the later years of his mother's life, and particularly of her last illness, Mr. Bethune has left a most touching memorial. It enters, however, too minutely into detail, to be as a whole fit for the public eye. What has appeared to the editor the more interesting portion, the reader will find in the appendix.

I was once happy, and among the remaining ruins of which I still wished to dwell. But all is now over: the last green spot around which memory, imagination, and fancy were alike fain to linger, has for ever disappeared, and an unvariegated desert remains behind.

'For near a fortnight previous to her death, my mother had been losing her appetite, and becoming gradually worse; and after four days and four nights of great restlessness and suffering—during which she never once lay down though she was frequently in bed—at ten minutes before two on the morning of Monday the 21st curt., her spirit fled to those scenes above, from the contemplation of which she had derived her chief enjoyment through life.

'With the exception of the corn-fields, which had begun to lose somewhat of their freshness, the summer was in its very prime when she was first taken ill. She lived to see the sickly hues of autumn succeed its gorgeous colouring—the crops cut down and secured—the trees stript of their verdure—and the fields prepared for the snowy mantle of the season; but before the full dreariness and desolation of winter had set in, her spirit fled, we trust, to the bowers of an unchanging spring. Yesterday her dust was laid to rest beside that of her husband and son; and she now sleeps at the left hand of her latest born, whose untimely death she continued to lament till within a few hours of her own. Hoping that you still continue to enjoy health, and praying that the blessing of God may rest on you, I remain, in the midst of affliction, Yours truly,

A. B.'

In a letter to another friend he says, 'Her dust was laid down to rest beside that of her "dear John," as she frequently called my brother after he was gone. And now, father, mother, and son, slumber side by side, in Abdie churchyard!—the three little mounds forming what may very appropriately be called, "The graves of a household." On the present occasion I feel even more desolate than when my only brother died. Then, I had his mother, and my own, beside me; and when my heart was full I could turn round to her and speak of the subject: but how can I expect that any one should now have patience to hear me tell my tale of sorrow.'

I give the following letter from the friend in England referred to at the end of last chapter, both from its value and appropriateness in regard to the occasion on which it was written, and as an indication of the not altogether rare attainments of natives of our country who have to earn their subsistence by their daily labour:—

' BEDWELL PARK GARDENS,
HATFIELD, HERTS, Dec. 31, 1840.

'My Dear Friend,—I have allowed three full days to pass away since receiving your note with the melancholy intelligence of your beloved mother's decease. You may perhaps think me careless in thus permitting such a length of time to pass before answering it, but, to tell you the truth, even now I scarce know how I am to do so. The tenor of some of your preceding letters was entirely such as might have led me to expect the sorrowful event; yet, while there remained even the bare possibility of recovery, hope was not extinguished, and I could not sometimes help thinking that she might yet be spared.

'I lament that it was not in my power to assist in bearing her remains to their final resting-place. It would have been a satisfaction, although a sad one, had I been able to do so. Well do I remember her parting words to me when I left Leafield: "Fare-ye-weel, Davie: I shall never see you again in this world." I thought upon these words after I had left her, and could scarce refrain from weeping. I have thought upon them a thousand times since; and even now I can fancy that I hear her pronounce them. It would have been much pleasure once more to have met her in this world, but it will be infinitely more to meet her in the world above, where she now is. She was one, and I might say the only neutral one in such circumstances, for whom I ever felt the same sort of attachment. So far back as I am capable of remembering, she was to my mind the object of veneration and affection. I have often endeavoured to trace these feelings towards her to their origin as connected with some circumstance in early life, but I have as often failed. I have no remembrance of their commencement. Doubtless her disinterested goodness of heart, the deep anxiety which she at all times manifested for my welfare and the welfare of all, were amongst the causes which produced them. She is now no more! and although it be some consolation to think she is now enjoying, in a better world, the society of those she loved in this, the mind has still to struggle with that sorrow occasioned by the consciousness that she is not with us. Yes, she is gone —and one tie less now exists of those that bound me to my native land. Every year, as it rolls past, carries with it into the bosom of eternity some one intimately connected with the heart's best affections; and, ere that which a few short hours will usher in has sped, it is very probable that the number of those who are only to be sought for in the remembrances of the mind will have been increased. But it is only adding to the present sorrow to anticipate others.

'You know better than I can tell you the only source from which comfort can be derived. Any attempt on my part to afford you consolation were far worse than useless. I am a partaker of your sorrow—I sympathize with you in your sufferings; and, were it in my power by word or deed to alleviate either, the being is not in existence that would more willingly do so.

'I shall be very anxious to hear from you. Do

write the first spare moment you have, let it be ever so little.—Most truly Yours, D. R.'

The following appears to have been Mr. Bethune's answer:—

'MOUNTPLEASANT, *Feb.* 6, 1841.

'My Dear Friend,—By this time you may well accuse me of carelessness; but, though I did not answer your last, as I had intended, I have not forgotten you. Indeed, when the dark and downward tenor of my fortune for the last three years is considered, I may perhaps be excused though I should not be very punctual in these matters. From the 8th of Feb. 1838, to the 21st of Dec. 1840, was, as you will perceive, little more than two years and ten months; yet within this short period I had seen the whole of the little family to which I belonged, one by one, seek their last resting-place in the cold grave, from which no effort and no care of mine could save them. It seemed as if each had been in haste to follow the other who had gone before; and, at the last mentioned date, I found myself alone in a world which had become to me emphatically "a desert!" But enough—they are gone, and every hour is lessening the distance between us.

'Your last letter was soothing, and accorded well with the melancholy state of my own feelings when I received it. Indeed, the manner in which you speak of my mother could hardly fail to be gratifying to any one in my circumstances. With perhaps her own share of those failings which "flesh is heir to," she was certainly a true and a warm friend where she professed friendship; and I believe she had all along regarded you with as much affection as it was possible to bestow upon any one beyond the circle of her own little family. This being the case, you may easily conceive that it was pleasing to the only individual on earth whom she had left to mourn her loss, to find that you had not forgotten her.

'Some time ago I was told by your mother that you were then busy in furnishing your house, and that the whole of the funds which you could muster had been required for this purpose. These are not her words, but they imbody her meaning. The thing is probably done now; but, had it been to do, at the risk of being deemed presumptuous, I should have advised you to do it in a plain style, and to encumber yourself with nothing more than what was necessary to your present comfort and convenience. Fair and smooth as matters may now appear, a storm may soon darken around you; and a good seaman will always endeavour to keep his vessel in sailing trim, whatever weather may betide. You have already felt somewhat of the mutations of fortune: in my own limited experience I could number more of them than is known to the world, and what has been before may be again. At all events, it is well to be provided for such occurrences, whether they should or should not come. To be prepared for the future cannot, in the smallest degree, detract from the enjoyment of the present; and I hope this is the principle upon which you act. I trust you still stick to temperance, and that the cause is prospering in your neighbourhood.

'A. B.'

The following letters and extracts, imbodying friendly suggestion and caution, show that Mr. Bethune's opinion and advice on the most important concerns of life, were valued and looked to with deference by those who had intimately known him long. The first two extracts imbody some very judicious observations on the proper combination of dependence on Providence, in a humble and submissive spirit, with the exercise of individual judgment and enlightened personal exertion in the concerns of life. The letters from which they are taken, are addressed to his friend, the tutor above referred to :—

'MOUNTPLEASANT, *July* 21*st*, 1840.

' Dear Sir,—Most sincerely do I sympathize with you in the unpleasant situation in which Providence has at present placed you; and I only wish it were in my power to communicate something like comfort. But, alas! in this respect I am a bankrupt myself, and can have but little of the kind to offer to others. All I can do is to add my amen to your own prayer, " that your way may be opened up," and, "that God may cause this shortly to work for good." Yet, while we pray to him for his aid in all things, we should also try to avail ourselves of such means as he may have placed within our reach, and to use that understanding with which he has endowed us, to lighten our trials and shorten those seasons of affliction which are caused by men. While endeavouring to imitate the "harmlessness of the dove," we are enjoined to aim at, "the wisdom of the serpent" also. The nature of your reception appears strange; and yet if you could contrive to bear up under it, neither overacting nor underacting your part, things might soon come round again to their old channel. When people experience coldness, it is certainly wise to avoid, as far as possible, giving any just cause for its continuance, and at the same time, neither to appear dispirited by it nor unhappy under it. There is, however, a sort of levity, and a propensity to make the conduct of others upon these occasions the subject of conversation, which should be shunned. When accident has thrown us into the company of one who has treated us coldly, if others be present, we try to laugh and to appear in very great spirits; if we are left alone with him, we are uncommonly dignified and silent; and, as soon as we get his back turned, we tell the first person we chance to meet, or rather every one with whom we converse, how little we care for him and his coldness, and that we should be sorry to waste a single thought on him. Now our doing all this, just serves to show how deeply we are cut, while it at the same time tends to perpetuate the uneasiness which we receive from such causes. On such occasions, you will find that nothing contributes more directly to restore one's cheerfulness, than the effort to be really cheerful, observing at the same time, towards the parties, such a bearing as to convince them that you can live without them, and that you can be happy either with or without their countenance. That you may be able to do this, say to yourself,—These men are in the hand of God; I have done them no wrong, and, unless he permit them, they cannot deprive me of the necessaries or comforts of life; why should they deprive me of my peace of mind?—I will not distress myself though others should look down upon me without a cause. I will spread forth my case before the Lord, and with his countenance and in his strength, I will endeavour to be composed and cheerful as I have been before. A. B.'

'MOUNTPLEASANT, *September* 2, 1840.

Dear Sir,—I trust the Lord will continue to bless you and your efforts for the good of others; and to be the joy and rejoicing of your heart, though seasons of sorrow and affliction must necessarily intervene. Clouds and storms form a part of the most propitious summer; and night must follow the sunniest day. It is even thus with human life: those who are most favoured have much to bear and much to suffer; but, as some one—Dr. Young, if I mistake not—has said of "crosses"—"Those who bear them best deserve them least." We must not look for unmingled happiness on this side eternity; nor hope to find aught abiding in the midst of a scene of perpetual changes.

'Before speaking of the change of situation to which you advert, pardon me if I should offer a few preliminary observations. And first—Though there are no doubt particular providences which frequently lead, or rather drive us, contrary to our own inclinations, in a particular direction where we are to meet some one to whom we are to be of use, or some one who is to be useful to us; still, in the ordinary concerns of life we must exercise our own judgments, and not run into hazardous courses in the expectation that God will work a miracle to rescue us from the effects of our own rashness. Paul " wrought with his own hands" for the things of this life. He no doubt knew that God could have supplied his necessities in a miraculous way, as he did those of the Israelites in the wilderness, had it been the divine pleasure so to do; but he knew also that "in the sweat of his brow" man was to eat bread; he knew that labour, according to God's appointment, was the way in which the greater part of mankind must procure their subsistence,—and therefore he was willing to use the means and look for the end in the ordinary course of events, without expecting a miraculous intervention of Providence in his behalf. Taking this view of the matter, I would have you to drop all thoughts of "giving in your resignation, and expecting that Providence will interfere to direct its acceptance or non-acceptance." You have doubtless read of the ancient custom of uncaging a bird and directing the march of an army according to its flight—as also of shooting an arrow into the air, and as it pointed onward, when it fell, or the reverse, proceeding with an expedition or returning home. To me it appears that there is too much of the ancient spirit of divination—too much of a wish to pry into futurity—in your project, to be in strict accordance with a sound christian philosophy. The question at issue is simply this, If you do not like your present situation, have you another in view where you would expect to be more comfortable? and if you have not, could you make out to live for a year or half a year upon your previous savings till something of the kind should come in the way? If you can answer neither of these questions in the affirmative, then it would almost appear to be your duty as well as your interest, if your present situation is at all tolerable, to try to make the best of it for at least a time.'

* * * * * * * *

'Were we to consider what every one would say and think of us upon every occasion, we would scarcely ever move a single step. There is a degree of firmness which is necessary to enable a person to go through with even the most trifling un-

P

dertaking: and that firmness when regulated by a discriminating sense of right and wrong, and habitually practised [maintained,] will in the end rarely fail to call forth the respect of those who can lay no claim to it themselves, and who at first might be inclined to censure it in others. In short, firmness is an indispensable ingredient in the character of all who would wish to reform either public or private abuses. A. B.'

The following is his opinion of a notorious weekly newspaper, which, to the disgrace of the English nation, it seems obtains a very wide circulation:—

'MOUNTPLEASANT, *October* 27, 1840.

* * * 'By the way, I do not consider that "Weekly Despatch" a good paper. Although it possesses an overwhelming circulation—the greatest, it is supposed, of any newspaper in Britain—from what I have seen of it, it appears to have no principles, but to cater through thick and thin for the prejudices of the most ignorant class of society, merely to keep up its popularity. For instance, the "Poor Laws," and "The Poor Law Amendment Act," are with it inexhaustable subjects of declamation; and, from what you say in a former letter about "whig bastiles," I believe that it has, in part, led even you astray. You must consider this subject again—consider what national wealth is, and what are its effects upon society; and you will find that the whole amount of the sum which goes to support paupers is taken directly from the fund which should give employment to independent labourers. No enlightened well-wisher of his country could have wished to see the Poor Laws remaining as they were. Previous to the Amendment Act, they literally gave a premium upon indolence and improvident marriages, while they placed honest industry and independent feeling at a most terrible discount. A. B.'

The following is from a note accompanying a snuff-box which had belonged to Mr. Bethune's brother, as a memorandum to a friend:—

'MOUNTPLEASANT, *July* 23, 1840.

'My Dear Friend,—I now enclose for you a small white-iron snuff-box which belonged to my brother, with a very small quantity of the last ounce of snuff which was ever bought for him. Had you not requested it, I should have been ashamed to send you such a homely article; but, to quote a verse of his own, which you will shortly see in the book,

"'Tis not the value of the gift,
　As valued in the world's esteem,
Which makes the boon by Friendship left,
　A thing of such importance seem."

Had he been in the habit of fawning upon great men, and flattering them for his own interest, it is probable I might have been able to send you a silver-mounted snuff-box, which had been presented to him by Mr. This, or Sir Somebody That, or my Lord Something-else; but whatever his few wants required, it was his wish to purchase for himself, and, to the honour of "a discerning world" be it told, he was allowed to do it. No one ever thought of presenting him with anything which would cost them a halfpenny; and he had himself too much of the reflecting principle to squander his scanty earnings upon useless finery. But, let others think what they may, I now feel prouder of his stern and uncompromising independence—far prouder—than I should have done had he been in the receipt of favours from half the great men in Fife. A. B.'

CHAPTER VII.

CORRESPONDENCE WITH MRS. HILL, EMBRACING OPINIONS ON GENERAL EDUCATION, PAUPERISM, POOR LAWS, PRISON DISCIPLINE, POLITICAL ECONOMY, &c.—VISIT TO GLASGOW—SITUATION OF TURNKEY THERE—ILLNESS—RETURN HOME.

I HAVE now to introduce to the reader portions of a very interesting correspondence between Mr. Bethune and Mrs. Hill, the lady of the Inspector of Prisons for Scotland, which appears to have originated from a desire on Mrs. Hill's part to introduce him into what she conceived would be a situation of less hardship and greater usefulness than that which he had hitherto occupied. But her views in opening this correspondence will be best explained by a portion of one of her Letters. After expressing deep sympathy with his mother's sufferings, (then in her last illness,) and making enquiry whether there was any way in which she could contribute to their alleviation, or to the promoting of her comfort by cordials, warm clothing, &c.—which, like all similar proffers, Mr. Bethune declined—she proceeds;—

'I do not know whether chance has ever brought before you any account of the exertions that my husband, as Inspector of Prisons for Scotland, has made for the reformation of "our criminal brethren." Although his wife, I have no hesitation in saying, that during the five years he has been Inspector, the good that has been effected in the prisons of Scotland, with limited means, has been surprising; but now the operation of the New Prison Act, under the especial control of a General Board, (of which he is a member,) insures an active and able management over the whole country. There are some highly-talented as well as benevolent men at the head of some of the larger prisons, or applying for the Governorship of them; and many able, good, and efficient men over others. Excellent instructors are also being appointed to all prisons where the prisoners are detained a considerable time. Everything is being done to teach new habits of industry, self-employment, and honourable feelings to the poor individual whose ignorance and recklessness, or wretched early training, have made him the inmate of a prison. Many are the delightful anecdotes that the enlightened and benevolent Governor of the Glasgow Bridewell, Mr. Brebner, can give of the effect of such discipline, and most interesting it is to hear them.

'Would you like to aid in this good work? Of course, till a personal communication, we could not tell what precise situation would be most suitable for you; but do you feel, that to help to snatch the unfortunate from guilt and misery, is a great and noble employment? Perhaps you are not aware, that the order and arrangement of a well-conducted prison, is wholly different from all our old ideas of a prison. In the separate system, no swearing, quarrelling, or displeasing conversation assails the ears. The prisoner in his cell, is in the best condition to avail himself not only of the solace of industry, but of books, instruction, and sympathy. This latter motive is almost wholly wanting when prisoners are together; but, when separated from their companions in vice and misery, they gratefully feel the value of the kindness of a judicious governor or warder. I speak from the experience of the best informed. Perhaps you may think, that your habits of life having been so contrary to the habitual, control, zeal, and watchfulness necessary in an officer of a prison, you might not be able to adapt yourself to so new a position. This is, however, no objection. It is desirable for all the new officers, however high may be their position, to go through a regular training in the Glasgow Bridewell, for a few weeks at least, where they may practically see the working of a good system of management, where kindness and good discipline take the place of harshness and disorder.

'Mr. Hill begs me to tell you, that should he succeed in obtaining a situation for you, we are aware that you could not afford to lose so many weeks' salary, but that we will undertake the necessary expenses of your residing at Glasgow, while daily attending the Bridewell, as well as your travelling expenses.

'I do not call your attention to any one particular situation—in the state your poor mother is in, you could not immediately avail yourself of one—but I wish to know your general opinion. The requisites of a good officer are manifold. From your works, and the high character we have heard of you, we have no doubt whatever of your excelling in high integrity, and moral and intellectual worth, all which qualifications are so truly desirable for the cause which we have so deeply at heart; and we have very little doubt that the other requisites will not be wanting. These, however, can but be judged of by an interview. Our first object is, to secure an efficient officer in the public service; our second, to benefit an individual who has at once excited our respect and our sympathy; and happy shall we be, if we can combine the two objects.

'In answering my letter, will you be so good as to mention any kind of labour that you think you can superintend; and whether, besides your love of literature, you happen to be fond of music or drawing. Weaving, I remember, you are acquainted with.

'Hoping, dear Sir, notwithstanding the sorrowful cloud that is yet hanging over you, that life has many cheering years of happiness and usefulness still in store for you,—Believe me to remain, Yours, very sincerely,   MARTHA HILL.'

'EDINBURGH, 25*th November*, 1840.'

The following letters to this lady imbody some very interesting references to Mr. Bethune's personal history and habits, as well as his views on some very important subjects connected with the improvement of the condition of the people:—

'MOUNTPLEASANT, *Nov.* 30. 1840.

'Dear Madam,—Three days ago I received your long and very interesting letter; and in acknowledging it I can only say—as my poor brother did when shown some trifling presents which had been sent him as he lay dying—" that I could not have believed there was so much benevolence in the world!" I should have returned an answer sooner had it not been that I wished to delay doing so, till I could read the whole of the " Report"* with which you were so kind as to favour me. I have now read the greater part of it attentively; but, though this is the case, I find that at present I cannot command resolution to enable me to advert to its particulars in such a manner as I could have wished. My mother is just now considerably worse than she has been for some time past; and after a

* Mr. Hill's 5th Report on Prisons.

night of much suffering to her, and of sleepless and painful anxiety to me, I have so much to distract my attention, that I scarce know what I am writing. Indeed, I begin to feel somewhat weary of a world in which my efforts to benefit myself and others, have been so often frustrated; and were it not that I would wish, if possible, "To keep a while, one parent from the grave," at this moment I could almost sigh for that "place of refuge and repose" where, in the language of scripture, "The wicked cease from troubling, and the weary are at rest." If you only knew how limited are my wishes, and how little I can now expect to enjoy, you would turn your benevolent efforts to some other quarter, where they were more likely to be rewarded with that success which they so eminently deserve.

'But, to indulge no longer in useless generalities, —though I could not possibly leave my poor debilitated parent, with whom, as it seems, I have exchanged relationship, and who now looks up to me for assistance and support with all the helplessness, and—from the circumstance of her mind being affected, as well as her body—with all the simplicity of a child; yet in the event of my surviving her, if for nothing else than to show how ready I was to adopt the course which you had pointed out, I should be inclined to go to the Glasgow Bridewell for the purpose of ascertaining what were the duties of an efficient prison officer. While I would pause here to thank you and Mr. Hill for your generosity in offering to bear my expenses, I would humbly beg to say that I should consider myself bound to bear these myself. They would not amount to any very great sum; for my habits are still almost as unexpensive, and my wants almost as few, as when I was a boy. As an evidence of this, I may be allowed to say, that a pound of oatmeal made into porridge, and a pennyworth of milk, serves me regularly for both breakfast and supper; my dinner is even still less expensive; and beyond a draught of cold water, I never required any intermediate meals. In short, my ordinary fare has seldom cost more than the cheaper kinds of what is called prison diet. After having seen the "working of the system," if I thought the duties were such as I could perform, I should then be ready thankfully to accept of a temporary appointment to some subordinate situation; and if I could succeed in performing the duties of that situation in a more creditable way than they had been performed by others, I would naturally expect to be advanced. But, on the other hand, if I had good reason for suspecting that my own experience and abilities were not such as to qualify me for the task, I would certainly be doing wrong were I to allow any prospect of pecuniary advantage, or even the overweening kindness of a patron to weigh with me in accepting a situation where I could not ultimately give satisfaction to my employers. These are simply and briefly my views of the matter: and I hope you will pardon the abrupt manner in which circumstances have at present compelled me to state them.

'Though a natural propensity for trying everything which came in the way, and a somewhat checkered fortune, have contributed to make me partially acquainted with various kinds of work, I fear there are only a few, and these the least available, which I could "superintend." With the blasting of rock, stone-breaking, hedging, ditching, the forming of roads, wood-cutting and pruning, sawyers-work, and gardening I have been familiar since boyhood. At some of these occupations, I have occasionally directed the operations of twenty men—without, however, receiving a farthing more for my trouble, than the least responsible labourer of the gang—and I do not think I should find much difficulty in superintending any to a considerable extent; but they could be of no service in the case under consideration. When I was a boy, with the odd halfpence which children usually spend at fairs and in toy shops, I bought wright's tools, with which I made chairs and tables; and of these, that upon which I now sit, and at which I now write, are specimens. To oblige, and at the same time save the money of some poor neighbours, I was also in the habit of working during my leisure hours, as a cooper; and there is not at present, a single wooden vessel in the house, which I have not at some time or other repaired. From having devoted a portion of my spare time to mending shoes, I had once some little fame as a cobbler;

I never indeed attempted to make new ones, but, with a little attention, I could have repaired the old almost as well as most shoemakers. After I came to be engaged in the quarries, when the smith chanced to be from home, I sometimes endeavoured to supply his place by sharpening the quarry tools myself; and at this branch of the business I had acquired a tolerable proficiency. By far the greater part of both the mason and wright work of the house in which I now live was performed by myself and my poor brother. We succeeded, however, more by patient and unwearied perseverance, than by that despatch which should characterize a good tradesman; and it would be utter folly in me to lay claim to anything like a perfect knowledge of any of these businesses. From the foregoing it will be seen that my occupations have been as varied and as numerous as those of most other men. In so far as regards the subject under consideration, most of them could be of no use; but I once had great confidence in my own ability to learn anything, and, though it is highly probable that passing time may have impaired the quickness of the capacity, in an emergency I still think I could learn a little. Lest it should be supposed that I might have made a fortune, I must here be permitted to say, that the little skill I possessed in these crafts, was, in most instances, exerted for the benefit of others, and very rarely brought any advantage to myself beyond the pleasure of having surmounted difficulties which others would not attempt to overcome.

'Of music, when supplied by others, I was always fond; but I could never either sing, or play upon any instrument myself. Perhaps my ignorance of these accomplishments may be partly attributable to the circumstance of having had so much of what some one has called, "sterner work to do." I was wont, moreover, to consider music as a mere amusement, and, when carried to excess by those who had to earn their bread with the sweat of their brow, as a sort of dissipation of time; and, as I always wished to be engaged in something useful, I never thought of following after it. To drawing I can advance no claim. I beg to enclose for your inspection the only trial I ever made in my life. As you may see by comparing it with the frontispiece to my brother's Poems, it is an attempt to take a sketch of that group of old houses in one of which my best and happiest years were spent. I had no teacher or assistant. I soon found that I wanted that accuracy and delicacy of touch which would have been necessary to finish a picture upon which a lithographer could proceed, and after working upon it for half an hour, I gave it up in despair. I should say, however, that I have drawn plans of fields, plantations, and roads, upon a given scale, with no other instruments for taking angles &c. than such as I had constructed myself. My life throughout has been a busy one; and, with respect to getting forward in the world, the result holds out but small inducement to others to follow my example. Yet it was not in my nature to be idle. With me, to be employed upon some new undertaking, and to find that I could succeed in it, was frequently to be as happy as mortals need ever expect to be in the midst of what has emphatically been called " A Vale of Tears!" and perhaps if I had got less to do, I should only have had more time to muse on those melancholy subjects of which enow have been in my way. A. B.'

'Moutpleasant, *Jan.* 6, 1841,

* * * * * 'The works which we were able to purchase were neither very numerous nor very important, at least during the early part of our career. Some time afterwards I shall beg to give you a list of them. The mass of reading, however, which passed through our hands, was by no means inconsiderable. After it became known that we were readers, the whole of our acquaintances, far and near, and even some people whom we could hardly number as such, appeared eager to lend us books. It was soon discovered that we could despatch a pretty large volume in a very few evenings, and that we never suffered a book to sustain the slightest injury while in our possession; and thus people lent us books which they had themselves borrowed, without the slightest hesitation. So punctual were we in these matters, and so unwilling either to break faith, or return a book unread, that on one occasion I recollect perfectly having gone through the whole of one of Sir Walter Scott's novels, a work, so far as I can remember, of upwards of 400 closely printed pages, between night-fall and four o'clock next morning. The work was one of the first uniform issues, with the author's notes. Though we used to read alternately, dividing the labour between us, upon this occasion, from my brother having caught cold, nearly the whole devolved upon me; and well do I recollect the strange feeling of exhaustion which crept over me before I had reached the end. In addition to the books with which we were thus favoured, for a series of years, commencing with its very first appearance, we got regularly "Chambers' Edinburgh Journal," and this of itself served to keep up a degree of activity and a constant succession of new ideas in our minds. Indeed I have often thought since, that it was well we were readers then; for afterwards our time for such pursuits became very circumscribed, and we were glad to devote almost every minute which could be spared from works of necessity to writing, in the hope—a vain one so far as we were concerned—that we might thereby be able to better our fortune.

* * * * * *

'It affords me very sincere pleasure to see the subject of "Houses of Refuge" so warmly taken up, both in the Report, and in John Wigham's tract. Such institutions, when once fairly established, with economical management should support themselves

—a very important feature in a country like this; and I have not the slightest doubt that they would be the means of confirming good and virtuous habits in the bosoms of thousands who otherwise would inevitably fall back to their former vicious courses, and ultimately become the subjects of criminal legislation. If the thing were possible, though I know it is not, I would strongly advocate the necessity of the whole of our young men and young women belonging to the humbler ranks of society, undergoing a regular course of training in some school of industry similar to these Houses of Refuge, before they were allowed to settle in life. It is truly distressing to look upon that mass of poverty and wretchedness which is at present eating into the very vitals of society; and it is equally distressing to think that this mass of poverty and wretchedness has been in a great measure brought on by the idleness and early improvidence of the very individuals who are suffering from it. I feel confident that the general diffusion of industrious and economical habits, added to an ordinary degree of foresight, would, in the course of a single generation, go so far to banish from our land those appalling scenes of misery which are constantly harrowing the heart and the eye of humanity; but hitherto, with the exception of the feeble and rash attempt made by my brother and myself, an attempt which fell still-born from the press, no practical effort has been made to beget or to foster such habits.

Dr. Chalmers has spoken of making the poor support the poor, according to some plan which he adopted in a parish about Glasgow, and Dr. Alison (if I have not mistaken the meaning of a paragraph which I saw in a stray newspaper) has advocated the necessity of the rich supporting the poor; but no one has endeavoured to prove to the poor that, with proper management, it might be possible for them individually to support themselves, and that it is alike a duty and an honour for them to do so. Yet, unless this can be done, as society now stands in this country, I think it almost admits of being proved that we must go on from bad to worse, till we arrive at a state of things resembling that which prevails in Ireland. As an auxiliary and nurse to the great principle of self-dependence, I know of no means likely to be more successful than Savings Societies, as sketched in " Practical Economy." If a man can only be persuaded to save one pound, by a sort of instinct he almost always wishes to add another to it; and, having once been accustomed to consider himself somebody, he has ever after an aversion to the idea of sinking into nobody. Such hard-earned savings, moreover, are always estimated more highly and guarded with infinitely greater care than an unearned fortune. Hence it were but fair to infer that if young men generally could be got to make a beginning, they would be inclined to pause and consider before they ventured to incur the responsibilities, which, if incurred without a proper provision, must necessarily plunge them deep in the gulf of poverty and misery. We all see the wretchedness that prevails, we are all in the habit of lamenting over it, and we often talk of financial and commercial embarrassments as the causes from which it proceeds; but when we have done these things, and perhaps endeavoured to lend some temporary relief, we think we have done enough,—no one thinks of probing the sore to the bottom. Yet if this were done, it would at once be seen that the youthful improvidence of our manufacturing population, their early marriages, and the rapid increase of their numbers which is thus occasioned, are the plague-spots of modern society—the worm which is preying on the root of every comfort; and till these evils are so far remedied, no palliation will ever do much in diminishing the amount of national suffering. Could not Robert Chambers take up the subject?—he has done much already to enlighten the minds of his poor countrymen—and fairly institute a Savings Society under his own eye, as a model for others to proceed upon. Originating with him, and backed with the influence of the Journal, the scheme would certainly find favour and support, although it emanated from too obscure a quarter at first to attract any notice. With but half the influence which some people derive from their annual thousands, I have often fancied that, in some respects, I could mould society to my will; but with only the influence of a poor individual earning his daily bread with the sweat of his brow, I have all along felt that I was a nonentity, and could do nothing.

'When I began to write, I had not the slightest intention of touching on this subject, but having been led into it, and having thus got upon one of my hobbies, it seems I could not easily get off again.

'I was much pleased with an article in the "Australian Record," entitled, "Self-Taxation and Emigration." The philanthropist may rest assured, that he cannot minister more effectually to the comfort of his poorer brethren, than by affording every facility for freeing the country from the surplus population which is at the root of Irish misery, and which is every year making both English and Scottish misery more distressing. But upon this subject I must not enter. * * *
I have long been of opinion, that the first essential to reforming any one, from the petty wrong-doer to the abandoned blackguard, is to secure his affections; and this, in general, is easily done, though few people ever think of making the attempt. Assist a boy with his top, or his kite, or enable him to get through with some favourite scheme, and he will do almost anything you please for you in return. In these matters, full-grown men are often mere children; they have only to be convinced, by your conduct and general bearing toward them, that you do take an interest in their happiness and would willingly make them better

men if it were in your power—taking care, however, to show, at the sametime, that you are not to be duped by any artifice to which they may have recourse—and then there is, at least, a chance that they will listen attentively to whatever you may have to say; and, should your character be such as to command the respect of others, there is also a strong probability, that they will endeavour to follow your example. I am again an invalid, and this is the only excuse I can plead for the length of the present letter—the writing of it having been my only amusement, and, indeed, all that I have been able to do, for the last two days. My complaint, however, is nothing more than a second cold. From having been, for some weeks previous to my mother's death, constantly in a room which was kept warm for her sake, the wintry winds seem now to pass through me as if I were a withered leaf; and I feel that it will require some care to harden me, before I can face the storm as I was wont to do. A. B.'

'Mountpleasant, *January* 18*th*, 1841.

'Dear Madam,—

* * * * * * * *

'My warmest thanks are due to the patriot who introduced the penny postage, which has been the means—I had almost said—of saving me from ruin. If the hundreds of letters which I have received within the last twelve months had cost, as was usual, fron 7½d., to 1s. each, I know not where or what I should have been ere now. I am getting better, and endeavouring to take the best care of myself I can. In a short time I expect to be able to acknowledge at greater length your kindness. In the meantime, I remain, Dear Madam, Your much indebted, very humble servant, A. B.'

'Do pardon me for returning the stamps, which, I trust, will not be required. This is unnecessary, you will say; but it is only following out a principle which you have taught me to respect more than ever. A. B.'

'MOUNTPLEASANT, *January 31st*, 1840.

* * * * * * * *

'While the thing is in my head, I must not forget to tell you that I received a letter the other day from my unknown friends, enclosing £15 *—requesting me to acknowledge receipt of the money "in a sealed note," which the Messrs. Black would address—

---

* This sum, as well as that mentioned below, was contributed by Mr. H. F. Chorley, author of "Music and Manners," and a few friends, and transmitted anonymously, through Messrs. A. & C. Black. Mr. Bethune used every effort to find a clue to the donors, in order to return the money, but without success. In these circumstances he lodged it in the Bank, and so far as I have been able to ascertain, continued to decline applying any of it to his own use. Whether any of it was applied to the erection of the monument to his brother, as some thought of doing so is indicated in the present letter below, I have not been able to ascertain.

and stating that if there was anything else in which these friends could assist me, to correspond with them through the same medium, &c. It immediately occured to me that this was a way of reaching these friends which I had not before thought of; and I accordingly acknowledged the money, and returned it at the same time—thanking my benefactors in the best way I could—assuring them that I was not in want—that, upon principle, I considered it the duty of every man to provide for his own necessity as far as his ability would go—and begging to be made acquainted with the name of the gentleman who had interested himself so much in my behalf, &c. &c. The first £10 is still in the Commercial Bank as a deposit in my name, but I intend to send that also as soon as I get an answer to my last communication. No mention was made of the money having been sent for the purpose of erecting a stone to my brother's memory. For this, however, I have now made arrangements with a tradesman. It is only a plain stone, somewhat larger than the common size, with the name of the deceased, the date of his death, and his age, at the top; and below this, the last verse of the first of his own "Hymns of the Churchyard." On the opposite side, or back of the stone, will be the words, " Erected by an only brother to the memory of the ' poor inhabitant below.'" I have now applied for liberty to enclose the three graves with a wall not exceeding two feet in height—a liberty which it seems

I cannot obtain till a meeting of the heritors takes place, and which may perhaps be denied even then;* but if it is granted I intend to place another small stone on the eastern side of the square, with the words, " The graves of a household," engraved upon it. These are my plans, and the accomplishment of them, I am told, will cost between 10 and 11 pounds —a sum which I am glad to find I can still afford.

'Though not habitually a very great egotist, I would beg your permission to say a few words concerning myself. Since a little after my mother's death, I have been the sole inhabitant of a house which, by the road, is at a distance of more than a hundred yards from any other; and there I cook and eat my solitary dinner, and days pass in which I never see " the human face divine," or once try my voice at speech. To some this would be the consummation of misery, but to me it is nothing. Indeed, the day always appears to be too short. I am now so far recovered, that I have only a slight cough, and I should have been willing to go to Glasgow immediately, had it not been for the following reasons :—As far back as 1826, while engaged in harvest work, I slept in what was called a stableloft. From the breath of the horses, which had free access to ascend, the place was frequently like an oven; but then, if a gale chanced to spring up— from the vicinity of a large hole in the wall, through

---

* It was denied.

which the fodder was introduced, and which had no door or other provision for closing it—it was no uncommon thing to have the bed-clothes ruffled with the wind. In other respects I liked the place well enough, because it freed me from the noise of the rabble with whom I was connected by day; but the changes of temperature were often, in a single night, very great, and, as a consequence which might almost have been expected, I caught a severe cold. For months afterwards it was entirely neglected, till at last it seemed to bid fair for terminating in consumption.* With the constant exercise in the open air, however, which my work afforded, and a constitution otherwise unimpaired, I did recover; and more recently I have recovered from the effects of accidents which, in the estimation of others, rendered my case alike hopeless and desperate; but since then I have always been more subject to catch cold, particularly from travelling and changing my bed in severe weather. To avoid the last-mentioned circumstance, I have sometimes walked between forty and fifty miles in the depth of winter, that I

---

* I have no other information regarding this case than what the above statement affords; but Mr. Bethune's employer, whoever he was, was culpable to a degree not easily estimated, in sending any human being to sleep in such a place. Immediately above horses is a very unwholesome situation to sleep in, however well protected the place may be from the weather. But in such a place, with a large open hole or door in it—we hardly could have believed such barbarity to have existed,

might reach home the same day on which I had left it.

* * * 'I am glad that you sent me the "Abstract of Dr. Alison's pamphlet." I have now read the whole of it with deep interest; and I must say that the facts which he has brought forward—facts with which I was before wholly unacquainted—have tended considerably to modify my ideas with regard to Poor-Laws. The prevailing and regularly increasing amount of national misery certainly does call for prompt measures to check its progress. Education, in time, might obviate a part of the evil; but then it would be inhuman to stand by and see thousands on thousands perishing in the very lowest abyss of wretchedness and crime, while this slow remedy is in the course of application, without making an immediate effort to rescue them from their fate; and for such an effort—made upon a scale sufficiently extensive—voluntary charity will not supply the means. I am now convinced that if any thing deserving the name of relief is to be attempted, assessment is the only alternative; and as it would equalize the burden, making it bear alike upon the unfeeling and the benevolent, it seems to be the best course which could be adopted. But it is easy to see that the measure will be opposed by at least two-thirds, if not three-fourths, of the whole landed interest in Scotland; and unless the English members carry it through in defiance of the Scotch, it must be lost to the country. Work-

Houses, of which I had not before thought, evolve an excellent principle. In them it is easy to recognize a sufficient check upon imposture, and at the same time the means of effectually relieving real destitution. But perhaps the best feature of the whole is, that they *do not tend materially to break down the independence of their inmates so long as it is of any importance to the community to have that feeling preserved.* If I understand the system properly, every " able-bodied" man and woman who is admitted into these institutions is set to work in one shape or other; and so long as an individual is constantly employed, he has reason to believe that he is providing for his own wants, the only circumstance being the overseer's furnishing him with work. Thus the feeling of independence is left to operate in the natural way as long as people are fit for labour; and when this ceases to be the case, society can suffer nothing from its being dispensed with. The only danger seems to be, that the prospect of a legal provision against old age, might make individuals less careful to provide for this season themselves; but practically it would appear that the confinement and strict discipline of a Work-House in a great measure counterbalance the evil to be expected from this quarter. It may also be fairly admitted that very few ever think of making a provision for old age in the time of youth, which, with most, is the only time at which it could be done; so that, view the matter as you will, very little can be lost. I myself have known more than one family who have been brought to the very verge of starvation by a fictitious want of employment which, so far as I could judge of the matter, was a premeditated plan among their superiors; and nothing could move these superiors to stir hand or foot in their behalf; nor was it till after an interval of three months that the men, three in number, succeeded in procuring employment. The thing occurred in the winter of 1832-3, when a spirit of dissension seemed to exist between some of the ultra-conservatives in this neighbourhood and the industrious classes, in consequence of the passing of the Reform Bill. From having endeavoured to interest myself in the cause of these poor men, I could still detail the whole story to the minutest circumstance; but into these details it would serve little purpose to enter. Suffice it to say, that I did consider it barbarous, to a degree, in these gentlemen thus to wreak their party spleen upon a few unoffending day labourers, who had never in their lives attended a single political meeting, and who could not possibly, in any way, either forward or retard the measure which then kept the county by the ears. The scene was truly distressing to those who had an opportunity of hearing the complaints and desponding thoughts of the suffering individuals, as I did; but with Work-Houses and a properly administered Poor-Law, such a scene could not have occurred. What Dr. Alison mentions about the simultaneous ejectment of the poor people from whole estates—a thing which, when indispensable, should always be done gradually—is also revolting to humanity. This circumstance alone would make it appear that checks upon the rich are, in some instances, as necessary as checks upon the poor; and therefore, I would say, let us have Work-Houses if we can get them. For myself, I can only bid Dr. Alison, Mr. Hill, and every other gentleman who is engaged in the cause of humanity, God speed.

'With all this, I would spare no effort to keep poor rates within as narrow limits as possible; for whenever a large amount of charity is required, it may at once be inferred that something is wrong, and that society is in an unhealthy state. It should also be remembered, that there are serious evils inseparable from a large amount of charity, in whatever form it may be bestowed; and not the least of these is the circumstance of every half-penny which is given in charity, being abstracted from the fund which otherwise would have gone to employ independent labourers. It may indeed be said, that the rich can well spare a few luxuries for the support of the indigent poor; but then, there is scarcely a single article which either rich or poor can purchase, upon which labour has not been bestowed, and the purchase of which does not tend directly to create a demand for more labour. Take foreign wines for an example:—At first sight it would appear that the consumption of these could not in any way benefit the British labourer; but with a little investigation, it would perhaps be found that a large proportion of these very wines had been brought home in exchange for articles of British manufacture. I do not say that the drinking of wine is the best way in which a man can spend his income, but, that this branch of expenditure is not wholly without its use. Of course this argument cannot be applied to ardent spirits, the drinking of which I think, almost admits of being proved to be positively injurious to the community, in every sense of the word. Now, if the above doctrine is correct, and if there be any truth in Political Economy, the rich cannot curtail even their luxuries—unless they save the money for other purposes—without diminishing, to a certain extent, the demand for labour, and producing a consequent diminution in the wages of the labourer. Take what most people would be inclined to consider the very worst view of the matter, by supposing that all the rich were to become misers, and hoard up their money with the very greatest care; and still they could not do even this without conferring a positive benefit upon society. To derive any advantage from spare money, people either must employ it themselves, or place it at interest, in both of which ways, by an immutable law, it must find its way into the pockets of the industrious classes; and, by creating a demand for their labour, tend to improve their condition. In short, it would appear that we really want more misers than we have; and upon reflection it would appear that the Wise Governor of the universe has regulated it upon a principle of benevolence, which makes even men's selfishness minister to the good of their fellow-creatures. From natural stupidity, I may have failed to state the matter so as to make you understand it, or, what is still more probable, you understood it a thousand times better than I do, before you had read one word of what I have written; and thus, like every one else whose heart is open to the calls of benevolence, while you are willing to sacrifice so much good to get rid of a pressing amount of evil, you will see the propriety of keeping both principles in view, and endeavouring to lessen misery in both ways, namely, by a well administered Poor-Law, and by endeavouring to communicate to the poor a knowledge of those immutable laws which regulate their income, and those principles upon which their prosperity and the prosperity of nations must ever depend.

'Here, if I might venture to express an opinion upon so momentous a question, I would say, that it might, perhaps, be advisable to make the rudiments of Political Economy a subject of instruction in every school and seminary of education, from the highest to the lowest. Political Economy is a most important science—imasmuch as it may be denominated, without a figure—the science of the prosperity of nations, and the comfort of their inhabitants; and it might be taught with a great deal more advantage than Geography, and some other things with which the children of the poor often dissipate their time at school to little purpose. A knowledge of some of the leading principles—such, for instance, as the theory of wages, and the manner in which population and capital act and re-act upon each other, &c., &c.—would in every case enable the labourer to trace the hardships of his condition to their real causes; and, by enlisting his selfishness, which, with the greater part of mankind, is the most powerful of all the passions, on the side of true reform, prove a most efficient engine for removing many of these hardships. It might also be presumed, that such a knowledge would free us from many of those wild and impracticable theories with which the Chartists of the present day distract their own heads, and distress thinking individuals. So long as the great mass of the labouring poor consider that they are " unjustly deprived of their rights," (I use their own language,)—that " it is the selfishness of their rulers by which they are oppressed," (a principle, by the way, which is as powerful in the lowest, as in the highest of the race,)—and that " the rich, if they were actuated by proper motives, could make them perfectly happy,"—they will always be ready to indulge in day-dreams about reforming the government, and to grasp at every thing they can lay their hands on in the shape of charity; while it were almost unreasonable to expect them to do more for themselves than what the lash of misery compels them to do. But if it were proved to them in a popular form, and upon the clearest evidence, that while charity may do good to some, it is almost as great an evil to others of their own class—that the root of bitterness lies amongst themselves, and that they only have the ability to eradicate it—that their employers, in truth, have no more power in regulating the amount of their wages and comforts, than *they* have in regulating the luxuries of their employers—and, in short, that the social system can never be greatly amended unless they lend the whole force of their own individual efforts, scientifically and steadily directed to one great purpose,—it were at least reasonable to suppose, that in time we might have a better state of society, and that, ultimately, the demands upon charity might be greatly reduced.

'This process of improvement must necessarily be slow; and to afford any hope of success, it must be begun with the young; for it is easy to see that the heads of the old are already filled with a set of notions which it would be very difficult either to efface or alter. This throws us once more back upon the schools, where I think classes might advantageously be formed, for instructing the elder boys in the principles of Political Economy; while at school examinations &c., it might even be advisable, to award the highest prizes for the greatest amount of knowledge in this science. In our Scottish parochial school system, however, which is far from good, no reform of the kind could be expected, unless the government interfere, and positively enjoin that such and such qualifications be henceforth deemed indispensable in all candidates for the office of a parish schoolmaster. But here again there is too much reason to fear a determined opposition from the clergy, as well as from the whole host of those whose hobby is " Religious Instruction." If such a parliamentary enactment could not be obtained, or, what were still better, in addition to it, it might be of the greatest importance to have a set of " Easy Lessons" upon Political Economy, mixed up with the whole catalogue of school books. This could hardly fail to familiarize by degrees the mind of the pupil with those subjects upon which his thoughts were to be afterwards engaged. Another advantage which would result from the adoption of this plan, deserves to be mentioned. From the circumstance of almost every one endeavouring to send his children to school, for a longer or shorter period, according to his ability, these books may be frequently seen among agricultural labourers; and, in short, in the families of our whole rural population, where no sort of literature, and no book besides, is to be met with. Now, if the plan noticed above were acted upon, the parents might sometimes stumble upon useful instruction, when mere curiosity prompted them, as it frequently does, to look into the books of their children. I had almost forgotten to say, that with a view to ascertain how far a Poor-Law operates upon population, it might be of some importance to obtain accurate returns of the relative increase of population in England and Scotland—the one country being with, and the other without, a Poor-Law; and for this purpose it might be desirable in making the next census, to have the natives of both ends of the island, distinguished from the Irish and other emigrants. Dr. Alison is perfectly right in concluding that misery forms no check to population, among what may be called the "dregs of society;" but then, every brief season of prosperity gives it a decided impulse among the whole of those classes situated immediately above the lowest. This fact, if I mistake not, would be satisfactorily established by a reference to the register of marriages for 1825, and and 1836, the seasons when a sort of feverish commercial prosperity prevailed. This seems to sanction the opinion, that, unless the industrious classes can be taught to form a more correct estimate of the causes of misery, by a rapid increase of themselves they will always neutralize any effort which can be made greatly or permanently to improve their condition. With double the extent of territory which we possess, double our commerce, and double our manufactures, we might all have the means of living comfortably;* but in 30 years we would, in

---

* This is an exaggerated supposition, and not in harmony with our author's economical principles. We require no such extra-

all likelihood, double our population also, and then we should be exactly where we were.

'In conclusion, I must now beg your pardon for what I have written. I cannot very well excuse myself for having thus dragged a lady over such a length of dry and dusty road. But I know that you are an enthusiast in the cause of humanity; and as I have no other means of making myself heard, you may perhaps be induced to pardon my impotent attempts to help forward a most important movement. I have no room to say how glad I was to hear of the new system of training adopted in some of the English schools. Could we have nothing of the kind here?—With warmest thanks to you and Mr. Hill, I remain, Dear Madam, Your much indebted, very humble servant, A. B.'

ordinary extension of territory and commerce as this, in order to all being furnished with the means of living comfortably. Our present resources are, in spite of injurious commercial restrictions, adequate to this, were they economically applied. But while there is so much luxury and frivolous dissipation among the rich, and so much improvidence and recklessness amoug the poor, national distress cannot justly be referred to over population as its direct principal cause. Distress could be charged to that cause only if it continued to prevail after our resources were generally frugally applied. Our distress, as yet, arises not from any inevitable law of society, but from a too prevalent misapplication of our resources. But evil is often overruled in some way for good; and Providence seems to be making the pressure of distress here, the means of forcing off large numbers of our population to distant lands, carrying with them the blessings of religion and civilization, and giving them extended localization in every region of the globe.

'MOUNTPLEASANT, *February*, 20, 1841.

'Dear Madam,—I have now to thank you for your very kind letter of the 18th inst., and, while I am afraid that I am only destined to disappoint your expectations, I must say, that I am now willing to strain every nerve to comply with your friendly wishes. Perth is a place which, of all others, I should like, both on account of its scenery and its proximity to the scenes among which I was bred. By the steamboats, it is only about an hour's sailing distant from Newburgh, and even the house in which I now write may be seen from the hills in its immediate neighbourhood. In a fortnight or so, I may be able to leave this quarter, and then I would beg to have the honour of thanking you personally, as I pass Edinburgh on my way to Glasgow. I need not trouble you with an account of the little matters which must detain me here till the time mentioned above. I feel that it is better to be endeavouring to obviate difficulties as fast as possible, than to sit still and either write about or think over them. The moment I have got things in readiness I will apprise you of it; and in the meantime, I remain, Dear Madam, Your much indebted, very humble servant, A. B.'

According to the intention indicated in some of the preceding Letters, Mr. Bethune went to Glasgow early in March. He had not high or sanguine anticipations we may suppose; but he felt bitterly the degradation of being, on his arrival there, put into the place of a common turnkey. In such a situation, he felt that he could not, in any circumstances, have long remained; but his departure was hastened by a severe cold, which he caught a few days after his arrival in Glasgow. As soon as he was able to move, he hastened away from a position so repugnant to the entire current of his feelings. He walked the greater part of the way home, and, on arriving there, found himself so much a sufferer from this ill-advised adventure, that he had to keep within doors for some time afterwards. The following extract which has been furnished me, is from a Letter to Mrs. Hill, written shortly after his return home to Mountpleasant. I give it with a note appended to it by Mrs. Hill prefixed :—

['Mr. Bethune went to Glasgow, and had scarcely time to become accustomed to the duties of a warder in the North Prison, when he caught a severe cold, and was quite incapacitated for any labour. Mr. Brebner, the benevolent Governor of the Prison, was anxious to show him every kind of humane attention, and, indeed, had a room prepared for him in the Prison, but Mr. Bethune was too ill to be any where but in his own home; and this conviction made him take the immediate step of returning to Newburgh, after only a week's trial. From all that Mr. Brebner saw of Mr. Bethune, he believed he would make a good officer, and he most kindly offered to receive him again as a warder, if he were inclined to return; but Mr. Bethune's health continued far too impaired for such a step to be taken, even if his mind had not been made up against holding the office of warder, or keeper of a prison.']

'MOUNTPLEASANT, *March* 23, 1841.

*　*　*　* 'Jailers and turnkeys are indispensable to the very existence of the present state of society—nay, farther, we are told in scripture, that "The land shall not be cleansed from blood, but by the blood of him who shed it;" which proves that hangmen are indispensable also. yet there are thousands on thousands of individuals who would rather have the rope put about their own necks than put it about the neck of a fellow-creature, whatever might be his crime—and I am only one of these. I would almost as soon be hanged myself, as be either a hangman, or the keeper of the commodity upon which he is to exercise his craft. As I once hinted before, (were health restored,) I still think I might be of some use as a teacher or librarian—or rather, I should like to be one or other of these. In such a sphere, the little knowledge of human nature I have already picked up, might perhaps be turned to some small account. But unless I could obtain some situation which would afford something like leisure for conversing with the prisoners, and trying to ascertain what had been their thoughts, springs of action, and causes of crime, together with opportunities of offering such advice as the case seemed to call for, I would at once and for ever relinquish the idea of having anything to do with prisons. While I would beg your pardon for the freedom with which I have spoken, I would also beg to say that to me it has always appeared best to speak definitively upon such subjects. Let me once more request you not to trouble yourself with writing till you hear from me again; and in the meantime, believe me as before &c. &c.,

A. B.'

A good while afterwards, we find him thus writing his literary friend in reference to this affair:—

Mountpleasant *March* 21, 1842.

'Dear Sir,—My coming to Glasgow was not, as you seem to suppose, occasioned either by destitution, or "some new misfortune." The cause of it was simply this:—A copy of my brother's Life and Poems had, it seemed, fallen into the hands of Mrs. Hill, the lady of Frederick Hill, Esq., Inspector of prisons; and she wished to procure for me what she conceived would be a comfortable situation, as a teacher, or something of that sort, in one or other of these dens for evil-doers. In this I must give her full credit for being actuated by a sincere wish to serve me. The Glasgow Bridewell was considered as the pattern of such institutions; and thither I was requested to go that I might be there initiated into the mystery of managing wild beasts of the human species. Without being very sanguine in my expectations, I was not displeased at the prospect of a situation where my earnings would be uniform; and I accordingly went. But on getting there, I came to learn that, if I would consent to officiate as a turnkey for a year or two, or till such time as I had made myself thoroughly master of the science of " prison discipline," I might have a chance of being promoted to the situation of a jailor in some country town, with a salary of forty or fifty pounds a year. For such promotion, I had no great relish; and besides, I could not help disliking the society of the other turnkeys, some of whom, notwithstanding the very great praise which had been bestowed on them, I soon came to regard as the very pink of puppyism and self-conceit. Sometimes, however, I was not a little amused by discovering the most sublime ideas which these " rare specimens of humanity" had formed of their own knowledge and importance, as compared with the ignorance and utter insignificance of my own very unimportant self. In the midst of duties which were not very pleasing, I had, nevertheless, determined to remain for a month or two, to please my patroness, and then beg to be allowed to retire from a situation for which I did not consider myself qualified. But, on the eighth or ninth day after my arrival in Glasgow, I caught a very bad cold, which laid me aside from these duties altogether. For some time previous to my mother's death, and throughout the winter, my health had been in a very tottering condition; I could not help thinking that this cold might do for me, what the cold which he had caught on the 28th of January, two years before, had done for my brother; and, after having been confined to my lodgings for one day—during which my only resource was an almost total abstinence from victuals,—toward noon on the second day, I felt somewhat relieved—wrote a note to the " governor of the prisons," giving up the situation, and got into one of the canal boats, with which I proceeded as far as it went on the way to Stirling. The rest of the journey I was able to perform on foot; and when I had again reached my own solitary habitation, this "wild-goose chase" was at an end. Altogether the thing was an unfortunate speculation, in as much as it occasioned me a good deal of expense, and an illness from the effects of which, together with the journey which followed, I did not recover for three or four months. A. B.'

His friend's opinion of the situation is expressed in the following extract:—

'*April* 26, 1842.

'My Dear Sir,—The account you have given of your trip to Glasgow certainly adds another hue to the already chequered page of your history. Of all conceivable occupations, that which you undertook was certainly the least adapted to your habits and character. "Misery makes a man acquainted with strange bed-fellows," quoth the poet; but I rejoice in the good fortune which did not compel you to keep such company longer than you found it agreeable. I have been through all their dens here; and certainly there does not appear to be much to choose, in the way of comfort and liberty, between the jailer and his charge. Indeed, the difference is, in my opinion, in favour of the latter. His term of durance vile is limited; and he is often kept from absolute despondency by the hope of ultimate liberation. The turnkey's imprisonment, however, is perpetual; and although it be voluntary, it is scarcely less rigorous than that of his charge. Besides, the very nature of the office is revolting to every feeling of humanity; and jailers are often as great rogues as their prisoners. The motive, however, which induced the lady to put such a situation in your power, is exceedingly creditable to her; and this circumstance, taken in connection with those voluntary offers of aid which the publication of your work has excited, must be very gratifying to your feelings, although you could not avail yourself of them. They are decidedly proofs of the popularity of the work among a class of people whose good opinion is certainly worth having; and I am glad to think that you are thus induced to continue your literary speculations, and in a way which cannot subject you to any pecuniary risk.'

To those friends who understood his character best, his escape from such a situation was matter of sincere congratulation. Another thus writes:—

'While I am unfeignedly sorry for the suffering you have undergone, I cannot help feeling glad that you have abandoned the situation of a turnkey. Verily, had I guessed a hundred years, I should never have guessed that as an office likely to be yours; and had I been told by any person but yourself that you had made trial of it, I would not have believed them. Not that I consider any dishonour attached to such an office; but, knowing something of your habits and disposition, I would consider you the most unlikely person in the world to fill a situation of the kind with either pleasure or satisfaction to yourself.'

In these views of the case we entirely concur; and while we accord to the lady who interested herself on his behalf, full credit for benevolent intentions, and for the deep concern she evinced for Mr. Bethune after, as well as before, his visit to Glasgow, we yet feel called on to add a few remarks of our own. The case, then, on which the preceding extracts bear, furnishes us with an illustration of the estimate put on literature, apart from wealth and other extrinsic distinctions. Even though allied with high virtue, and the truest refinement of character, if it present itself under a

Galasheils coat, and with the horny hands of labour, what is it worth? Only the lowest function about the most degraded of mankind—a function which any one possessing delicacy of feeling would wish that the spirit of mechanical invention might altogether supersede. Would a situation of this sort ever have been thought of for the merest clodpole trained under exemption from manual labour? But it seems it was the indispensable initiatory in the training of a prison officer. Indispensable in order to what? Mr. Bethune would have been willing to have become a teacher or librarian: what relation had turning bolts, and keeping guard on cells to either of these? Would he have been fitter for the one or the other, after a year or two's training at such an occupation? If he was not to receive a situation in some degree congenial to his feelings, and in some measure worthy of his genius and attainments—far better have allowed him to remain where he was—enjoying the freedom of his hard-earned independence.* It is not in its

---

* We cannot altogether acquit Mr. Bethune himself of blame in the affair. In one of his earlier letters to Mrs. Hill, he had thus written:—' Once more, let me beg you to think of me as one in no way superior to the common race of day-labourers who are to be met with upon our public roads. The appearance of many of these would indicate far higher attainments than mine; and, had they chosen to exert themselves, it is highly probable that they would have outdone me in the few things I have attempted. I should be most willing to submit all to the judgment of Mr. Brebner; only I would have him to regard me

individual aspects and relations on either side, however, that we attach the greatest importance to this transaction, but as an exponent of the sentiments which pervade cultivated society generally in regard to such men as Mr. Bethune. Were they not estimated much more by the rank in life in which Providence has ordered that they should have their birth and training, than by their mental qualities and attainments, would a case like that which has called forth these remarks ever have occurred? There were persons who, in the most praiseworthy spirit, would have assisted Mr. Bethune, but he uniformly declined gratuitous pecuniary assistance; and seeing this was the case, it may be asked, what then could be done for him? We are prepared not only to justify Mr. Bethune in doing this, but to accord him high admiration. The spirit actuating those who offered such assistance, as contrasted with the apathy pervading the public generally, merits high praise; but until literary men, situated as Mr. Bethune was, come to be regarded in quite another light than as objects of charity, we shall rejoice to see them acting as he did—so long as their own exertions can at

with suspicious scrutiny before he decided upon my fitness for even the humblest situation.' We should never profess a measure of humility which we are not conscious that we really feel; nor express an estimate of our powers and relative importance which we would not like others to entertain and act on in regard to us.

all procure for them the means of supporting existence. When persons whose distinctive services have, to say the least, a very equivocal relation to the good of mankind, receive the highest honours and rewards of the State; while *they*, if not treated with utter neglect, are offered only the very meanest situations in the public service—it is refreshing to meet with such instances among them of lofty and stern independence.

At this hour, while we write, thousands are assembled to enjoy themselves, (if the elements would permit them,*) under the name of commemorating the genius of Burns; while he, when living, after having been lionized for a winter or so, was discarded, and allowed to seek a scanty subsistence for himself and family in a situation which drew from him the bitter doggerel :—

" Searching auld wives' barrels,
  Ochon the day
That clarty barm should stain my laurels!
  But what'll ye say ?—
These muving things, ca'd wives and weans,
Would muve the vera hearts o" stanes."

Ah! but had he lived now, how differently would he have been treated! Good, living public, you would fain cheaply enjoy this credit. Writing pa-

* On the 6th of August last, the day of the Burns Festival, it poured out torrents of rain.

negyrics, getting up fetes and festivals, if nothing more was necessary to establish your reputation for sympathy with genius how it would shine! But unfortunately there are other tests. What have you done for men (we compare them not with Burns as to genius, but of no mean capabilities and of the highest virtue,) who lived, toiled, struggled, sunk amid the very echoes of your plaudits over the genius of Scotland's great poet? You reproach the public, and the dispensers of patronage who preceded you—that, when Burns made his appeal to them, they heeded not, but allowed him to drag out his brief life in the ungenial and degrading capacity of an exciseman. Well: Alexander Bethune—a far worthier, if not such a highly gifted man—made his appeal to you, and there was proffered him the situation of a turnkey! But here he had the advantage of the great peasant-bard. By reason of his high virtue and self-command he was in a condition that did not impose on him any necessity of accepting a situation repugnant to his feelings.

The following letter to Mrs. Hill, while it discloses more fully Mr. Bethune's views and feelings, shows the critical state of his health after his return from Glasgow, and imbodies some very remarkable premonitions of his approaching end:—

'MOUNTPLEASANT, *March* 31, 1841.

'Dear Madam,—When you heard of my leaving

Glasgow, you would probably think that I acted very childishly in quitting a situation which it had cost so much trouble to procure, for what some would deem nothing more than a passing cold; but when you know that a large blister has been applied to my breast, that it is still raw, and that I have done nothing since, you will perhaps think less hardly of me. What I considered the worst symptoms of the case are now gone, and I am at present a good deal better; still, my own conviction is, that the machine is nearly worn out, and that it would be vanity to make any great exertion to procure new employments for one for whom fate, at no very distant day perhaps, will provide a permanent situation. Indeed, I did not know that I was so much enfeebled, till I had made an attempt to be stronger, and felt that I was so weak. After having been nearly deprived of sleep the greater part of half a year, previous to my mother's death, and being mostly confined to the house throughout the winter, I am now convinced that the mere circumstance of having every faculty of both mind and body tied down to a round of duties with which I was unacquainted, for sixteen hours out of the twenty-four, (as was the case in the bridewell,) had it been persisted in for any length of time, would have placed me above patronage. Though the discovery was perhaps an unwelcome one, I feel that "I am not what I have been," and there is no use in dreaming that I shall ever be so again, or in attempting to deceive others with such a belief. I am not now ashamed to own the circumstance, although I might have been so once. With the same discipline, and the same amount of tear and wear, perhaps few men had lived so long as I have done; and now some little exercise in the open air, and some little relaxation—things which could not possibly have been obtained in the situation I occupied at Glasgow—seem to be indispensable to my existence; and therefore, whatever others may think of the step, I feel no regret, except for the disappointment it must have occasioned to one who had taken so much interest in my fortunes. It was only sacrificing that, which, for reasons already stated, could have never been more than a prospect. I am now inclined to look upon myself as "a doomed man," who may be reprieved from time to time for a number of years, perhaps; but after having experienced the effects of confinement, I do think that to have shut myself up in a prison for sixteen hours a-day, could have hardly failed to ensure the speedy execution of the sentence. My idea is that I am not as yet exactly consumptive, but that my lungs have been injured, that recent events have not tended to repair the injury, and that it wants only an exciting cause to develop that fatal malady. With all this, in justice to myself, I must be permitted to say, that had I been allowed to enjoy only an ordinary degree of health, out of respect to yourself and Mr. Hill, I had determined to remain four or five months in Glasgow, and then beg to be allowed to retire from a station (that of a turnkey I mean) for which nature had not fitted me. * * * * 'As teachers and librarians have nothing to do with the lighting the cells in the morning or locking-up at night, their hours of attending are shorter than those of a turnkey, while their duties incur less responsibility, or, at least, less risk of getting into errors. A short interval might thus be obtained every day for attending to what George Combe has very appropriately called "The Laws of Health;"—laws which I have long disregarded, because I could not do otherwise, but which it seems I cannot disregard much longer and continue an inhabitant of this earth. * * * * *

'I have no sinister motive in view when I mention such a situation as one which I would like. When the additional expense of living in a town is considered, I do not expect to be a pound richer at the end of the year by going to Perth than I would be by staying at home; but in the course of conversation, by pointing out passages in books, and buckling them with representations of my own, I might perhaps be able to do a little in diffusing a spirit of humanity, as far as it was consistent with the regulations of a place of punishment, among the other officers. As yet you can have no idea of the very limited extent to which this spirit prevails. No farther gone than Saturday was a week, when suffering from disease, and worn out with travelling, I was within a hair's breadth of having to take quarters for the night by a dyke-side, because no one, whether "publican or sinner," or righteous man, in the village where I then chanced to be, would give me a bed, though I had money enough in my pocket to pay for at least ten times more than I required, and told the good people that this was the case.

'I have already ventured to say that I should like the situation which I have mentioned, if it could be easily obtained, at Perth; and what would render such a situation still more desirable, is the ease with which it can be reached from this quarter.

'A. B.'

Mrs. Hill still continued to interest herself in Mr. Bethune's behalf, and now with the more definite and suitable object in view, of procuring for him the situation of teacher or librarian in the Penitentiary at Perth. With this view, she communicated with the Governor of that establishment, endeavouring to give him a just impression of Mr. Bethune's character and acquirements. The result was, that this gentleman desired Mrs. Hill to communicate to Mr. Bethune his wish that he should meet him at Perth. Mr. Bethune's answer to Mrs. Hill, on writing him to this effect, is characteristic and instructive, as indicating very distinctly that he felt there was something else due to him than a commiserative and patronizing regard:—

'Mountpleasant, *May* 15, 1841.

'Dear Madam,— * * * * Having no engagement of any moment, I will be in Perth early in the week—Monday or Tuesday, perhaps; and, as soon as I conveniently can, I will not fail to apprize you of the result of my interview with Mr. D.——. From the tenor of your letter, I almost infer that you are not very sanguine in your expectations of my being successful; and I must say, that I do not anticipate much myself. I am, however, perfectly free from everything like anxiety on the subject—a consciousness of power to provide for my own wants, in a number of other ways, sets my mind entirely at ease; and should Mr. D—— start any serious objections, as to my leaving Glasgow so abruptly, or the like, I may perhaps let him know, that it will depend as much on *my* accepting, as on *his* preferring, whether or not I shall ever darken the door of the Penitentiary at Perth with my shadow. The whole, however, will depend upon the elevation from which he may choose to look down upon his very humble servant. What pleased me particularly, during the very short time which I passed in your presence, was the total absence of that galling condescension with which the rich in general treat the poor whom they may think proper to patronize. I would scarcely have patronage upon such terms, as long as I could patronize myself to a breakfast of porridge and milk, and a supper of potatoes and salt. But of this, "somewhat too much," as Byron would have said.

'Ever since I left Glasgow, I have had an intention of communicating some particulars which I think I have picked up respecting the character of turnkeys in general, and the characters of those who are likely to be most forward in their attempts to get into such situations. Something of the kind might be useful; and for arriving at the truth, persons in my station have many facilities which never can be enjoyed by gentlemen, whatever may be their acuteness of penetration. But this I must defer till I write again; and it is questionable if even then I may be able to accomplish my purpose. In the meantime, I remain, with the greatest respect—dear Madam, Your much obliged, very humble servant, A. B.'

Notwithstanding much negotiation and exertion on Mrs. Hill's part, nothing ever came out of this Perth business. The Governor had to be removed—it was long ere a Chaplain was elected; and, so late as November, 1842, we find Mrs. Hill writing Mr. Bethune—that the question as to whether the Governor or the Chaplain was to have the superintendence of the instruction department was still undetermined.

The following extracts from Mr. Bethune's answer to the communication just mentioned, imbody some of his views in regard to prison discipline. His impressions regarding the character of some of those in the situation of turnkey with whom he came in contact during his brief sojourn in Glasgow, the reader will perceive to have been anything but favourable. But Mrs. Hill states in a note, that two of those then in that situation, were only engaged on trial; and that they "were dismissed for want of that kindness and benevolence of feeling so necessary in a good prison officer." The Report referred to, and commented on, is Mr. Hill's Report on Prison Discipline. The date of the following extracts rather outruns the narrative; but I give them in this connexion, as the conclusion of Mr. Bethune's correspondence with Mrs. Hill in regard to Prison situations :—

'MOUNTPLEASANT, by NEWBURGH,
FIFE, *Nov.* 22, 1842.

'Dear Madam,— * * * * To deserve the good opinion and the esteem of the more intelligent part of the community, has always been one of the objects of my ambition; and, though I would not wish to overtax their benevolence, still I must say, that my appreciation of their regard is not lessened by such efforts as you have made to improve my worldly condition. To come at once to the point—my sentiments relating to the situation at Perth are still unaltered. I should like it, if I could give satisfaction to my employers. I am, however, in some respects, an unfavourably constituted animal. To seek employment, or thrust myself upon the notice of others, are things which I could scarcely ever do; and unless you were to allow me to show your letter to Mr. M'Lean,* or to favour me with a few lines as an introduction, I fear I should appear before him with a very bad grace. * * * * * * * *

'At the "Report," with which you have favoured me, I have as yet had only time merely to glance; but most sincerely do I add my amen to what Mr. Hill says, (page four, near the bottom of the page,) concerning Prison Officers. From the little which I saw, during my short residence at Glasgow, I feel quite confident that there are among them individuals who, in the estimation of their superiors, pass for efficient men, " good hands," " smart lads," and all that sort of thing, who are at bottom coldhearted, selfish, tyrannising sinners. It is quite a different thing to see an individual for a few minutes, going through a routine of duties in the presence of his employers, or of one he wishes to please, and showing off his dexterity to the best advantage—and to watch him in moments when he supposes himself unwatched, and see all the cracks and flaws of his character coming out—his littlemindedness, insolence, and vanity manifesting them-

---

* Chaplain of the General Prison, Perth.

selves in a number of ways which those who have never seen such scenes would not have dreamed of. Hugh Miller, in his work on Geology, mentions "the advantages of a wandering profession;" and, I think, I could almost point out a counterpart to these, and which I would call, "the advantages of being born to a lot so humble, as to be utterly below the notice and consideration of the world;" at least, to this circumstance I am certain that I owe a sort of acquaintance with people's real characters which I should have despaired of obtaining from the most classical education. And now, if I might venture to state my own sentiments, I would say, that the out-and-out, hackneyed, professional turnkey will, in general, be found a person with very little true benevolence—how much of the affected quality he may have, it were difficult to say —such a share of cautiousness as to enable him to conceal his own faults and delinquencies, and a large measure of self-esteem; together with a consciousness—forced upon him, perhaps, reluctantly, by previous circumstances—that his own attainments, and the range of his intellectual faculties are not such as to command much attention from his fellow-creatures in ordinary circumstances. The natural consequence of his self-esteem, in connexion with the above-mentioned consciousness, must be a wish for opportunities to exact submission and respect from others, in such a way as that they must, of necessity, yield to his desires—

with the further conviction, that this combination of circumstances is only to be met with in a prison, where men are not free agents. Hence his attachment to a profession which, to a truly humane individual, with a proper sense of the dignity of his own nature, would not be very agreeable—that is, unless a wish to be the means of reforming others, (which, after all, is a thing of rather rare occurrence,) made it so. The foregoing is something of the same sort as the intended Essay on Turnkeyism, to which I alluded in a former letter. It is, I readily acknowledge, a dark picture; but still, I think, in some instances, a pretty correct one. I have not, however, drawn it for the purpose of throwing suspicion over the whole of the profession—far less those who endeavour conscientiously to do their duty; but simply to corroborate Mr. Hill's opinion, that the greatest care should be exercised in choosing Prison officers. I do think, also, that in every instance where "prisoners complain," it should be deemed a subject for the strictest investigation; and that whenever a turnkey shrinks from such investigation, or "wonders" why his superiors "should receive, as deserving of any credit, the declarations of any of the prisoners," he should be regarded with suspicion, and sharply looked after. Let a turnkey only take care to tell a prisoner, mildly and firmly, but, at the same time, clearly, and in such a manner as that he may comprehend it, the rules of the place;

and then, should he continue refractory, let him address him in some such manner as the following: " John," or " James,"—as the case may be—" I'm sorry for you—sorry to think that you cannot regulate your conduct so as to avoid punishment; but you already know the discipline of the Prison: I cannot shield you from it; and, if I could, it would not be my duty to do so." Let him then bring a fair and impartial statement of the whole before the Governor; meeting everything the prisoner may have to say in his own defence in a candid and straightforward manner, and there will scarcely be such a thing as complaints from prisoners. A. B.'

CHAPTER VIII.

PUBLICATION OF THE SECOND EDITION OF THE 'LIFE AND POEMS OF JOHN BETHUNE'—INTEREST EXCITED IN REGARD TO MR. BETHUNE IN TWO LADIES, MEMBERS OF THE SOCIETY OF FRIENDS—CORRESPONDENCE WITH THESE—MR. BETHUNE'S KINDNESS TO A FRIEND IN ILL HEALTH—LETTERS—MARKS OF INTEREST IN MR. BETHUNE ON THE PART OF DR. ANDREW COMBE AND MR. GEORGE COMBE.

In the early part of 1841, a second edition of 'The Life and Poems of John Bethune' was published by John Wright & Co. Bristol.* It was at first intended to extend the work to two volumes, but from this the publishers were dissuaded by James Montgomery, to whom they applied for an introductory essay. Mr. Montgomery, however, declined attempting this in a letter, the greater part of which has been prefixed to the second edition, and which imbodies a very just estimate of the character of the Bethunes. The publication of the work in England, brought it under the notice of not a

---

* This edition is inscribed to Mr. Dalgleish, who had taken such an interest in, and done so much to promote the success of, the first.

few, in whose minds its perusal excited much sympathy and admiration. Among these were two excellent ladies belonging to the Society of Friends, one of which proved a most indefatigable and successful agent in promoting the sale of our author's works; which she soon found the only method in which he would allow her to confer a pecuniary benefit on him—a way in which, it may be remarked, it was open to many to have promoted his interests, at once sucessfully, and most gratefully to his feelings. This lady opened her correspondence with him, by a proffer of the sum of three pounds, of which she begged his acceptance, as a "token of grateful remembrance of the pleasure afforded her by the perusal of 'The Life and Poems of John Bethune.'" The following is Mr. Bethune's answer, declining of course the acceptance of the money:—

'MOUNTPLEASANT, *near* NEWBURGH, FIFESHIRE, *December* 16, 1841.

'Dear Madam,—I have this evening received a Post-Office order for three pounds, from you, and, in acknowledging it, I know not well how to express my feelings. To me it is gratifying in the highest degree to know that my humble endeavours to preserve a memorial of the name and the virtues of a very dear friend, now gone to his eternal rest, have been appreciated by one at so great a distance—gratifying, too, to believe that his simple story had interested you so much as to make you think of extending your generosity in the manner you have done, to his only remaining friend. But, alas! to those, who, like me, have survived their kindred, even money cannot recall the past, nor can it fill the void which death has made. With no living thing to care for, or to care for me, I should be but ill justified were I to draw upon that benevolence which has been so liberally and so generously extended towards me. I had once an ambition to rise above poverty; and solitary as I am, I should still like to provide something for sickness, (old age I must not expect to see,) but even this must not be done at the expense of others; and though I should die poor, as there is a strong probability that I will, it will still be a consolation to think that if I have not in any way benefited the world, neither have I during my brief space, been a burden to it. For these reasons, dear madam, and with a gratitude fully as warm as if I had remained your debtor for the full amount, I now humbly beg to return a Post-Office order for the sum, three pounds, as it was sent. To have excited your sympathy, and—might I add —to deserve your esteem is enough, and more than enough for me.

'I should now conclude, and yet I feel as if my motives might still be liable to misconstruction; but after having read my poor brother's story, I think you will not misconstrue them. It is not the pride of an increasing fortune which makes me averse to availing myself of the benevolence of others: for

—apart from the profits of the first edition of my brother's posthumous works, which await the finishing of a monument to be placed over his grave, and about five pounds which I have drawn for copies of the second edition which I have sold for the publishers—I have at present, only thirty shillings which I can fairly call my own; and my earnings, when the weather allows me to be abroad from morning till night, are only one shilling and fourpence a day, with scarcely half work. But from boyhood, I have all along considered it the duty of every man, to the very uttermost of that ability which God has given him, to endeavour to provide for his own wants, and to be satisfied with that station, however humble, which Providence had assigned him—provided he could not better it by his own honest industry. Should the all-wise Disposer of events see meet to spare that measure of health which I am still permitted to enjoy for a little longer, though I feel that my constitution is sadly shaken, it is possible that I may yet be able to save something. The second edition of the book, too, as I feel pretty certain that it is in honourable hands, should produce a little—that is to say if it sell, a matter which is still questionable. Whatever be the result, let me beg you to lie under no apprehension for my comfort. I have at present, everything which I really want, and I have often fared far harder before than I do now. My work might have been as steady perhaps, as that of other men, had it not been that for the last three or four months I have been keeping myself free from any lengthened engagement in the prospect of obtaining a sort of situation where my rewards would be somewhat better than those of a day-labourer, the settlement of which, has been delayed from time to time, and which I now begin to suspect will produce nothing for me. As soon as this affair is finally concluded, I have no doubt of being again able to get into steady employment, and that, with health, I shall be at least above want; and I must not expect to find the world, which had been strewed with thorns for my few friends, a path of roses for myself.

'During the evenings, and those intervals of leisure which I could command, I have lately copied and prepared for the press, with some additions of my own, a Memoir of my grandmother, which was written by my brother in 1836; and if I succeed in getting it printed, as the work will be of a kind which may be easily forwarded by post, I should be most happy to present you with a copy, as a small token of my gratitude for the notice which you have been pleased to take of me, and of my much lamented brother's literary remains. In that case, I hope you will pardon my once more intruding myself upon you; and otherwise, I must ever remain Your much indebted, very humble servant,

A. B.'

I cannot deny myself the pleasure of inserting

his friend's rejoinder, which I doubt not will be welcome to many readers, as indicative of the refined spirit, the sweet humility, the serenity of soul, and active benevolence, which characterize many of the members of the Society of Friends :—

'My Dear Friend,—Thy letter, covering the returned Post Office order, was received this evening, and I am much obliged by thy candour, and truly admire the motives which induced thee to maintain that independence so commendable in those who feel the will and the ability to maintain it; but surely it may be carried too far. Thy dear brother appeared to be of my opinion, in his sweet poem, "The Wish;" but what can be the use of wealth, if it be refused by those we wish to serve. I did not see the letter to which thine is a reply. It was written at my request by a young person who is my companion. There was nothing in it, I hope, that could wound thy feelings. I should indeed be grieved if there was. Nothing could be farther from my intention; yet I fear it must seem to imply a want of delicacy in the offer, which, I am sure, was not considered as a gift, but simply to acknowledge the pleasure and instruction received from the perusing of the volume of John Bethune, and to claim some sympathy with the noble mind of his brother—a brother not by consanguinity only, but so in heart and in mind. I am, it is true, a stranger, and situated at a distance; and though of the middle class like thyself, have all my lifetime—and I am now advanced in years—been blessed with such a competency as afforded me the very responsible means of helping those on whom the ills of life had been permitted to press more heavily, either from sickness or other causes; and this as due from a partaker in human suffering—a fellow-pilgrim and friend. It is new to me to be refused; but this, I fear, must have been my own fault, and I am still in hopes thou wilt point out some way in which I can serve thee. Is there any other medium more agreeable to thee than the Post Office? I have sold a considerable part of the books I purchased, and am in want of more. Canst thou supply me with twenty or thirty copies of the Life of thy excellent brother, so as to ensure a better profit than that from the booksellers? If not provided with the books, wilt thou please to order them from the booksellers, to be sent to me; and receive the money thyself. But remember I will pay the full price for the books, which I consider very low.

'I was much interested by the account of thy venerable grandmother, in the printed volume, and am glad to hear that a Memoir of her is likely to be printed. I am a visitor to a society here for the relief of aged women; and such a publication might be highly useful to them. Surely thou couldst have no objection to my contributing towards the expense of printing it. Again I would repeat, that it would oblige me much if I could know in what way I could serve thee.'

The zeal and success with which this lady, who proved a real friend, prosecuted the labour of bookseller and book-distributer on Mr. Bethune's behalf, will appear from the following letters:—

'Mountpleasant *by* Newburgh,
Fife, *April* 29, 1842.

'My Dear Friend,—I have just been favoured with a letter from your young friend, enclosing a Post Office order for £5, and requesting an additional twenty-five copies of my deceased brother's "Life and Poems." These I have ordered from Bristol to-day, by the same letter which accompanies a proof of the Memoir of my grandmother, sent here for correction; and I now hope they will reach you in safety. Of your past and present kindness, in this respect, as well as of the exertions which you have made, and are still making, not not only to gratify my wishes concerning the memory of my brother, but to put money in my pocket, I may well be ashamed, inasmuch as I have done and can do nothing to deserve them. At another time I might have said that I was afraid that you were only making the "demand for the work" a pretext for bestowing your own benevolence upon one who has, perhaps, too much of what has been called the "pride of poverty" in his disposition; but, at present, for the following reason, among many others, I can scarcely feel otherwise than gratified in the highest degree. In the course of the current year, if Providence bless me with health, I shall have the manuscript of a volume of my brother's "Letters, Prose Essays, and other Papers" ready for the press;* and, if the present edition of his poems could be disposed of, I have good hopes that the firm of "Wright, Allis, and Bagnall," late "Wright and Albright" might be induced to add a second volume of prose works, in bringing out another edition. It is not but that the little celebrity which my brother's name has already acquired might, perhaps, enable me to find another publisher; but I am most desirous that the whole of his writings which may be given to the public, should issue from the same press and be published by the same house, which I think would ensure a wider circulation;—and thus my thanks are due to you in no ordinary degree for the very great number of copies which you have taken off the publishers' hands. I must not press them in this matter, however, but wait patiently till I see how they can clear themselves of the risk which they have already undertaken.

'My health—and for this I have reason to thank God—is now tolerably good. Two months of hard labour in the open air, has greatly improved my strength and given me a power of resisting fatigue

---

* This volume was not published during Mr. Bethune's lifetime. The copyright was by him bequeathed to the 'Free Church,' but I have as yet heard nothing as to its publication.

which I did not expect ever to possess again. By a wise arrangement of Providence, the very toil by which the greater part of the human race must subsist, has a tendency to strengthen the body; and in numerous instances it will invigorate a frame which ease and inactivity would certainly destroy. While God shall be pleased to give me strength, I should never wish to be idle, though there are times when I could almost wish the drudgery to which I am occasionally subjected, less severe; and if I am spared, I begin to think it possible that even in this I may obtain my wishes. With about £80 in money, together with the advantages which I possess, I could put up another house here, which would draw £9 yearly. This, added to the rents of part of the house which I now inhabit would make my income, independent of labour, nearly £15 annually; and with such a sum I should feel myself as independent as the greatest landed proprietor in the country. Though I am a member of the Church of Scotland, in which I was born and bred, you would hardly believe how much of Quakerism there is in my manner of living. In dress, and almost every thing else, I have all along endeavoured to study the greatest plainness which was consistent with ordinary comfort—a thing which has often enabled me to get honestly through, where otherwise I should have hardly been able to do so. I must also say that that feeling of friendless desolation, which, after my few relations were called away, had rendered me nearly callous to every thing, has now in a great measure passed away, and there are seasons at which I can reflect upon my departed friends with a sort of melancholy interest which has in it more of pleasure than of pain. From this you will see that my circumstances and prospects are not at all disheartening. If the new work* sells well, and I can dispose of the 300 copies, which, in that event I am to get, I will be in possession of £15; and before the expiration of the year, if Providence should bless my endeavours, I may, perhaps, be able to make this sum £20 or £22 which will be at least a fourth part of the money required to make me independent.

'To give you some idea of the contents of the proposed second volume of my brother's posthumous works, (though years may elapse before it can be published,) it has just occured to me that I may send you an "Essay on Poetry." I have not yet had time to read it since I finished the copy, and it is therefore probable that it may contain some errors, but I flatter myself that the spirit of some parts of it will not be displeasing to you. If the reading of so much manuscript would not be fatiguing, I should be much gratified by your looking over it; and, as I have promised to send it to another acquaintance in Aberdeenshire, I would

* Memoir of Annie Macdonald. The sale fully answered his expectations.

beg you to return it in three weeks or so; by which time I hope you will have received the books safe.

'For all your kindness, as well as for that of your friends, to whom I am now indebted for a number of interesting letters, I can only offer you my thanks in return, praying that God may reward you with his richest blessings; and, with much respect, I am Your very humble friend and servant,
'A. B.'

'MOUNTPLEASANT, *by* NEWBURGH,
'FIFE, *July* 8, 1842.

'My Dear Friend,—I have again to acknowledge the receipt of your bounty, in a Post Office order for £2 10s, making altogether no less than £17 10s of your money, which I have now received for myself and others—£10 for my departed brother's "Life and Poems," and £7 10s for "Cottage Piety," of which the bookseller's profit upon the former of these sums and the whole of the latter, is my own. I must believe you, when you say that you are a "Bookseller." That you are incomparably the best book circulator I ever knew, is unquestionable. Long may you be spared to pursue your benevolent labours for the good of your fellow creatures, and may you reap abundantly the fruit of these labours, both here and hereafter,—is the sincere wish of one who owes much to your kindness, and who now begs to subscribe himself, Your very humble friend and servant, A. B.'

The following letter was addressed by Mr. Bethune to the other lady of the Society of Friends,* referred to at the commencement of this chapter, in answer to one from her which she had been induced to write by the perusal of his brother's Life and Poems, expressing much generous and appreciatory sympathy, and making many kind inquiries, such as only a spirit finely alive to the beauty and worth of the character of the Bethunes could prompt. 'This time four years, my husband and myself,' she remarks, ' were travelling in Scotland, on our wedding journey; and we visited the residence of Sir Walter Scott. Thy very estimable brother was living at that time; and had we then known him as well as we now do through the medium of his Memoirs, how much I should have preferred seeing him to viewing the dwelling of the great Sir Walter! and even now, if again in Scotland, how much more interest should I feel in seeing what was once the residence of thy brother, and also in seeing his grave, than in looking at any thing at Abbotsford! I admire John Bethune's character much more than Sir Walter Scott's.' And in regard to many of the higher moral elements, and those features which will outlive time, who can doubt but it was more worthy of ad-

---

* Neither of these excellent ladies has allowed me the pleasure of introducing her name to the reader; but in regard to this last, I may be permitted to say, that she is the sister of a gentleman well known to the public, and one of the most distinguished living ornaments of the Society of Friends.

miration?* The lady's husband having joined with her in writing Mr. Bethune is the cause of his addressing in the plural:—

'MOUNTPLEASANT, *by* NEWBURGH,
FIFESHIRE, *September* 19, 1842.

'Dear Friends,—Deeply as I may and do regret the circumstance of your very interesting letter of the 8th of last month having remained so long unacknowledged, it is with unmingled satisfaction that I now take up a pen to reply to it. The harvest in this quarter is now wholly completed, the greater part of the crop secured, and I have again taken up my abode in that humble domicile which had been reared with so much toil and care for the accommodation of a little family, the whole of whom, with the exception of the present writer, are now in the dust. In a certain sense of the word, my "path" may be said to be "smoother" now than it once was, inasmuch as I have no friend for whom to provide—no one for whose sustenance or comfort to be anxious—in short, no living thing to care for, or who could care for me; and my own wants are

* No reader will be so obtuse or perverse as to suppose that any comparison of literary merits can be intended; or that the editor is insensible to the many fine and noble traits of character evinced by Sir Walter Scott; more particularly to the heroic spirit, and almost self-sacrificing efforts of the last years of his life, under a pecuniary calamity so tremendous as would have quite unnerved any ordinary man.

easily supplied. This, however, is a state of things which I believe few would covet; and, had such been the will of Providence, I should have certainly preferred those little anxieties, with which my mind was once occupied, to that solitude and exemption from care with which I am now surrounded. Yet it must not be supposed that I am melancholy or unhappy. Time has a strange influence in reconciling people to almost any circumstances, and it has now somewhat worn off the depth and poignancy of those feelings with which I was wont to ponder over my departed friends. I must also say, that I believe I should have no difficulty in finding friends in this neighbourhood who would be ready to assist me with money, if that were necessary, or whatever else I might require; but this was a sort of assistance which it had been our uniform endeavour to dispense with, and, as I do not need it now, it would be meanness to take it. The natural wants of a single individual may be at all times easily supplied: I have scarcely any artificial ones; and it is certainly the duty of every one to provide for himself honestly and independently, so long as Providence may spare him the ability to do so. As to that other sort of friendship which consists in mutual confidence and reciprocity of feeling, I should almost despair of finding it. Indeed, I can easily conceive that I may be, in this respect, myself to blame; and that as I do not readily repose confidence in others—perhaps from having found it oftener than once abused—others will not place confidence in me, except when placed in circumstances over which they suppose, whether right or wrong, I may have some control: and thus it is perhaps probable that "the world" and one of the obscurest of its denizens may part as they met, upon "fair terms" and nothing more. I have sometimes thought that because I do not join very heartily in the gossip and tattle of the working people around me, they have come to regard me as a creature altogether different from themselves, and therefore not to be trusted. Be this as it may, I would still wish to sympathize with them in their sufferings, and to promote their happiness to the extent of my little abilities; and for the rest I have little care. While speaking of gossip, I fear you will be inclined to think that what I have just written is a sad specimen of that commodity, and to myself I must say that it appears nothing better; but I cannot help it now.

'You are perfectly right when you suppose that I had "intimately shared in the various trials and sufferings of my brother." I could not be said to be his preceptor; but I was his elder by five years and some months, and the greater part of the little instruction which he received in early life was communicated by me. Afterwards the whole of our little schemes were prosecuted together. I was to have taken a part in almost the whole of his literary projects, had they succeeded; while he was to have done the same in some others in which I failed: and it was trusting to some little experience which I had acquired in building dykes, that we ventured upon the task of putting up a house. We had been all the world to each other from infancy; and when he was taken away, what remained appeared to be but a worthless wreck. Even now, I am sometimes tempted to think that the dispensation which called him hence was a hard one; but such was the will of God, and I must not murmur, though I cannot cease to lament.

'The five shillings I retain, not without some upbraidings of conscience, for the purchase of " Hydropathy," which I shall order the bookseller in Newburgh to get me to-morrow; and when I have got it, I shall paste the card bearing your name upon the cover, and regard it as a present with which I have been favoured for the purpose of making it do as much good to suffering humanity as possible. This, as you will see at a glance, is the manner in which I am endeavouring to reconcile myself to the idea of taking money for which I can give nothing in return.

'In the hope that it may not be wholly uninteresting to you, I also enclose a rude lithograph of Lochend—the place where my brother and myself had lived so long. It was given as a frontispiece to the first edition of his "Life and Poems;" and as I rather think it must be a copy of the second edition which you have seen, it will at least have the recommendation of being new to you. Should the book ever be reprinted, I agree in thinking that the frontispiece might be restored, and other "views" added. If it would not be deemed impertinent, some time afterwards I should be happy to send such a sketch as I could myself take of the simple monument which was erected last spring over the grave of its humble author.

'I should still have much to say, were it not that the time which I can at present spare is exhausted; and I cannot think of delaying this sheet any longer. I am aware, however, that I have done almost nothing in the way of answering your very interesting letter; but the only thing that I can do more at present is, to beg you to excuse, in the best manner you can, the foregoing hurried scrawl, from one who is, with much respect, Your very humble servant, A. B.'

In answer to subsequent communications, inclosing some interesting narrative tracts, and requesting a sketch of his present habitation, &c., we find him writing as follows:—

'MOUNTPLEASANT *by* NEWBURGH,
'FIFE, *October* 22*nd*, 1842.

'Dear Friend,—I beg to present you with two rude views of the house in which I now live, and a rough sketch of the monument which I was at last able to place over my brother's grave. For the

badness of the "drawing," the only apology which I can make, is to say, that I never got a single lesson in the art from any one, and never read a single paragraph upon the subject. Having little wherewith to pay an artist for taking a sketch of Lochend—the picture which I sent you before—I tried it myself; and this was my very first attempt at drawing. I failed, however, and had to pay for the thing after all. But I found that I could make out a sort of rough likeness of the place, and it was a recollection of this which emboldened me to speak about sending you a sketch of the monument. The present is I think only my third attempt at drawing. I have read with deep interest both the tracts which you sent me—in the case of the last, not unmingled with indignation at the Americans for their treatment of the noble-minded and disinterested E. P. Lovejoy.—My best thanks to you for both. I remain Your very humble friend and servant,
A. B.'

Though declining all assistance himself, Mr. Bethune was forward in proffering it to others; and, as was to be supposed, ingenious in devising modes of doing so, the likeliest not to wound delicacy of feeling—as the following communications to a worthy friend of his, dependent on the labour of his hands for the support of himself and family, and who was threatened with consumption, will show:—

'MOUNTPLEASANT, *Nov.* 24, 1840.

'Dear Sir,—I have been a good deal concerned about you since I heard from Mrs. Ferguson that you had caught more cold. Let me beg you to be as careful of yourself as you possibly can: in the humble, but highly useful and creditable sphere which you occupy, you are one whose services we could ill spare. Numbers have felt the comforting influence of those prayers which you have offered up by the bed-side of sick and dying relatives. These have been sought after and valued, when the world, with all its emoluments and schemes of ambition or enjoyment had shrunk into nothing. Among others, I hope you will allow me to express my gratitude for your attention to my much-lamented brother, when near the termination of his earthly career. For the sake of your own family, and for the benefit of society, I am anxious to have you well again, as soon as possible; and, therefore, I must be pardoned for again repeating my injunction to be careful of yourself. Above all, try, if possible, to get that sort of victuals which agrees best with your stomach. So long as the irritation is kept up, the stomach can hardly recover its wonted tone; and while it is weak, the whole body must be weak also. Disease of the stomach has often a tendency to depress the spirits, and make people take gloomy views of their own situation, and of every thing around them. Against this you must strive, by endeavouring to keep your mind as cheerful and easy, with respect to the future, as possible. In answer to the foregoing, I almost think I can hear you saying, "All this is very fine, and comes with a very good grace from one who has nothing to do but give advice to his neighbours, and who knows nothing of what I have to think about!" Such, I doubt not, will be your sentiments. But, my dear Sir, I have felt much, if not all of what you feel, with a family of children to provide for, and cut off from your usual employment; and it is this that makes me sympathize with you the more readily and the more deeply. In the meantime, simply to save myself from being classed with those who say, "Be ye warmed, and be ye filled, yet give none of those things which are needful for the body," I have ventured to enclose a very small trifle, of which I would now beg your acceptance—or, to speak more properly, for which I would beg your pardon. I must also beg you never to mention the circumstance to any one—far less to myself, for we are enjoined "not to let our left hand know what our right hand doth." * * I trust that those whose ability may be greater, will be more liberal; and, though it is my earnest wish and prayer that you may be speedily restored to your wonted employment—if Providence, for wise ends, should see meet to lengthen out the period of your affliction for a little longer—still I would not have you to be too anxious; for I do hope and trust, that a deserving, and really good man, will never be allowed to feel even the fear of want. Hoping that you will never lack that comfort which passeth understanding, and begging your pardon for this hurried scrawl—I remain, dear Sir, Yours truly, A. B.'

'MOUNTPLEASANT, *Feb.* 6, 1841.

'Dear Sir,—Pardon me for venturing to offer you the enclosed trifle. I have not time to tell you how I came by it, farther than that it is the price of a story which I had intended to devote to your service. I had devised some means for conveying it to you, without letting you know that I had any hand in the matter, but they failed; and I am loath to lose time in forming new schemes. I hope you will pardon me for adopting the present plan. I can only beg you, further, never to mention it either to myself or any one else. I have now got some information on the respirator, which I will be glad to communicate. With best wishes, I am, dear Sir, Yours, very sincerely, A. B.'

As explanatory of the extract which follows, I transcribe a sentence or two of a letter to myself from the friend who was the object of Mr. Bethune's benevolent exertions and devices:—'I received this letter after he came home from Glasgow. He felt very anxious about my recovery, and hearing of the respirator as a preventive of the cough, he urged me to get one; at the same time putting one pound into my pocket. Quite overcome with his kindness, I accepted it, on condition that I would use it for that purpose, if I required it; and if not, it would go as part payment of some doors I had to make for him. On finding myself recovering, I wrote him to the effect that I would not need the respirator, and would only use the money I received as payment of the above-mentioned work—and this was the answer I received:'—

'MOUNTPLEASANT, *March* 29, 1841.

'My Dear Friend,—I received yours of the 26th to-day, and I cannot tell you how much pleasure it gives me to hear that you are getting better. Let me however, endeavour to impress upon your mind the necessity of still paying strict attention to yourself, and being particularly careful not to catch cold. In taking exercise, you must also be careful not to fatigue yourself; to do so must necessarily retard, rather than facilitate your recovery. But I need not trouble you with such injunctions; for by this time you must doubtless know what agrees with you, and what does not; and in these cases experience is better than a doctor. Though I was anxious that you should have got a respirator, I am glad to hear that you are getting better without one; and I trust the money which should have gone for it, will be useful to you or your family in some other way. You must not, however, think of applying it as part of the debt which I owe you for the doors—that I will pay you as soon as I see you. I can spare it, else I should not have offered it; and when I am called to a final reckoning, I shall have enow sins to account for, though hard-heartedness should not be among the number. Between the strongest of us and the grave there is but a span, and short as is the space, it must be greatly diminished with those whose constitutions, like mine, have been nearly worn out by accidents, hard labour, night watching, and anxiety.   A. B.'

Among those in whom admiration and sympathy for Mr. Bethune were excited by the perusal of the Life and Poems of his brother, were George Combe author of 'The Constitution of Man,' and his brother, Dr. Andrew Combe. Both of these gentlemen presented him with their works; the former doing him the honour of requesting his critical opinion of his "Moral Philosophy" and "Notes on America." The following extracts are from one of Mr. Bethune's to Mr. George Combe:—

'Mountpleasant, *March* 1, 1841.

'Dear Sir,   *   *   *   *   *   *
   *   *   I, or I should rather, say we, (for there were two of us,) were too sanguine in our anticipations of human improvement—but to be so is perhaps the fault of youth; and, with a little reflection, it might have been easy to foresee that it would take ages to accomplish the change which we

had supposed might be effected in a few years, or in a single lifetime at most. I should be glad if the period could be by any means shortened, and I know that "society" might possess the power of doing it; but at present, it puts forth its energies in a wrong direction. We almost uniformly bestow approbation, or what is nearly the same thing, homage, humble obedience, and even flattery upon riches and power: men see this, and almost every individual who has either talents or ambition, is anxious to get rich as fast as possible, that he may thereby make himself an object of respect to those who are below him. Riches, in most instances, can only be acquired by giving full scope to the principle of selfishness; and this principle, or organ, by being constantly stimulated by the love of approbation, and the expectation of obtaining it, appears soon to grow into a state of such activity, as to make men generally turn a deaf ear to every plan in which selfishness is not in some way or other interested. It is upon this point that my despondency, if despondency it be, rests: this I consider as the grand cause which retards the commencement of that condition of society which every philanthropist would wish to see established; and it appears to me that the strenuous efforts of enlightened individuals will be necessary for a length of time to make approbation run in the proper channel. I do not mention these things as if they could possibly be new to you —as a philosopher, they must have attracted your observation long ere now;—but simply to show that I have thought and pondered over your benevolent theory more than you had perhaps supposed; and I think I have been the means of communicating, at least, a partial knowledge of it to some quarters which otherwise it would have hardly reached. Besides lending the work to every one of my acquaintances who I thought could read and understand it, in the course of conversation I was wont to exert any little influence which I possessed, among my own class, in endeavouring to make people frugal and industrious; and in doing this I always began by referring them to that portion of " The Constitution of Man" where you speak of the strong probability that missionaries going out to convert the heathen, and embarking in a worn-out vessel, or with unskilful seamen, would be drowned; while a company of profligates, by prudently selecting a stout vessel and good sailors, might pass over the watery element in perfect safety. After having stated this powerful argument, and noticed briefly the tenor of the work from which it was drawn, I endeavoured to convince them that Providence, to which they were often in the habit of referring the whole of their good or bad fortune, wrought systematically, and by fixed laws—that the same causes uniformly produced the same effects; and that it was as vain for them to expect that Providence would make them comfortable, and enable them to live independently upon their own earnings, without being industrious and economical, as it would be to expect to escape drowning while they embarked in a ship which must unavoidably go to the bottom with the first gale. My poor brother was even more zealous in the cause than I was myself: so far as he had become acquainted with the Laws of Nature, when circumstances would at all permit, he was inclined to keep them even to punctiliousness; and when he died, I could not help coming to the conclusion that, in the present state of society, no man could keep these laws, so as to derive much benefit from his endeavours to do so. As to "infringement" and "punishment" being inseparably connected, his brief career affords several striking examples. The seeds of disease were first implanted in his system, by bathing in fresh water, which he persisted in through ignorance of his own constitution; and afterwards he narrowly escaped being sent to his grave by the consequences of having been employed at those sorts of work which were almost certain to prove destructive of health. In the last case, however, he had no choice, and no control over the selfishness of his employers; and therefore, he was not to blame. It was these circumstances which made him so anxious to teach others how they might avoid those errors from which he had himself suffered; and I had once some thoughts of noticing them in this point of view, but it occurred to me that as the rich would have been implicated, they might have construed the attempt into a wish to lessen the hardships of my own situation, and increase my own comforts—an idea which I could not brook; and therefore, I contented myself with a simple statement of facts as they were. You overrate my influence when you suppose that I could "shame the rich into improvement:" I can assure you that a writer in the very humble, and very obscure station which I occupy, would require to exercise the greatest caution to avoid drawing down their vengeance upon himself, instead of exciting shame for their own conduct. I will not, however, forget the hints which you have been so kind as to favour me with; and whatever I can do for the labourious poor, my endeavours, at least, will not be awanting. If the Laws of Nature are to be kept, in any thing like perfection, it must be by the concurrence of society as a whole—not by isolated individuals.

'I shall be most happy to avail myself of the order which you have sent me for your "Moral Philosophy," and I anticipate much benefit from it.

A. B.'

CHAPTER IX.

CORRESPONDENCE WITH THE EDITOR—VISIT TO ABERDEENSHIRE—EXCURSION TO DEESIDE HIGHLANDS—NOT ENTHUSIASTIC IN HIS ADMIRATION OF ROMANTIC SCENERY—DIFFERENT KIND OF TASTE, ILLUSTRATED BY EXTRACT FROM 'DAY DREAMS'—'THE RUIN'—RETURNS HOME BY ABERDEEN—PROJECTED STORY OF THE DON—HE VISITS EDINBURGH—PUBLICATION OF 'SCOTTISH PEASANT'S FIRESIDE'—CHARACTER OF THAT WORK—TALE OF JONATHAN MOUDIWORT—EXTRACT FROM 'THINGS AND THOUGHTS.'

My interest in Mr. Bethune was first excited by the perusal of an article in the Athenæum on his brother's 'Life and Poems.' On reading that article, I lost no time in ordering the book itself; but it was then out of print, and it was a considerable time ere I could procure it. The very strong interest excited by its perusal, induced me to address a short letter to Mr. Bethune, in which I made some inquiries regarding his brother's unpublished writings, particularly those of a humorous character, as well as in regard to his own situation in life, having heard some vague rumours of his being engaged somewhere in connexion with the prisons.

In a few days I was gratified by a note in reply, and afterwards by an answer more at length. The following are extracts:—

'Mountpleasant, *September* 19, 1841.

'My Dear Sir,—I have just perused your letter of the 14th inst., which reached this place two days ago. Had I been at home, I should have been proud to acknowledge it earlier; but, from being engaged in the harvest, at a place three or four miles distant, where, as a matter of course, I must stop throughout the week, this was entirely out of my power. My engagement will not be completed for, probably, a fortnight to come, and at present I can only write a few hurried lines to say that I have received your much esteemed letter, and that it is most gratifying to me to be thus taken notice of by a kindred spirit; but as soon as I can command leisure, I will endeavour to reply more fully, and, if possible, to send you a manuscript copy of one of the pieces which you mention. A. B.'

'Mountpleasant, *October* 19, 1841.

'My Dear Sir,—Having got through with the harvest, it is with much pleasure that I now take up a pen again to address you. You can hardly conceive the amount of satisfaction which it gave me to learn that you had been reading the story of my deceased brother, "with deep, sympathetic interest." This may proceed from a weakness in our nature; but, if it be so, it is one to which I at once plead guilty. From there being only two of us, and from the peculiar circumstances in which we were placed, we were all the world to each other: now, when he is gone, my world may be said to be annihilated; and the greatest satisfaction which I can enjoy, is to hear that others, and more particularly those who are qualified to form a correct judgment, can appreciate his humble virtues. For me, I have done nothing, save narrated a few simple facts in the plainest and simplest manner I possibly could—it having been my firm determination when I began to write his Life, that I would carefully avoid everything like "colouring," or an attempt to "make the most" of any incident. Had it been otherwise, from having had some little experience in the art of giving effect to a story by the manner of telling it, I might perhaps have contrived to throw more of what an ordinary reader would call interest, into the pages of his biography.

'In looking over those parts of my brother's papers which I had transcribed, and have still lying beside me, I find that I have not copies of the two poems which I had in my eye, when I mentioned his wit, and humour. These were "Love in a Barrel,"* and "Johnie Craigie's Wedding"—the first consisting of about twenty pages, and the last of ten pages, of manuscript such as the enclosed. They

---

* See Appendix, No. 2.

were sent to Bristol, to give the publishers—Wright & Albert—a choice of them in the making up of the second edition; and they, as well as a number of others, have not yet been returned. The two enclosed pieces, however, which are of a half humorous cast, will, I hope, convince you that what I said was not altogether without foundation.

'It would give me the greatest satisfaction to be able to publish these, and a great many more of his productions, in a third edition; but the sale of books, and more especially of poetry, at the present time, is a most precarious affair; and it is as yet very questionable if another impression will ever be be required. Publishers, moreover, must always be consulted in these matters; unless one were to publish wholly at his own risk. I should say, however, that the publishers of the present edition would have enlarged it to two volumes without scruple, had they not been dissuaded from it by James Montgomery in the same letter, a part of which is now published as an introduction to the work.

'If you should feel any curiosity to see specimens of his prose productions, you will find some of them in "Wilson's Tales of the Borders," to which he contributed the following stories.—"The Victim of Vanity;" vol. IV. No. 201; "The Bewildered Student;" vol. V. No. 220; "Mary Middleton;" vol. V. No. 247; "The Cruise of the Pibroch;" vol. V. No. 248; and "The Factor;" vol. V. No. 256. These stories were spoilt by an attempt to accommodate them to the nature of the work for which they were intended; and their interest still farther destroyed by being terribly cut down in proof, to bring them within the compass of a single number. In justice to his memory, I may be allowed to say, that their author was induced to try this species of writing, solely because it was the only means which presented itself of procuring a little money at a time when that was with us a very scarce article. Trifling as is the kind of literature to which they belong, I could almost wish you to see these stories; and, were it not that the carriage would exceed the price of them, I would send you copies.—I am, with the greatest respect, Dear Sir, Yours very sincerely,

A. B.'

The following letter may be acceptable to the reader, as furnishing at one view a bibliographical history of Mr. Bethune's various publications:—

'MOUNTPLEASANT, *Nov.* 3, 1841.

'My Dear Sir,—I again beg to enclose for you a copy of the two pieces* of my brother's, which I mentioned as having sent in my last; and which must have certainly been carried away by the wind, in the way you notice, for I am almost confident that they left this place under seal.

---

* Two of the humorous pieces referred to in a previous letter.

'I have done but little in a literary way of late. Three articles, which were printed in "Chambers' Journal;" together with three or four others, which were rejected, comprise the amount of my writing last summer. I must say, that I really have now more leisure for writing than I once had; but I feel, at the same time, that I want that restless and untiring activity of mind and body, which once enabled me to accomplish a good deal with but scanty opportunities. Indifferent health, and depression of spirits are not very favourable to literary pursuits; and that these should now be, to a certain extent, my portion, you will hardly wonder, when you know that I have been twice thrown into the air by gunpowder, and on both occasions narrowly escaped with my life—that for three months, during my brother's last illness, I scarcely ever enjoyed more than an hour and a half's sleep out of the twenty-four—and that for nearly five months previous to the 21st of December last, the time at which my mother died, my clothes had never been off, except to shift my shirt. Those feelings, too, which may be experienced but cannot be described, and that deep anxiety of mind which was inseparable from my situation—destined to watch in solitude, from hour to hour, and day to day, the downward progress of disease—the slow and sure decay of a last friend, struck speechless, and almost motionless, by repeated shocks of palsy,—these things, taken together, have told fearfully upon a consti-

tution which was not originally very feeble; and now I might almost regard myself as a "doomed man," who is only reprieved for short intervals. Still, however, I have plans in my head, which I only want time and spirits to prosecute. Last winter, I had copied, and prepared for the press, as many of my brother's "Letters and Essays" as would make, perhaps, about 150 pages of letterpress, the same size as the volume now published. There are still some pretty long Essays to copy, as well as a number of unpublished Stories; and, if I could get time to prepare as much Manuscript as would make a volume of 320 pages, or thereby, I would try some publisher with it. In the event of doing so, I need scarcely say, that it were folly to expect to realize anything; but still it would gratify those feelings with which I am inclined to regard the memory of a departed friend. * * *
* * * * * * * *

I have, besides, nearly as many unpublished Stories of my own as, with some slight corrections, would make another volume of "Tales and Sketches of the Scottish Peasantry;" and a pretty long didactic poem, in blank verse, entitled, "Confessions of Convalescence,"* which, along with some others, might be published separately. The preparation of such a mass of matter, is a work which I can scarcely

---

* Another title for 'Day Dreams,' as the reader may recollect being mentioned at the commencement of extracts from that poem.

expect to live to accomplish. Had I been as I once was, the task would have been an easy one; but I now find, that a short time of confinement to the house, and close application to these pursuits, would entirely destroy the little remains of vigour which I possess. A considerable portion of my time, moreover, must be devoted to earning my daily bread, in one way or other; and even though the whole were ready for printing, the greatest difficulty of all would remain to be surmounted—namely, that of getting publishers to undertake the risk of such speculations. The entire copyright of "Tales and Sketches," &c., which is now out of print, was disposed of for fifty copies of the work. "Practical Economy," as stated in my brother's "Life," was literally given away for nothing; and still the publisher will probably be a loser. Concerning the first edition of the "Life and Poems," an acquaintance, who was himself connected with a printing office, gave me distinctly to understand, that no publisher would undertake the risk of bringing it out; and so it was published at my own expense, and cleared somewhat more than twenty pounds—the greater part of which will go, in a few weeks, to place a monument over the grave of its poor author. The second edition is brought out by the same house which published "Foster's Essay;" and it was at one time proposed to include it in the series of which the above-mentioned work forms a part. This idea, however, was ultimately given up; and the publishers have the copyright, upon the principle that I am to have one half of the clear profits, which, after deducting publisher's and bookseller's commission—the expense of material and workmanship in printing and binding, advertising, &c., &c., from the selling price—may be, as nearly as I can guess, about three halfpence per copy. I have now tried to make you acquainted with as much of my history, plans, and concerns as I could possibly cram into a single sheet; and, hoping that you will not be offended with the freedom which I have taken, I should be glad to hear, in return, how you contrive to get on with your publishers—that is, if you have no particular reason for keeping it a secret. I had almost forgotten to say, that I still live in one of the rooms of the house to which you allude, where my habits have almost become those of a hermit. I should have told you, too, that the Bristol company opened a communication about the publishing of the book, of their own accord. But for this, I should have never thought of applying to them. You cannot regret the distance at which we live from each other more than I do. I can seldom find the time and the means for travelling together; but if ever I should take a "jaunt," it will be to Aberdeenshire. Begging your pardon for this long and hurried scrawl, which I can scarcely find time to read without losing the post.—I remain, dear Sir, Yours, very sincerely, A. B.'

The first of the following extracts will explain what is stated above (page 205) as to one of the reasons why Mr. Bethune did not derive more pecuniary advantage from the first edition of his brother's 'Life and Poems.' Most readers will, I believe, regard it as an instance of honesty carried out to the romantic :—

' MOUNTPLEASANT, *January*, 22, 1842.

'Dear Sir,—Being now two letters in arrears, I gladly seize the opportunity of a bad day to pay, at least, part of the debt. On the evening of Monday last, I received, and read with deep interest your account of your literary career—in some respects, how like my own! though in others it is somewhat different.

'Though the first edition of my brother's " Life and Poems" was a four shillings book, the price mentioned in the prospectus was only three shillings, and at this it was sold. But a Mr. Dalgliesh, who, between himself and his friends, had undertaken to dispose of 100 copies, charged four shillings for the book; and I believe he must have got some trifles beside, in the way of charity—at all events I got £22 from him instead of £15. This I accepted, being at the time eager to have the means of ministering to the comfort of my poor paralytic mother, whose life, I had flattered myself I should be able to prolong by unremitting care and attention. But after her death I determined to return every farthing which did not exclusively belong to me; and I have now returned four pounds, and three still remains. This may appear an extremely trifling affair; but, from my earnings being only between sixteen-pence and eighteen-pence a day, and what with want of work in these dull times, intervals devoted to writing—that most profitless of all employments—and a summer of indifferent health—really I get on but slowly in these matters. Had I chosen it, however, I might have been in comparatively easy circumstances; for various sums of money, some of them from England, have been forwarded to me by benevolent individuals who had read the book; but these I have uniformly returned, thanking my intended benefactors, and assuring them that, as I could still provide for my own wants, I should not consider myself at all justified in becoming a burden on society.—The only excuse which I can offer for this long chapter of egotism is, that part of it is an excuse, as you will see, for my own parsimony; and for the rest, like John Bunyan,

" Having got my story by the end;
Still as I pull'd it came, and so I penn'd."

'I have not left myself room to tell you how much I was gratified to hear that you were pleased with my departed brother's humble attempts at literature, both in prose and verse. Poor boy! he knew, from experience, but too well what it was to live in a house pervious to "the drift."*

'May I ask, if ever you have read "Physiology applied to the Preservation of Health," by Andrew Combe, M. D.? or "The Physiology of Digestion considered with relation to Dietetics," by the same author? If you have not, I wish I could send you a reading of the copies which I have myself. These are works which, I think, should be not only read but studied and acted upon by every human being who sets any value upon that greatest of all temporal blessings, health. Perhaps you may find them in some of the libraries in your neighbourhood; and if not, the next time you are inclined to spend seven shillings and six-pence upon books, I would have you to buy "Physiology applied to Health." The mere knowledge of the animal economy which it is calculated to confer, is worth the money.

'I did see the "Chapter from the Life of a Poor Man," in Chambers' Edinburgh Journal, and read it with a feeling of deep sympathy for its unfortunate author. Even now, when better times appear to have arrived, I can still pity him. Ten to one but his present patrons will some day hold themselves entitled to exact a debt of humility and gratitude, under which he may yet wince. This is no world for poets, particularly poor ones, to live in.

* See 'The Bewildered Student.' Border Tales, No. 220.

I have only room to say farther, that I am,
Yours very sincerely,   A. B.'

The following letter, as it discloses some of the effects of severe manual labour, in connexion with the comfortless solitude of Mr. Bethune's dwelling, will no doubt excite the sympathy of the reader :—

'MOUNTPLEASANT, *April* 3, 1842.

'My dear Sir,—I now feel quite ashamed of myself. Your last letter, dated Feb. 15th, has been in my hands somewhere about six weeks, without one word of acknowledgement or reply. A few days ago too, a copy of your "Moral Agency" was handed to me : so that being at present, in so many respects your debtor, I am glad to lay hold of even a portion of the day of rest, as you will perceive from the date at the top of the sheet, simply to acknowledge my obligation. This silence on my part has not been altogether a willing one. It is long since I had intended to send you " The Orphan Wanderer,"* which I now enclose, together with some manuscript productions of the same author, (not sent at present,) and a few verses of my own which were composed beside the lifeless remains of that brother to whom they refer. But of late I have been constantly employed, and when this is the case, with respect to writing in the evenings, I now find that it is widely different with me from what it was when

* By his brother.

my friends were alive. Then, everything was prepared to make me as comfortable as circumstances would admit of at my return from the toils of the day,—and the evening, whether short or long, was available for any purpose to which I might choose to devote it; but now when I come home, after travelling two or three miles perhaps, from the place at which I have been employed, I must get in water, go for milk, kindle fire, prepare my supper, and do such other things about the house as are indispensable; and by the time I can get through with these matters, the evening in general is so far advanced that I am good for nothing save going to bed. I have, moreover, always been subject to chopped, or in Scotch phrase, *hackit* hands during the spring season: they are always worst at night, and of late the evil has increased to such an extent, that in the very few attempts at writing which I have been forced to make, I have found considerable difficulty in wielding a pen, besides running a great risk of being wholly unintelligible. These things put together have made me delay writing from time to time, and have at last driven me upon the expedient to which I have now resorted. For some time yet I expect to be busy; but as soon as the gardening season is over, digging being at present my principal occupation, I shall probably have more leisure than will be altogether desirable, and then you may expect to hear more of me.

'I must not forget to thank you for the copy of

"Knockespock's Lady," by W. Thom: I had seen previously "The Mitherless Bairn." There is true poetry in both, but the last is, I think, better than the first. Mr. T.'s principal fault, I apprehend, is being too locally Scotch: such words as "litheless,* litheness," and "meen,"† would I fear, hardly be generally understood. But this subject too, must be postponed to a future opportunity. By and by, I will be able to give you some information about

---

* *Lithe*, is any out of door shelter, such as a bank, a bush of furze or broom, &c., and is peculiarly associated with the experience of a herd, or tender of cattle in a cold blustering day. To the natives of Aberdeenshire and the contiguous districts, most of whom in early life have been employed in the capacity of 'herds,' this word and its derivatives have a peculiar expressiveness and pathos. I do not know a truer stroke of the pathetic, than the line of the poem in question—

'And litheless the lair of the Mitherless Bairn.'

a pathos which I conceive, it would be quite impossible to transfer into English, there being no corresponding word.

In the dialect of the south-west of Scotland, *bield* comes near to it in meaning; as we find Burns addressing the mountain daisy as springing

'Beneath the random bield
O' clod or stane.'

But *lithe* has the advantage over *bield*, of being used as an adjective as well as a substantive; as for instance, it is quite common to say in regard to a place that has a better shelter than another—' It's lither here.'

† Moon.

a memoir of my grandmother, written by my brother in 1836, which I expect will be printed in the course of the coming summer. The manuscript which was mentioned in my last, I will send when I next write.—I remain, most respectfully and sincerely, Yours, A. B.'

About the end of July, 1842, Mr. Bethune paid his contemplated visit to Aberdeenshire. On his way he called on John Ouchterlony, Esq. of the Guynd, near Arbroath, a gentleman who had taken a great interest in the success of his works, particularly of the "Life and Poems;" but Mr. Ouchterlony was from home. Having taken the Perth boat from Newburgh to Dundee, and the railway thence to Arbroath, Mr. Bethune, I think, walked almost all the rest of the journey, a distance of upwards of fifty miles. One could not but value a visit from such a man, involving so much physical exertion, and it was no small gratification during Mr. Bethune's short stay with us, (only about eight days,) to take him about to see some of the most remarkable scenery in the neighbourhood. One day we drove up Deeside to the foot of Lochnagar, intending to have made the ascent of that celebrated mountain; but the boisterous state of the weather prevented us—a matter of very great regret both to my friend and myself,—though, even without the accomplishment of that object, the ride supplies almost at every point the most intense gratification to one whose soul is capable of being fired by romantic and sublime scenery. Mr. Bethune, though he enjoyed the scenery much, did not seem susceptible of a very high degree of this enthusiasm: his taste lay rather among the quieter beauties of nature, and the varieties of human character. I recollect, on another day, when driving from Alford to Auchindoir, and remarking on the striking and picturesque views afforded by that delightful ride, he remarked with a sigh, how much his brother would have enjoyed such scenery;—and when, as illustrative of the effect which such scenery had upon some minds, I recited that noble passage in the first book of the Excursion beginning:—

" What soul was his, when from the naked top
Of some bold headland, he beheld the sun
Rise up and bathe the world in light !*

he could not enter into its spirit—could indeed hardly regard it as other than a piece of senti-

---

* He looked—
Ocean and earth—the solid frame of earth,
And ocean's liquid mass beneath him lay
In gladness and deep joy. The clouds were touched,
And in their silent faces he did read
Unutterable love. Sound needed none,
Nor any voice of joy; his spirit drank
The spectacle: sensation, soul, and form
All melted into him: they swallowed up
His animal being, in them did he live,
And by them did he live—they were his life.
In such access of mind, in such high hour
Of visitation from the living God,
Thought was not—in enjoyment it expired."

mental raving. So true is the observation of Coleridge, the productions of genius tend only to raise uneasiness and irritation in minds not endowed with a susceptibility of corresponding impressions. But that Mr. Bethune had, as we have just remarked, an eye capable of being charmed to a high degree, by the more subdued beauties of nature, and especially by those associated with, and suggestive of rural quietude and enjoyment, no one acquainted with his tales can doubt. An instance of this has just presented itself to me, in a passage of the "Day-Dreams," not hitherto cited; where some of the moral associations suggested to a pensive spirit, by a fine sunset in late autumn, are impressively brought out:—

Time speeds him onward with unwearied wing.
* * * * *

The sun hath westered, and is near his setting—
Man pauses—loiters in the task of life,
Nor sees, nor heeds the shadow's solemn march
Which measures out his time upon the stone,
Which knows no moment's pause, but circles on
From year to year and age to age the same.

The sun hath almost reached his journey's close,
The ray he sheds is gentle * * * * and
Pure as the pensive light from woman's eyes
When kindled up by retrospective thoughts,
Wandering to former scenes of love or joy.
* * * * * * *

But yet there is a melancholy tinge
In that rich radiance—and a passing thought
Of things departed, and of days gone by,
At such an hour insensibly will weave
Itself into the texture of the scene.
Nothing departs alone—the dying day
Bears with it many to their last repose;
The setting sun so gorgeously arrayed
In beams of light, and curtained round about
With clouds steeped in the rainbow's richest dyes,
So fair—so full of light and living glory—
That with the ancient Persian one might deem
Him God of all he looks upon below.
His setting ushers in a night to some
Which morning shall not break.

* * * * *

The hour of evening hath a solemn voice
Which seems to woo the soul to meditation—
And I will meditate awhile to-night,
Or rather dream my idleness away.

* * * * * *

In the course of our journey up Deeside, I remember, speaking of early recollections, I proposed that he should give me a sketch of the development of his mind and literary tastes; which he agreed to do in a series of Letters. Since commencing the compilation of this volume, I have often had cause to regret that he should not have lived to carry this into effect; and have sometimes felt inclined to reproach myself that, during the period which elapsed between this and his being taken ill, short though it was, I had made no direct effort to induce him to make a commencement. —' Whatsoever thy hand findeth to do, do it with thy might.'

My late friend was keenly alive to the evils, both social and moral, connected with the extinction of small farms, which, for a series of years, have been undergoing a process of absorption into the larger, until what has hitherto constituted the worthiest and most virtuous part of the rural population is threatened with utter annihilation. It would be quite out of place here to institute any inquiry as to the causes which have led to this system, or any exposition of the evils it induces. We are glad, however, to perceive that these last are beginning to attract the attention of a rising and influential party in the State— a party which, however wrong we may deem it in many of its theories and assumptions, has, we doubt not, an important sphere to occupy and part to act in counteraction of that inordinate spirit of gain-seeking, as well as of that growing separation of the middle and upper, from the labouring classes, which are among the most unhealthy symptoms of our social state.

To some of his impressions and feelings in regard to the system in question Mr. Bethune has given utterance in the following apologue, which I well recollect his reading to me during one of our excursions. My friend's elocution did not by any means tend to set off the merits of the composition;

as he had, especially in reading verse, a drawling, sing-song way of pronouncing; yet, now that he is gone, there is a charm connected with the recollection of the tones in which these simple verses were recited. And the piece has another affecting association, having been one of the very few he was able to give me from his own hand when I visited him on his death-bed. The reader acquainted with his two volumes of Tales, will recognise its affinity with several of the pieces interspersed through these —the principal charm of which is a simplicity approaching to the style of our early ballads. When my friend read the piece to me, I objected to some of the verses as flat, or of lame construction, and have now omitted several which still seemed chargeable with these faults:—

'THE RUIN.'

By yonder ruin desolate,
   Upon the mountain hoar;
Shaded in lonely solitude,
   By the tall sycamore,—

Musing upon this changing scene,
   I lingered on my way,
Till shadows of the eventide
   Announced the close of day.

It was a place where man had been,
   With all his hopes and fears;
And woman's gentler spirit there
   Had melted into tears.

It was a place where hoary age
    Had left the scene of strife—
Where youth had loved, and infancy
    Been ushered into life.

And there a thousand images,
    Of days and years gone by—
Like the illusions of a dream,
    Flitted before my eye.

There, as I stood in musing mood,
    Methought a spirit woke
Among the rustling leaves, and thus
    In deepest accents spoke.

" Stranger, I pray thee, pause a while,
    And listen to me now;
And thou wilt pause, I rightly guess,
    Even by thy thoughtful brow.

" Three centuries of sun and storm,
    Have o'er my branches swept,
Since first upon my infant form
    The summer sunbeam slept.

" Long, long above that humble cot,
    I broke the midnight blast;
And o'er the cottagers at noon,
    A pleasing shadow cast;

" And since all tenantless and lone,
    These ruined walls have been—
Full thirty years of solitude
    My hoary trunk hath seen.

" But though I ne'er again shall hear
    The clarion of the cock,
Which wont the morning watch to mark
    To those who had no clock;

" And though long years have o'er me passed,
    With weary steps and slow,
Since I have heard the lover's vow,
    Whispered in accents low;

" And though no more, with busy hum,
    The children round me play—
Though quenched the fire, and cold the hearth,
    And all gone to decay,—

" Still, in the memory of a tree,
    A long, long story lives,
Of things which to the heart of man
    Its pain or pleasure gives—

" A story of the ceaseless change,
    With never-ending flow,
Which marks the destinies of men,
    And their affairs below.

" In days, now numbered with the past,
    Which have been long forgot,
When the simplicity of truth
    Adorned each lowly cot

" With all a peasant's homely joys,
    And piety sincere,
And hopes of immortality,
    Which triumph'd over fear.

"Industrious, frugal, and content,
  From vain ambition free;
They cherish'd no unnatural wants,
  And feared not penury.

"Beyond their needful ' milk and meal,'
  And dress of hodden-gray,
Their humble wishes never roamed—
  Their thoughts ne'er learn'd to stray.

"As seasons rolled, the song of praise,
  Duly at eve and morn,
Rose from that lowly cot, and up
  To heaven's high cope was borne.

"Then rose the prayer for humble hearts—
  For fortitude to bear;
While secret sins, before their God,
  Were all acknowledged there.

"The look of conscious rectitude,
  Which beamed forth in the eye;
The heart which gave the smile or tear
  Of natural sympathy:

"These shed a charm around the place,
  Which even I could share—
The charm of nature and of truth—
  Of piety and prayer.

"And when the hoary patriarch
  Was near his journey's ending,
His children's children might be seen,
  In sorrow o'er him bending.

" By his example on their souls,
   Stern virtue was impress'd;
And firm resolve and fortitude
   Implanted in each breast.

And counsels, precepts, looks, and words,
   By them remembered long—
Uprose, like angel-sentinels,
   To guard their hearts from wrong.

" Here, also, have I seen the maid
   Dance lightly in the sun,
When Spring to deck the freshening fields
   In bright robes had begun.

" I've heard her sing, in heartfelt joy,
   With voice as wild and sweet,
As is the lark's when springing up
   The dappling dawn to greet.

" But soon her glee and frolic gone—
   Her laugh, by thought subdued,
Told that the ' elder tale of love'
   In her must be renewed.

" That ' tale' her altered mien betray'd—
   Her musings lone and strange;
Her fitful bursts of merriment—
   Her eye's expressive change.

" Whene'er a light, young step drew near,
   The blush her cheek would cover,
Her fluttering heart, half hope, half fear,
   Leaped instant to her lover.

"Pure as the snow-drop when it gems
    The green turf where it grows ;
And innocent as infant's dream,
    That maiden's blush arose.

"It was a heart to Nature true,
    That made her young cheek glow
Bright as the rainbow's crimsoning
    When seen on mountain snow.

"These were the times to which I cling—
    In which my memory lives—
From which my time-worn heart a glow
    Of pleasure still derives.

"But since the deadly curse of war
    Upon the land hath set
That incubus of all its sons,
    The everlasting debt ;

"And since the cot and cottar's rig,
    No more may offer charms,
Such as the landlord now finds in
    Amalgamated farms ;

"Since ' milk and meal' no longer here
    May bless the labouring poor ;
Nor house, nor home be left for them
    By meadow or by moor ;*

---

* In what it here says, the tree was not speaking without some reason right or wrong ; as an individual who lived at no very great distance from its supposed site, and of whom it must have no doubt heard, was known to state the circumstance of his having ' razed out thirty hearth-stanes.'

"I've seen the country desolate,
  Its cottages thrown down;
Poor labourer, artizan, and all
  Driven to the smoky town.

"There, forced to breathe an atmosphere
  Of stagnate, smoky air—
They turn their longing eyes in vain
  To where their fathers were.

"Far from the cooling, mountain stream,
  And fresh, green mountain slopes,
Their days are spent amid the dust
  Of factories and shops.

"There, oft, the hapless youth, ensnared
  By an unhallowed charm,
No longer feels the purer flame
  Which should his bosom warm.

"There, too, the blush of modesty
  Forsakes the maiden's cheek,
And leaves the heart it wont to guard,
  Unfortified and weak.

"In vain I mourn the roofless cots,
  And ruined walls around;
And waving corn upon the spots
  Where hearth-stones once were found.

"Gold is the god men worship now,
  With never-ceasing care;
Nor heed they who may live or die,
  While they the spoil can share.

" The rich, in boundless vanity,
    Spend every passing day;
The poor ape their fantastic tricks—
    Even all as best they may.

" And, save when dire necessity
    Their vain desires hath shorn,
None seem to have a higher aim
    Than butterflies at morn.

" Go, tell these words to such as they—
    Go, tell them they are sooth;
Though mankind men must flatter here,
    Yet I may speak the truth!"

The impressions in regard to the amiable qualities of Mr. Bethune's character, which his writings and some little correspondence with him had produced on our minds, were verified and deepened by the brief period of personal intercourse we were privileged to enjoy with him. It would have delighted us could he have prolonged his stay; but harvest being about to commence in Fife, he had to hasten away, being engaged as a shearer. He returned by way of Aberdeen, whither I had the pleasure of accompanying him. Through the kind attentions of one or two friends, to whose care I left him, and who deemed themselves honoured in having him for a guest, he saw the principal objects of interest connected with that ancient city; among others, the 'Auld brig of Balgownie,' renowned in traditionary prophecy, when he seems to have received impressions, which, had he lived, he would probably have turned to literary account, as the reader may see from the following hints for a

STORY OF THE DON.

'A young man in Aberdeen is warmly attached to a servant girl in the same place. In time they fall out. Shortly after, the girl goes abroad late of an evening and is no more heard of. Some hair, supposed to be hers, and apparently torn out in a struggle, is found below the bridge of Balgownie; and her lover is tried for murdering her, but acquitted. Shortly after, he becomes melancholy and enlists. When in the army, his curiosity is excited by a young and handsome officer of a half melancholy half ferocious disposition. At the battle of ———— this officer is mortally wounded, and when dying, tells him he was the murderer of his former sweetheart,' &c.

Our friend left us, we had hoped, somewhat recruited in spirits; but on his arrival at home his mind received a severe shock from learning of a melancholy occurrence which had taken place in the family of his nearest neighbour and worthy friend, Mrs. Ferguson—the same who had so sedulously attended to his brother during his last illness, and who was soon to have the same melancholy duties to discharge towards himself. The following is an extract from a letter Mr. Bethune wrote me the day after his arrival at home:—

'MOUNTPLEASANT, *August* 10, 1842.

'Dear Sir,—I now hasten to apprize you of my safe arrival at home yesterday afternoon. I should have been inclined to give you a half-ludicrous account of my voyage to Arbroath, and of the sea sickness, &c., of my fellow passengers, of which I should think there was something more than an average amount; but, since I left home, one of my nearest neighbours has been called to another world, and I feel that I am in no mood for indulging in such descriptions. Little more than four years ago, Mrs. Ferguson, with whose name you must be familiar, lost her husband, who was an elder of the Secession Congregation, and a most pious and exemplary individual. In the interval which has elapsed since then, her eldest son had grown up, and bade fair to supply his place as the head of the family. But on Monday was eight days—the day on which we were at Insch—he had gone, for a little recreation, with the salmon fishers; and, while bathing, stepped over the precipitous front of a sand bank in the river, and, sad to tell, was drowned! His body was not recovered till the following morning, when the fishers, after many fruitless attempts, and when they were just on the point of giving up the search, succeeded in dragging it ashore with a net. He had completed his twentieth year about two months ago, and for industry and sobriety had few equals. I need hardly say that his mother is bowed down by a weight of sorrow, from which it is questionable if she will ever recover. I am, Dear Sir, Yours very sincerely, A. B.'

When the harvest was concluded, Mr. Bethune paid a visit to Edinburgh with the view of making arrangements for the publication of 'The Scottish Peasant's Fireside.' Messrs. Adam and Charles Black agreed to publish the book, taking all the risk and engaging to allow the author half of any clear profits which might arise from the sale. The volume appeared in the month of February, 1843. It is of similar size with the 'Tales and Sketches of the Scottish Peasantry;' and as was the case in that volume, there are interspersed among the prose tales several pieces in verse. In distinctness of portraiture and interest, the stories, in general, are not inferior to those of the previous volume; but we are not sure that we recognise so often that peculiar delicacy of touch in the delineation of female character; and we sometimes desiderate the critical pruning knife of our author's literary friend, to whose revision it is rather to be regretted that this volume had not, like the rest of his writings, been subjected.

Of all the stories in the volume that entitled 'Jonathan Moudiwort' has taken the most hold of our imagination; and perhaps of all the characters Mr. Bethune has sketched, that of Jonathan presents the greatest distinctness of outline and boldness of individuality. The distinctive lines of the character of Mrs. Evergreen, too, are very happy; but the filling up is carelessly executed. Indeed, the whole story, though admirably conceived, bears marks of great haste, and of the want of any severe revision; exhibiting in several places a redundancy of words and unclassical modes of expression, which, under the well-directed exercise of a severe taste would have suffered excision. Yet, notwithstanding of these faults few stories give a deeper impression of reality. As a proof of this we may, perhaps, be pardoned for mentioning that when we thought of commending, as a very happy one, that scene in which Mrs. Evergreen is represented as scolding her servant girls for breaking the Sabbath by cleaning the shoes, dishes, &c. on the morning of that day, when this should have been done on the Saturday night, though it was two hours past midnight ere they received them from the parlour,—we felt a momentary misgiving lest our remarks should meet the eye of the lady and give her offence.

The character of the Stone-breaker in 'The Illegitimate' interests the reader deeply from its obvious relation to Mr. Bethune or his brother; but the story does not excite the same feeling of nearness to our every-day life as the one just commented on; the scene seems always laid in some *terra incognita* over which hangs the dim haze of remoteness.

To a pensive reader, however, no part of the volume will be more interesting than that entitled 'Things and Thoughts,' inasmuch as it brings graphically to view an interesting episode in the author's own mental history. The prospect of having soon to remove from the room which he then occupied, to another part of the house, led him to examine some old lumber and half useless articles, with the view of committing, what might appear, mere rubbish to the flames. In the course of this examination he came upon several articles which had belonged to his brother; and the feeling of their being relics, rose so affectingly in his mind, that, though quite insignificant in themselves, he could not help preserving them. He then lighted on some old magazines, the sight of which awakened a train of most interesting associations, and brought back to his view the evening on which, along with several more valuable books, they were purchased, with all the vividness which had characterized the consciousness and perceptions of the actual occasion, deepened by all the affecting occurrences which had since intervened.

'The first of the magazines in question was for May 1830; and, though more than ten years of toil and care, with all their obliterating influences, had intervened, I had scarcely time to read the title page when imagination had conjured up the whole succession of events connected with the evening on which they became ours.

'As already said, we had been eager to increase our little library; and in the autumn of the year last mentioned—it might be near the 1st of November—we got notice of an auction of books which was to take place in a village about three miles distant. Fortunately, as we then thought, we had saved about £2. It was nearly the first spare money which we had been able to command—but the vision of cheap books and an abundant choice was before us; and, as soon as we came home, hands and faces were washed, a hasty supper despatched, and away we hied, happy in the anticipation of the good things which we were to bring back with us on our return. These consisted of the five numbers of the work already mentioned; Johnson's "Lives of the English Poets," in four volumes; Goldsmith's "Citizen of the World," two volumes; "Byron's Works," four volumes; a copy of "Burns' Works;" and some other trifles of comparatively little importance. Some of the books were not exactly what we most wanted; these, however, we could not obtain, and so we took what we could get, rather than bring home our money. But I am giving a history of the transaction from memory, rather than an account of the scene which was represented to my imagination. There was, in the first place, a cloudy and somewhat dark autumnal evening, with a slight breeze from the north, and a long streak of clear sky in the same quarter, indicating the approach of northern lights—a phenomenon which, for a number of years previous to 1830, so far as I recollect, was but rarely seen. Then the road, and the open country—with its scattered trees, hedges, cottages, and farms—and the distant hills, scarcely visible to to the straining eye, amid the shadows that rested on them, were exchanged for the long, narrow street of a rather populous village, slippery from recent rain, with figures gliding to and fro, or hurrying past in perfect obscurity, save when they glanced occasionally into view, for a few seconds, in the light of a shop window. Anon, there was a large hall, dimly lighted at the farther end, where a large collection of books had been placed upon temporary shelves; with a motley crowd of variously dressed and careless looking people sauntering through it, or resting on the seats along the wall. In the middle was the auctioneer, with a clerk at his side, and two candles burning before him—his eye evidently acquiring new lustre as it caught a glance of a supposed purchaser, while a broad grin of the most exalted satisfaction never failed to brighten up his whole countenance as often as any thing like a competition could be got up. But what interested me most was a young man —apparently older, but in reality under eighteen— with a thoughtful expression of countenance—hair which had gradually darkened as his years increased, till it was now almost black—and a complexion which was evidently paler than it had once been, from the combined effects of unremitting toil by day, late evening studies, and indifferent health; who, though several years my junior, was taller than me by nearly the head. For a time he watched intently the progress of the sales; then he obtained permission to look over the books upon the shelves; and finally, he requested the auctioneer, if it were agreeable, to put up one or two of the works which he wished to purchase. His request was at once granted; and then, with a straight-forwardness of character but ill suited to the present state of society and the very humble sphere in which he was destined to move, he carried them, regardless of the price. Again the hall and the books, the auctioneer, the candles, and the motley crowd, were exchanged for the slippery street—from the lateness of the hour now completely dark—the public road, and the open country; and once more the acquaintances whom we passed, or spoke with on our homeward way—the deep hush of night—the aspect of the distant mountains—and the bright aurora, which, rising from the northern part of the horizon, streamed up to the zenith in long streaks of wavy flame, making the path before us almost as distinct as if it had been but the twilight of a summer's evening;—the whole scene was again before me, almost as vividly as if it had been reality.

'As the concluding part of this panoramic view

of the past, there were the musty walls and smoky rafters of a low, damp cottage, faintly illuminated by the flame of a rush-light, which burned in an iron lamp, suspended by a nail driven into the rustic frame-work which supported the clay vent, and which had been kindled with some difficulty from the embers of a nearly burnt out fire. Before that lamp sat the same young man, forgetful alike that he had to be abroad before six o'clock next morning, and that it was then considerably past midnight; so intent was he in scanning the contents of the books he had just purchased.

'This was the closing scene of that particular evening, from which, as already said, imagination had shaken off the shadows of more than ten years, But she did not stop here: many painful recollections were inseparably interwoven with the intervening period. These, at her command, were carefully collected by memory, and, when they had been invested with her most vivid colouring, placed exactly in the array in which the corresponding events had occurred. After having yielded implicitly for I know not how long to the various emotions thus produced, I put aside the things which I had been vainly endeavouring to examine, extinguished the lamp by which I had pursued these musings, and went to bed. As the consequence of previously excited feelings, a sort of imperfect and broken slumber soon came on; and then my dreams were of that brother, whom imagination had so recently placed before me in the various stages of his existence, from infancy up to manhood. If the impressions in the one case had been vivid, what may be called the perceptions in the other, seemed to participate in a still greater degree of reality. Methought it was a bright Sabbath in the very pride of summer—that we had been engaged in the services of the day, and had strayed, during the interval of public worship to the ruins of the old church, and the parish burying ground which surrounded it —a favourite haunt of ours at such seasons. There, as fancy deemed, we were employed in deciphering the moss-covered inscriptions and half obliterated names, engraved on the rude monuments which had been " erected to the memory" of individuals long ago forgotten; when he started off all at once, and, after running to a short distance, disappeared behind a tombstone, beckoning me to follow. I hastened to obey, but I had taken only a few steps when I stumbled over an open grave, which I had not before observed, and fell; and the fall, imaginary as it was, served to awaken me to a full sense of the cold and saddening realities by which I was surrounded—to a sense that that brother was no more!—that my few friends had sunk, in rapid succession, into their graves! and that I was alone in the world—the sole, and solitary inhabitant of a home which had once contained a whole family, of whom, myself excepted, not a single individual was now alive!'

CHAPTER X.

MORE CHEERFUL PROSPECTS—IS SEIZED WITH FEVER—ILLNESS AND DEATH OF ONE OF HIS AUNTS—PARTIAL CONVALESCENCE—ACCEPTS, CONDITIONALLY, THE SITUATION OF EDITOR OF THE 'DUMFRIES STANDARD'—VISITS KENNOWAY FOR CHANGE OF AIR—DISEASE MERGES INTO CONSUMPTION—RESIGNS EDITORSHIP—CORRESPONDENCE WITH ENGLISH FRIENDS—INCREASED ILLNESS—DEATH—BURIAL—MONUMENT—CONCLUSION.

UNTIL near the end of November, 1842, Mr. Bethune continued to enjoy comparatively good health, and considerably recruited spirits. His friends were gratified by perceiving a more cheerful tone of mind pervading his communications than formerly—as for example:—'My prospects on the approach of winter are not at all disheartening. In the course of a month, or so, I may perhaps be out of work for a time; but then I still have a number of my brother's papers to transcribe, and with these I can keep myself busy till something else comes in the way.'—But about the 29th of November, he was seized with fever; having, as it appears, caught the infection from the family which supplied him with milk. Of his illness, and those

unhappy attendant circumstances which induced a transition into that fatal malady which terminated his life—I have received the following account from his medical attendant, Dr. John Lyall :—
'It was an attack of fever, but rather of a mild description than otherwise. One of his maternal maiden aunts, who had come to be his nurse, also became affected with the disease, and in a severer form—in fact, she was ultimately cut off in a deplorable state from bed-sore. While Alexander got convalescent, his aunt was at her worst; and, by her restlessness, delirium, &c., prevented him from obtaining the quiet and rest necessary for his recovery; and at that particular time when quiet and sleep were especially requisite for his welfare. On this account, he never made a thorough recovery—sleep went from him—his appetite did not return, and a slight cough began to annoy him: in short, there was a gradual transition into pulmonary consumption. It was during this interval, that a gentleman* who knew his penurious habits, and was afraid lest any thing should be awanting in promoting his recovery—transmitted to me one pound to purchase wine for him, and medicate it with a little bark, or some such article, so that it might not appear an offering of charity. This good deed was done by stealth—for the donor's name was kept a secret between himself and me.'

* The late John Ouchterlony, Esq. of the Guynd, a gentleman who had shown great zeal and activity in promoting the sale of Mr. Bethune's works.

During the period of his partial convalescence, an offer was made to him by the projectors of a newspaper then about to be started in the Non-intrusion interest in Dumfries—of the situation of principal editor—he having been recommended by Hugh Miller. To this application he expressed himself inclined to have acceded, had the state of his health permitted; and the proprietors being anxious to secure his services, an arrangement was entered into conditionally—should his health so far improve as to warrant his entering on the duties of the situation within a specified period. His salary was to have been £100 a-year—a scale of remuneration which, though far from large for an editor, would have appeared almost princely to his humble ambition, and as compared with his former earnings and most economical habits. Then, for the first time during a life of drudgery, disappointment, and privation, there dawned on him the prospect of reaching a position in society somewhat more worthy of his genius and acquirements, than that which he had hitherto occupied. But, alas! it was never more than a prospect. He had removed to Kennoway, a village about sixteen miles south from Newburgh, for change of air, but derived no advantage from it; and from this place he wrote one of the projectors of the 'Dumfries Standard'—resigning the last hope of being able to enter on the duties of editor of that paper.

Though he had so far recovered as to be able to

enter on these duties, it may be doubted whether he would have found them very congenial to his temper of mind. He was no doubt conscientiously attached to the cause of what has now become the Free Church; but his attachment partook little of the heat of partizanship—a quality which, under the present prevalent mode of conducting the newspaper press, is, unhappily, a principal element of interest and success. Had he, notwithstanding of this, succeeded, we should have expected one important service from him, namely—an example of improved temper in newspaper writing; for it would have indeed surprised us, had we found him, for any consideration, like some others of his class—

'Narrow his mind,
And to party give up what was meant for mankind.'

Several of his English friends, who had become aware of his illness, manifested deep concern and sympathy with him, and were anxious to devise means for promoting his recovery. Rendered unable to do anything for his own support, and with but faint prospects of speedy restoration, he now, in one or two instances, so far relaxed the rigour of his independence, as to permit himself to receive a small sum or two, proffered and pressed on his acceptance with peculiar delicacy, by highly valued friends; yet not without the proviso that he would either repay the money, or devote it to the relief of others, should he ever be able to resume labour. I insert the following note from one of the ladies belonging to the Society of Friends, as a remarkable instance of such delicacy, as well as of the deep interest taken by the writer in Mr. Bethune's welfare. Having employed an amanuensis in the business part of her letter, which related to some of Mr. Bethune's publications, in promoting the circulation of which she still zealously employed herself—she adds in her own hand :—

'My Dear Friend,—I must add a few lines just between ourselves,—As during thy late protracted illness, much expense must necessarily have been incurred, I am inclined once more to solicit thy acceptance of a few pounds, which it will be a great pleasure to me to send. Thou knowest me better now than at a former time, and I am in hopes wilt shew that thou hast "respect enough" for me to accept my money. If that privilege be granted me, I will send a Post-Office order immediately, but cannot risk its being returned; as that from a friend would be too mortifying to thy sincere and sympathising friend.'

The following are extracts from Mr. Bethune's reply :—

'MOUNTPLEASANT, *by* NEWBURGH,
February 15, 1843.

'My Dear and much respected friend,—How shall

I thank you for that unceasing kindness which I have done so little to deserve? Albeit I can express myself readily enough upon most subjects, here I can find no words, and can only say, that I experience a feeling of which I can convey no idea to others. I am now humbled, and beg that you will send me a Post-Office order for one pound—not more. Yes; let me be indebted to one who so well deserves every feeling of esteem and gratitude which any heart can experience; and if I should never need it for myself, I will try to distribute it among the most deserving objects whom I can select. Though the All-wise Disposer of events saw meet to visit me with affliction, he had previously provided the means of supporting me through it, without knowing what it was to suffer the want of any comfort which money could procure. As respects myself, I have much for which to be thankful, and little of which to complain.

'I do not recollect if I mentioned in my last, the case of my aunt * * * She died here on the 8th of the present month. This event happening as it did, has been to me the cause of much anxiety and sorrow. It was my earnest wish and prayer that she might recover, and go hence in health, even as she had come; but the Lord had determined otherwise, and this it seems was to be the last stage of her journey. Nor to her did it matter much when or where the call came; for a great part of her life had been spent in endeavouring, as God might give her strength, to make a suitable preparation for death, that she might appear with joy, and not with sorrow, before the Judge of all the earth.—Your very humble friend and servant,

A. B.'

Among those who at this time manifested a deep and most anxious solicitude in regard to Mr. Bethune were several gentlemen belonging to the medical profession in Bristol, to one of whom (the one who generally conducted the correspondence) we had occasion to refer in an early part of this narrative. These gentlemen not only proffered to Mr. Bethune pecuniary supplies, and tendered him professional advice, but communicated with some of his friends in Scotland, in order, if possible, more effectually to secure to him the benefit of their benevolent intentions; and even, as the reader will see from a letter he will find below, volunteered the assumption of the entire responsibility of his removing for a time to some place enjoying a more equable and warmer climate.* The following extracts from a letter of Mr. Bethune's, in reply to one covering a remittance from these friends, imbodies some particulars of most painful interest, respecting his own and aunt's illness:—

---

* The Isle of Bute was thought of; but Mr. Bethune's increasing weakness seems to have rendered inadvisable his removal to such a distance.

'*March* 15, 1843.

'Though I have occasionally returned some little benefactions before, from a conviction that I did not deserve them, and had no right to live upon the benevolence of others, yet I will keep this beside me, and, if it can be at all useful to me, use it freely; but, should it please Providence to restore me to health, and place me in easy circumstances, or if I should be called hence before my own resources are exhausted,—in either case, I hope you will have no objection to its being restored.

'It was not over-exertion which injured my health. Ever since my mother's death, which happened on the 21st December, 1840, I had been careful of it—careful to avoid every thing which I supposed would lessen it; and, but for the fever and subsequent events, it seemed probable that my constitution might have improved. From the fever itself I believe I should have recovered within the ordinary time: but my aunt had come here on my being taken ill; she was with me only a short time when she caught the infection herself; the disease almost immediately affected her brain, and during the nine following weeks, at the end of which she died, I do not think that she was silent as long as would have made three days altogether. She scarcely ever slept herself, and it was quite impossible to sleep in the house beside her. I was thus entirely deprived of rest for a long period, at the time when I should have been recovering. This, together with the anxiety inseparable from such a state of things, and a severe cold caught during those seasons of night-watching, which, unfit as I was for the last, fell to my share, have left me with a cough, a quick pulse, and a degree of general weakness which the last five weeks have done very little to remove.

Whatever may be the termination, there is thus some consolation in thinking that my present ill health has not been brought on by my own imprudence; and, while I shall do every thing in my power for my restoration, I would at the same time desire to be resigned to whatever may be the will of God concerning me. I have still a number of reasons for wishing my life prolonged for a few years. In a few days, if the weather be favourable, I shall go about sixteen miles to the southward for a change of air. For, since the 29th of November last, I have not attempted work of any kind; and at present, it is as much as I can do to walk about three miles or so in a day, for exercise. The hour for my going out is just arrived, and I would now beg to conclude by simply saying that, with many thanks, and the greatest respect, I am, Sir, Your much indebted, very humble servant, A. B.'

The following is the answer of his medical correspondent, which I cannot refrain from inserting entire, as much for the high sense of what was due to Mr. Bethune's character and worth which pervades it, as for the generous and even munificent benevolence which it evinces:—

'*March* 21, 1843.

'My dear Sir,—I cannot deny that the receipt of your acknowledgement of our enclosure, though earlier than what we should have judged an advisable exercise of your writing, was very gratifying to us. By the cordiality with which we cherish the thought that we can in anywise minister to your comfort, you may guess of the regret it would give us if you did not, in the most unreserved manner, put to whatever use could most benefit you the trifle we offered. So long as any 'Bethune' could be advantaged, or their memory honoured by it, not a fraction could return welcome to us.

'I regret to perceive in what language you are obliged to depict your present symptoms: they alone prove that our donation can form but an inconsiderable part of what your expense *should* be. As a physician, I should say the measures you are pursuing are in themselves good; but, from the same cause, I must claim your pardon for giving a further opinion, that a judgment of your case, as directing to either what plan might be devised with well-grounded prospect of your recovery, or a greater degree of certainty to your own prognosis, should be founded on a careful examination by the stethoscope, and the treatment be arranged accordingly. If the provinces afford you such an authority, well; if not, the expense of your repairing to Edinburgh for it we should most cheerfully bear, and beg you to resort to. All such further work as you have, prior to the fever, been pursuing, I hope you will banish the thought of—for ever, it might be said, but at any rate, for an indefinite period. If the situation sixteen miles from you do not answer the intended purpose, and you can learn from any quarter of a milder and more suitable, give your English friends the credit to believe that they will gladly take on them the responsibility of its demand on your finances. Knowing what is required to defray travelling expenses, proper medical advice, nourishing articles (whether of animal food, or wine), and attendance, such as you *should* have, it would pain them more than you are aware, if you, out of scruple, forewent any of these things; for which, your own present fund they request you (however laudable in preferring to look to that first) to regard only as a *primary* competence.

'Do not reply immediately, unless you see necessity; but if, after a few weeks, God graciously crown our wishes with improved health to you, a line or two to that effect will truly gratify Yours truly in esteem,
——————.'

After his return from Kennoway, Mr. Bethune became gradually weaker. From that time he seems to have ceased to attempt writing, as the latest of his letters, with the exception of the fragment to myself given in the preface, are dated from that place. And indeed we find him taking leave of one of his most valued friends, in a note dated from that place, of which the following is an extract:—

'KENNOWAY, FIFE, *April* 1, 1844.

' My Dear and much respected Friend,—My warmest gratitude to —— for her good wishes— though in so far as this world is concerned, there is but little prospect of their being realized. Should my present complaints terminate unfavourably, you will be among the few friends at a distance who will be apprised of the event; and if it should please Providence again to restore me, though my own hopes of such a result are now fading in the distance, I will myself communicate the intelligence. —With the greatest respect, I am Your much indebted, very humble friend and servant, A. B.'

By this time I had got very anxious about Mr. Bethune. I had written him in January and had got no answer. I wrote again in May: several weeks afterwards I received the note containing the painful intelligence of his illness, and expressing his wish to see me. I hastened away immediately, feeling that there was no time to lose. On arriving at Mountpleasant, I found our friend in a very weak state. It was evident his end was near. He was quite sensible of his situation, yet felt, like all others affected with it, the peculiar deceptiveness of the disease: 'How difficult is it' said he, ' to persuade a man that he is dying when he feels no pain.' For several days previous to my arrival the disease had begun to affect his mind occasionally, and it continued to do so. For a short time he would converse quite distinctly and with all his wonted correctness and propriety of expression, and then his mind would begin to wander. His surviving aunt and Mrs. Ferguson attended him with the greatest solicitude and tenderness, doing every thing in their power to minister to the wants of decaying nature and smoothe his dying pillow. He differed in temperament from his brother John, in respect that he was not very ready to give utterance to his religious feelings. But to the inquiry whether he enjoyed comfort in the prospect of another state of being, he replied, 'that his mind was quite at rest on that subject.' When taking my leave, I expressed a hope that through redeeming mercy we should meet in another and happier world. In this hope he intimated his concurrence, and added, 'Seeing it is so, why should we part melancholy?—let us part joyfully.' I left him on the Monday afternoon; and he gradually became weaker, until his spirit took its departure about midnight of the following day, being Tuesday, the 13th of June. The funeral took place on the Saturday following. It had been his wish that his body should rest in his brother's grave: and this wish it was intended to carry into effect, but by some culpable inattention of the grave-digger, his friends on arriving at the church-yard found that another grave had been opened; into that his body was put, but so dissatisfied was his aunt, that she did not rest until she had it disinterred, and put, according to his desire, into his brother's grave.—'They were lovely and pleasant in their lives,' and their resting-place is in the dust together.

On the north side of the monument erected by him to his brother, which is a square pillar about seven feet high, with a cornice surmounted by a vase, has been put the following inscription:—

IN THE SAME GRAVE
WITH JOHN, REST THE REMAINS OF
HIS BROTHER,
ALEXANDER BETHUNE,
THE LAST MEMBER OF A WORTHY FAMILY,
WHO DIED, JUNE 13th, 1843,
AGED 38.
WITH SCARCELY ANY SCHOOL EDUCATION,
AND UNDER THE PRESSURE OF POVERTY AND
THE SEVEREST TOIL, HE PRODUCED SEVERAL
WORKS OF MUCH MERIT, ILLUSTRATIVE OF THE
CHARACTER AND MANNERS, AND CONDUCIVE TO THE
IMPROVEMENT, OF HIS OWN CLASS OF SOCIETY;
AND WAS AS REMARKABLE FOR HIS INDEPEN-
DENCE OF SPIRIT AND PRIVATE VIRTUES, AS
FOR HIS LITERARY ATTAINMENTS.

By Mr. Bethune's will, his aunt has the use of the house and garden, with furniture, during her lifetime. The money referred to above as forwarded by 'English friends,' and lodged in the bank, he left to be disposed of according to Mr. Dalgleish's discretion, who has, I understand, appropriated it to the use of the same deserving relative;—little more than an act of justice, as she had from her own limited funds paid a large proportion of the expenses incurred during her nephew's illness.

The reader will already have a more distinct conception of Alexander Bethune's personal appearance (*ante*, pp. 67—69, and 161, 162 in particular) than, by any description of mine, I could have hoped to have given him. His countenance wore the expression of serene benignity, and was all the more interesting from the many traces (they were not disfiguring ones) of physical disaster which it bore. It is much to be regretted that no portrait of him was ever taken: but the regret is now unavailing.

As in the preceding pages it has been meant to exhibit Alexander Bethune's character, quite as much as to relate his history, I am satisfied the intelligent reader would regard any formal attempt at portraying that, not only as superfluous, but impertinent.

The history of Alexander Bethune, and that of his brother, cannot but be fraught with a special interest to that large and increasing class of young men, who, while they have to toil for their daily bread, are striving to educate themselves; some of them with the yet further aim of being distinguished not only for their acquirements, but for their productions likewise. To those who are thus honourably impelled and occupied, the story of the Bethunes affords special instruction and encouragement. First, —from the sound and healthy tone of mind in regard to the concerns of every-day life which they exhibited. You see they never made their consciousness of superior powers of mind an excuse for neglecting any relative or social duty—they never talked or felt as if genius was too lofty a thing to be beset by the ordinary toils and cares of humanity. Then, their indomitable perseverance should furnish you with a high stimulus and encouragement. Few of you, probably, will have to hold a long combat with circumstances so adverse as they had. Yet, amid disappointments and disasters, in unpatronized obscurity, they held on, till they emerged before the world as writers and teachers worthy to be heard. Yet though thus honourably successful, they proved how inadequate, unless in a few lucky instances, are the rewards of literature; and what a broken reed* it were for any one to lean to who can labour for his support. Measured by its pecuniary results, their success was poor indeed. But there are higher elements and criterions :—The mental discipline— the range and precision of thought—the moral elevation, induced by such a career and such achievements as theirs,—these are the noblest results; and they are independent of the world's opinion, and

* Preface to 'The Scottish Peasant's Fireside.'

the world's favour. Success of this kind is open to all, and it is enduring. It will bless him who has achieved it, in a region where the loudest trump of mere literary fame is not heard. Though it may be amid ungenial circumstances, and through frequent disappointments, then tug and grind on. Your worth may not be appreciated; you may meet only with indifference or with scorn. Be not discouraged. Not only are you securing immense individual benefits—you are exerting an influence—though it may be unperceived by you—which will not be lost—an influence, the pulsations of which will be felt, extending and deepening, ages after your name is forgotten. Remember that spiritual and moral excellence is the first object, and that if steadily pursued, honour will follow—if not in this world, yet certainly in the next.

APPENDIX,

NO. I.

EXTRACTS FROM 'NARRATIVE OF THE LIFE OF ALISON CHRISTIE, RELICT OF ALEXANDER BETHUNE, FROM THE TIME OF HER LEAVING LOCHEND, TILL HER DEATH, DEC. 21, 1840.'

AFTER describing the very great reluctance with which the subject of the narrative left Lochend, and the sorrow occasioned by the death of her husband, which took place within two or three months after the removal of the family to Mountpleasant, the writer proceeds :—

'In the month of November following, (1838) her two sons had some expectations of being able to support themselves and her by writing; and to her this circumstance gave unmingled satisfaction. She had often lamented what she considered the stern necessity by which they were exposed to the rains and storms of winter; and the idea of having them always at home, and of their being thus kept warm and comfortable, was to her particularly gratifying. A breach had been made in her family, but the objects of her maternal pride were still around her, and in her affection for them, and the interest which she took in their concerns, her heart appeared in some measure to have closed over the wound occasioned by the death of her husband. Throughout the winter she was again busy with her wheel, and during those short intervals of relaxation which she allowed herself, she was even cheerful. But as spring, which was the season at which death had last visited the family, again drew near, an almost unaccountable foreboding crept over her spirit; and, as she afterwards stated, the words "*There is more behind!*" seemed as if they had been ringing in her ears. At least the impression was such, that whenever she was left alone the thought always occurred. This she took, or rather mistook, for a presentiment of her own approaching dissolution: yet there were seasons when she seemed to have some misgivings as to its applicability in this way. But to those attempts which her sons made to convince her of the folly of yielding to such impressions, and the propriety of endeavouring to forget them, her uniform answer was, " That she did not wish to forget it, for it had driven her to be more frequent in prayer, and more earnest in begging strength from God to bear whatever trials might be before her."

* * * * * * *

' A severer trial than any which she had hitherto experienced was now approaching. Early in June, her son's illness began to assume a threatening appearance; and though she continued to toil on at her wonted employment with unremitting diligence, that she might neutralize as much as possible her own expenses at a season when the other resources of the family were almost entirely cut off, she all along complained of an inexpressible weight upon her spirits, which was often accompanied by a degree of pain about the region of the heart. Afterwards, when the fatal nature of his complaint had become more manifest, and the dark and hopeless certainty of his approaching fate seemed to close in on every side, she said frequently, "that it would be no wonder to herself if the indescribable weight which was upon her spirits should bring her to the grave before him!" Such feelings, it may easily be conceived, were carefully concealed from the sufferer; but this did not lessen their poignancy. Still, to use her own words, " she was earnest in prayer, that the evil day might either be averted, or that those who were to be called hence might be prepared for that solemn event and those who were to be left behind strengthened to bear the pang of separation." On the 1st of September, 1839, her son died, at the early age of twenty-seven; and this was the crowning wreath of her misfortunes. She strove to be resigned to the will of Providence; and said " that she had great reason to be thankful for the strict integrity of his life, and the hope which he had evinced at death—that he was a blessing which God had lent her for a season—and that what God had given he certainly had a right to take back." Sometimes too she would address her own heart in the language of scripture: " Be still and know that I am God!" In this manner she used to commune with herself and to converse with her friends; but still the yearnings of a mother's heart would not be repressed.

' The affliction of a mother for a son is proverbially strong; but in her case a number of circumstances had contributed to strengthen it. Unlike most young men, he had never left the house, nor had he ever been out of her sight for two days at a time, except during the short interval when he was learning the weaver business; in addition to the ordinary ties of such a relationship, she had cared for and watched over him throughout the whole period of youth and early manhood; and when years and increasing infirmities partly unfitted her for the task, he had returned her care and her affection, by providing for, and endeavouring to watch over her. When the humble station in which he was born and bred, and his total want of what is commonly called education, were taken into account, he was, moreover, a highly promising character. After a series of years passed in the severest drudgery and the most profound obscurity, during which he had been silently and assiduously endeavouring to cultivate his mental faculties, he had at last forced his way into notice; and it seemed that only a very few years more would have been necessary to enable him to establish his reputation in a literary point of view. In all this there was much for maternal feeling to feed upon and rejoice over; for who is so ready to appreciate the triumphs of a son, as the mother to whom he owes his existence? The links which bound her to him were thus doubly strong—admiration, esteem, and gratitude were twisted around maternal love;—and who can wonder if the bursting of such a chain should produce all but a universal wreck?

' His death did, accordingly, have an indelible impression upon her heart; a complete change seemed to have passed over her, and she never was like her former self again. After this event she was rarely seen to smile; and if, in the forgetfulness of the moment, her features did at any time relax, it was almost always followed by a heavy sigh, and a deeper shade of solemnity in her countenance and manner. "My dear John! my dear John!" she would sometimes exclaim, after a long season of silent musing; "how I could cry out in the greatest bitterness of spirit, if it would bring him back! But he is gone for ever from his home, and from the mother who would have gladly bought his life with her own." At other times she would try to soothe her wounded feelings, by endeavouring to contemplate the happiness which his spirit was enjoying. "It is vain and sinful," she would say at such seasons, "thus to mourn over him; for crowns, and kingdoms, and the richest prizes which earth can afford would not tempt him back to this vale of tears; and why should I repine at his happiness, or mourn over a separation which, at the longest, can be but for a few days? What is loss to me is to him unspeakable gain." Occasionally, too, she was heard to say: "I have been endeavouring to sum up my mercies, and to thank God for their vast amount. The good Halyburton said long ago, 'that he had a father, a mother, and ten brethren and sisters in heaven, and he would soon be the eleventh,' and I, in like manner may say, I have a father, a mother, a husband, and two sons, which make five, in heaven, and I shall shortly be the sixth! Why should I complain though I am separated from them for a few days?"

'Her efforts to comfort her only remaining son, the writer of this narrative, were more touching than even her own sorrows. On these occasions she sometimes tried to draw a comparison between the supposed actions of an earthly potentate, and the decrees of Providence. "If some great king," she would observe, "had called him away to place him in a situation near his own person —a situation in which riches, honour, and every earthly enjoyment would have been his portion, then you would have rejoiced at the change; and why should you mourn when he is called away from the disappointments, the toils, the weariness, and the pains of earth, to be near the person of the King of kings, and to enjoy the unspeakable happiness of heaven—a happiness to which all earthly enjoyments are but as a drop to the ocean?"

While she spoke thus, the tears which flowed fast down her own aged cheeks told too plainly that she was offering to another the cup of consolation which she could not take to herself. The christian strove to be resigned, but nature asserted her reign, and the woman and the mother was forced to mourn.

' As might have been expected from the tenor of her fortune and the desolating strokes with which she had been visited, at times she was inclined to take gloomy views of the present state. "I have been looking through the world," she said several times, "and endeavouring to sift it that I might see what was in it; and now I must confess, in the language of the prophet, that it is at best but ' a Bochim—a place of weepers!"'

'As the props of the house, one by one, gave way, and sunk around her, she seemed to lean the more confidingly on that which remained. Of her whole family but one son was now alive, and upon him that affection which had once been divided among the rest of its members was now concentrated. During the early part of the winter, being engaged in copying and revising my brother's papers, and preparing a sketch of his life for the press, I often continued writing till a late hour; but through the whole of these vigils she kept me company, and never once could be prevailed upon to go to rest till she had seen me in bed. Her reasons for doing so were, that she might be ready to *beet* the fire when it became low, lest I should suffer from cold, and to see that I did not prolong those studies so as to injure my health. In vain did I assure her that I could keep a good fire for myself, and name the hour at which I would retire to rest: nothing could persuade her to leave me.

' When I had gone to bed, and her little household

duties were finished, she would come to my bed-side to see that I was comfortable;—and I think I can see her still as she stood before me—her aged form bending gently forward—with the lamp in one hand, and leaning upon her staff with the other. Late as the hour often was, she always appeared loath to retire herself to rest, and she seldom did so without some attempt to comfort or instruct. On these occasions she would recount the anxious thoughts with which her mind had been perplexed, and her fears lest my constitution should give way under the task which I had imposed upon myself. "Recollect," she would say, "that though your father and brother are gone, you have still your poor, aged, and infirm mother to look after, and for my sake, if not for your own, spare yourself as much as possible; and do not be too anxious about the little debts which were contracted on our dear John's account. God will yet enable you to pay them honourably, and in good time. And oh! whatever you do, or whatever you leave undone, do not forget to seek His aid and His strength continually; for without Him we can do nothing. From the frailties and sorrows which are now weighing me down, I cannot be lang an inhabitant of this earth; and I may not be able to speak to you at death, but what I say now is what I would say at my dying moment, if the power of utterance were spared." It may be here noticed, that she mentioned frequently, and in a number of different ways, the possibility of her not being able to speak at death. The circumstance seemed to be impressed upon her imagination; and, by a strange coincidence, the event against which she was so anxious to provide actually happened.

'In the course of these parting conversations, she sometimes alluded, in the most touching manner, to her own weakness. After noticing the labours which she had been able to perform in her better days—" I have lang been an incumbrance upon you," she would continue, " and now I am a greater incumbrance than ever; yet I am sometimes afraid lest I should be ta'en awa' at a time when ye may be ill able to bear the expenses of my funeral; and thus, though I am but as one of Job's comforters, I could e'en like to linger on beside you for a season, like a withered leaf clinging to a tree after the whole of its fellows have been swept away by the wintry storm." Though she was previously well assured, that the individual whom she addressed was very far from considering her " an incumbrance," and that he would have willingly made any sacrifice to increase her comfort, or prolong her existence—it always seemed to give her a degree of satisfaction to hear that assurance repeated; and thus she sometimes gave the conversation a turn such as that just noticed. More frequently, however, her discourse was directed to the things of another world, and the importance of endeavouring to provide a better inheritance than the perishing things of time. So earnest was she in inculcating these matters, that I was frequently compelled to remonstrate on the necessity of her retiring to give her wearied body and wo-worn spirits their wonted repose, before she would go to bed. " I maun e'en leave you, then," was almost always her parting salutation—" but may the Lord give you the sleep of his beloved; and when you awake, may you be satisfied with his likeness."

' Let me here pause, to pay a tribute of grateful remembrance to her memory. However far I may go astray, I have had at least the advantage of the example and the instructions of a pious mother—of one who, with some frailties and imperfections, such as flesh is heir to, was certainly a christian, if there is one on earth. So diligently had she read, and so well was she acquainted with her bible, that it was almost impossible to mention a single text or passage, in any part of the sacred volume, which she could not turn up upon the shortest notice. She did not, indeed, recollect chapter and verse, but the tenor of the whole of the inspired writings was imprinted upon her memory; and from the nature and import of the subject mentioned, she always knew within a little of the place where it might be found. So well was this known to both my brother and myself, that if at any time we had occasion to quote a few words from scripture, and did not happen to know the exact reference, it was uniformly our custom to inquire at her, and, in general, she was able to give us the necessary information in a few minutes.

* * * * * * * * *

'A large bible, which had been left her by her mother, was almost her constant companion; and when not employed with it, she might have been seen walking slowly through the garden with her staff, or leaning upon this support and extracting the most luxuriant weeds from a small plot of onions, in the culture and growth of which she still continued to take an interest. From the beneficial effect which they produced upon a peculiarly constituted, or rather a diseased stomach, onions, for a number of years, had been a favourite article of diet with her deceased son; as such, she had been particularly careful to keep them free from weeds while growing, and to do everything in her power to ensure a luxuriant crop, at her former dwelling; and thus, though he was gone, and the motive no longer existed, the habit which had been formed still continued to manifest itself. When not employed in one or other of these ways, she might have been found in a retired situation, where she considered herself safe from the prying eye of strangers—upon her knees; and, as the season advanced, this exercise became with her more and more frequent.

* * * * * * * * * *

' Previous to this time, her deceased son's Poems were in the press. She had often expressed her regret at the delays of the printer; and she now began to manifest a more than ordinary degree of anxiety for their appearance, and frequently requested me to urge him on with the work—assigning as her reason for doing so, that she wished " to have the satisfaction of reading her dear John's Poems in print, before she left the world." Whenever any of the proofs arrived, she had always her spectacles in readiness, and was waiting eagerly to read them the moment I had done making the necessary corrections. While thus engaged, her tears frequently manifested the feelings with which she perused the effusions of her departed son; and in this way, with the exception of the concluding half-sheet, she did read the whole of the work in print; but before it made its appearance in a connected form, her sight and other faculties were so much deranged by the disease of which she died, that her reading was for ever at an end.'

The rest of the Narrative is occupied chiefly with details respecting the progress of the disease of which she died, (paralysis,) and the devices which filial affection prompted for its alleviation.

NO. II.

'LOVE IN A BARREL.'

' Sconced in the corner of a park,
Whose shady trees make noonday dark,
Whare scarce a beam has room to twinkle,
Stands the abode o' Sarah Wrinkle;
A modest domicile I ween
As e'er in Scotia's isle was seen.

 ' Secluded there from love and strife,
Sarah hath lived a serious life—
And still she lives (let none upbraid)
A venerable vestal maid;
Within whose heart Love never ventured,
But once—and cursed the day he entered.
 * * * * *

 ' Know then, she is a moving steeple,
And far o'ertops the neighbouring people—
A perfect giantess—but slim
As you could wish in bust and limb.
 * * then for her features—
She seems the best of mortal creatures:
Her eyes are dark, and o'er her nose
Superbly rise her arched brows,
Retiring far, while twinkling under
The fiery orbs seem full of wonder;
Her cheeks are lean, of iron hue,
But striped and streaked with red and blue;
Her nose is long, and hooked, and pointed,
And glows as if by oil anointed.
 * * * *

 ' Next, with your leave, her mental graces
Shall figure in their proper places.

Blest with a mind of quick discerning,
And stored with much recondite learning,
* * * *

Her glance is critical and tasty,
In judging puddings, pies, and pasty;
And even the slightest impropriety,
Draws down her censure on society.
Skilled in decorum, she is able
To point each person's place at table.
* * *

She can propound with zeal most fervent
The duties of a female servant,
And with unrivalled skill can handle
A serious text on country scandal:
You'd think her an inspirëd teacher,
And swear she might become a preacher.
She loves the church, but chiefly twines
Her laurels for the old divines,
Because, she says, in their discourses
The truth is drawn from purer sources
Than human pride and human knowledge,
Those idols of the modern college.
' She has a taste for cats and birds,
And loves the creatures' simplest words,
And into English verse can render
Their curious converse, sweet and tender.
She warmly hates all romping boys,
Who stun the studious with their noise,
And gives good hints to those who keep them
On the necessity to whip them.
She quite abhors all rural meetings,
And rustic junketings and greetings;
And reprimands with due severity
The timid maids for their temerity.
Even her white lips will writhe and redden
In wrath upon a penny weddin'.

APPENDIX.

But it would take a folio ponderous
To set forth all her virtues wondrous:
These are but an inferior sample
Of Sarah's graces rich and ample.

* * *

* * Her female servant.

Deborah is a different creature
From Sarah, both in form and feature:
Her face is full, and round, and ruddy,
And then, Heaven bless her! what a body!—
'Tis a substantial mass of matter
As e'er came from the hand o' Nature;
And though apart from my intentions
To sketch you out her full dimensions,
Yet I shall briefly try to show her,
That when you meet her you may know her.
  'Unlike those fashionable misses

* * * *

Whose swelling breasts and slender middle
Must still remind you of a fiddle,
Deborah has a goodly back,
Even thicker than a barley sack,
And her high shoulders, round and broad,
Might bear a horse or horse's load;
Her massy arms are plump and yellow,
Sun-burned, and soft as any pillow,
Though there, alas, Love never laid
His sunny cheek and curly head;
Her neck and chin, as next in order,
Claim notice from the just recorder.
The first, though short, contains, at least,
Materials for a moderate waist;
The second is the most uncommon
Appendage to a common woman.
Would I could show you but a section
Of such a manifold projection,

With all its burly butments swelling,
Like barbican in ancient dwelling!
I fain would paint it, but despair
Of painting justly, and forbear.
Around her mouth, but late appeared,
Blest symptoms of a glorious beard.

* * * *

I'll not expatiate on her nose,
Nor dwell upon her cheeks or brows,
But simply say, that when contrasted
With Sarah's, none would think she fasted;
For while the lady's cheeks are thin,
Deborah's almost burst the skin.
And then, for Sarah's meagre pimples,
Deborah has her buxom dimples.

'Such is a picture of the pair
Of ancient virgins good and fair,
Who long have lived in close connexion,—
Though not from mutual affection,
But that they knew each others failings,
And better bore their mutual railings.
'Sarah, as I have said above,
Had ne'er but once been given to love;
And as she could not find a mate,
Her passion settled into hate;
But every day that fleeted over,
Deborah was a constant lover.

* * * * * *

Did no poor wight or wanderer orra,
Return the love of good Deborah?
O yes! she had a host of suitors
Who would have waded through the gutters
To visit her by night or day;
But Sarah scared them all away—

For Oh! the frowns of Mrs. Sarah
Were worse than all the plagues of Pharaoh.

* * * * * *

But tho' Deborah's charms were wasting,
And tho' her marrying days were hasting;
Yet while her rosy cheeks were withering,
Her hoarded wealth was yearly gathering,—
And faded forty blest with plenty,
Is better far than dowerless twenty;
And thus Deborah's charms renewed,
Made her more worthy to be wooed.
But still the suitors kept their distance,
Deterred by Sarah's fierce resistance:
Until at length a lucky quarrel
Made love a lodger in the barrel.
  'Alas! that it should be recorded—
Good Sarah and her maid discorded,
And as Deborah thought, (tho' blindly,)
Her mistress treated her unkindly.
She swore with fearful resolution,
That there should be a retribution;
And well she knew if she could catch
Some moidered wretch to make a match,
Sarah would die of perfect spite
Upon her merry marriage night.
And luckily before a week
Elapsed, she met with Andrew Breek.
Now Andrew was a man of valour,
And both an elder and a tailor,
And by the powers of his profession
Had ruled the members of the Session;
And Andrew even in his devotion,
Had long been haunted with a notion
To wed for better or for worse
A woman who possessed a purse.

And he was marvellously delighted
When good Deborah him invited
(With a most gracious smirk and leer,)
To " Come some e'ening o'er an' see her."
Andrew went home so light with love,
He scarcely felt his body move ;
And he that night was so enamoured
That all his senses seemed beglamoured,
And awkward cuts and crooked seams
Attested his romantic dreams ;
For he attached with active stitches
A coat sleeve to a pair of breeches.
And drab, and cassimere, and kersey
Were mingled without care or mercy,
Till Andrew fixed upon to-morrow
For his first visit to Deborah,
And ere the hour of assignation,
He bore his love with great discretion.

' The morning dawned—the mid day passed—
The longed for evening came at last.
* * * * *
' He reached Deborah's blest abode
Just as her mistress walked abroad,
And he was previously instructed
How matters were to be conducted—
And watched awhile his opportunity,
Then boldly entered with impunity,
And in an instant more, the stranger
Was garreted, and out of danger.
Deborah, like a practised jailor,
At once secured the amorous tailor ;
And then the pair with souls sedate
Held their delightful tete-a-tete,
Until at length a thunder shower
Made gentle Sarah seek her bower ;

And soon, alas! in deep despair,
They heard her footsteps on the stair:
What could be done? the door was locked,
But must be ope'd when Sarah knocked,
And then the mistress must discover
The maiden and her luckless lover.

'Deborah strained her powers inventive
For remedy or for preventive :—
And what dilemma e'er was laid in
Too hard for an ingenious maiden?
A cask is fixed on Sarah's wall
To catch the rain-drops as they fall
From off the roof, and downward trunnel
To fill it, in a leaden tunnel;
And soon Deborah's blest invention,
Contrived a passage of suspension
Between the window and the barrel,
Upon whose top the amorous carle
Might free from danger rest a space,
Or leap to earth without disgrace,

'Some trifle Sarah's steps delayed
Till the proposed descent was made;
But sadly was the precious water
Polluted by that vile avatar—
For the dread cask's unfaithful cover
Gave way beneath the faithful lover!
There was a splash—and then a gushing—
A sound of many waters rushing;
It reached the attic of the maid—
And Sarah on the stairs was staid,
While her poor niece in sad condition
Came with a terrible petition—
"Oh auntie, auntie! come to me,
The kitchen's sailing in a sea—
The cat upon the hearth is drowning,
The very dogs for fear are running!"

' Sarah descended like a falcon
To save her favourite old grimalkin;
But guess how flashed her fiery eyes,
Starting with terror and surprise—
When, foaming fiercely through the entry
To kitchen, closet, press and pantry—
She saw an inundation dreadful
Which would have made an Arkwright needful;
A flood (with reverence be it spoke)
To which good Noah's was a joke!
 * * * *

Yet boldly waded to the door,
To learn the cause of such uproar.
 ' There was a splash, a groan, a snarl—
The devil was drowning in the barrel!
 * * * *

The cask sent forth a mighty river,
Which roared as it would run for ever.
But Sarah prayed that it might cease,
And thus addressed her trembling niece:—
"Run lassie! run for doctor Dover!
And say I beg him to come over;
Bid him prepare himself for evil,
And bring his books to lay the devil."

Meanwhile Andrew,
 Sometimes scolding, sometimes mourning,
Still kept up a perpetual churning;
His voice now sank in low lamenting,
Of his unlucky love repenting;
Now rose in louder tones and longer,
As love grew weak and wrath grew stronger;
Now madly quick, now softly serious,
Made a commotion so mysterious,
That you had thought some deadly quarrel
Was settling in the haunted barrel.
 * * * *

"O dear Deborah, d'ye hear me,
Is ony livin' creature near me?"

* * * *

"Na; nae a word—I might as weel
Cry to a monument o' steel,
Or lippen to a lion's paw,
Or summon help frae Largo Law—
Aweel, aweel! we e'en maun dree
A' that is fore-ordained to be."

* * * *

'By this, the Reverend Dr. Dover,
In holy armour had come over;
Prepared by faith to go to battle,
With fiends, or fools, or horned cattle.
And, when he heard the amorous carle
Bumming and bubbling in the barrel—
He kindly turned the cock about,
To let the element run out;
And, when the waters were subsided,
The reverend Doctor was provided
With a strong ladder, and ascended
With caution and with courage blended—
Resolved to summon the surrender
Of Sarah's cask from its defender;
And, looking o'er the wooden battlements
On Andrew in the inner settlements,
He shouted with a lordly air
And lofty tone—" Ho! who is there?
"Whase there—whase here!—guid Sir, its me!"
Said Andrew, glimmering up to see—
"Its me—its thee! and what art thou
That dared to raise up such a row?"
"Hoot, Doctor; wusht! mak' nae profession;
Ye ken the members o' the Session:—
Yer ruling elder claims assistance,
An' charity forbids resistance.

Ye ken me noo, ye ken my worth—
Come, bear a hand, an' help me forth."
  'The merits of the good divine
Demand at least a faithful line;
For he exerted strength and reason,
To rescue Andrew from his prison;
And risked his life in lith and limb,
By struggling o'er the barrel's brim.

  'Know then, the elder did inherit
By birthright a most patient spirit;
And tho' he'd been inclined to snarl
At his dear mistress in the barrel,
He was no sooner out of danger,
Than Love returned like an avenger;
And he had neither peace nor rest,
Till his contrition was confessed;
And, ere a fortnight had passed over,
His kind deliverer Dr. Dover
Was called upon, and came to eke
Deborah Dumps to Andrew Breek.'

The preceding piece I have given, about one half abbreviated, from a small manuscript volume of poems by John Bethune, entitled, 'Pictures of Poverty,' which the reader of his Life will recollect being mentioned there. I give it as supplying an important element, indispensable in order to form a just estimate of John Bethune's mental character. The sense of the ludicrous is a susceptibility of the higher order of minds, those of the poetic temperament especially, which gives to their movements and exercises a graceful flexibility and range; and which, when under proper discipline and control, contributes, perhaps, more than any other, to the highest measure of refinement.

I am also tempted to give some excerpts from a piece in the same volume entitled 'Johnny Craigie's Wedding,' particularly the 'gathering,' which, for distinct and graphic portraiture, has rarely been exceeded:—

* * * 'Johnny
Was a fiddler good and gay,
And had been from his earliest day.
* * * *

''Mid music Johnny passed his life,—
His fiddle was his friend and wife;
He'd played at many a harvest feast
In Scotia's isle from west to east;
Had seen the smiles of ladies bonny,—
But nought could move the heart of Johnny—
Nor maid, nor widow, high nor low,
To him seemed worth his fiddle-bow.
But Time, that old officious meddler,
At length o'ercame the hardy fiddler;
And, waggling thro' this world of trouble,
His legs began to fold and double;
But, when they fairly failed to move,
Then Johnny turned his heart to love,
And courted Maggy i' the glen,
A stately dame of five-feet-ten.
'Maggy, in forty years of life,
Was thrice a bride, and thrice a wife;
And thrice in weeds of blackest hue,
Had wept the old and won the new.
* * * *

Thro' walls that have been often breached,
The citadel is easy reached:
Thus Maggy, unprepared for siege,
Conducted by experienced age,

After an hour of strong temptation,
Made fair and full capitulation.
  ' The day was set and trusty pages
Sent forth to summon in the lieges.

 * * * *

  ' All he loved or knew were bidden
To dance at his propitious weddin';
And when the appointed morn of pride
Arose on Johnny and his bride,
On every road a lengthened train
Was seen approaching Maggy's glen:
Shepherds from neighbouring hills arrayed
In bonnet blue, and tartan plaid,
With country lasses from the farm,
Came gaily laughing arm in arm;
With these appeared in moleskin jackets,
And shoon well shod with iron tackets,
With fustain breeks, and furrowed stockings,
A host of ploughmen from their yokings;
And with each gallant in the throng
A buxom maiden bounced along,
With ribboned hair, and muslin gown,
Which gaily swept the gowany down.
Sailors rejoicing in the sport,
Came flocking from the neighbouring port,
In canvass trousers tightly braced
Around each much diminished waist;
And giggling girls from Borough bowers,
In bonnets graced with knots and flowers,
With flapping shawl, and flowing veil
Came scudding on before the gale.
From reeky Frantlam's crowded streets
Weavers appeared in troops and fleets,
Their dingy night-caps red and blue,
Thrown by for hats of blackest hue,

Gave an appearance brisk and smart
To each bold youngster's upper part;
With these, their pirn-winders drest
And dizzened in their very best,
Glad to escape from swifts and wheels,
To rax their limbs in rustic reels,
Came featly forth and thronged the road,
Altho' it was both long and broad.
Tinkers poured forth from camps and tents,
Where they had lodged on moors and bents,
And gaily left unclouted kettles,
Forgotten 'mid unmelted metals,
With grim but friendly smiles to cheer
The fiddler's feast, and taste his beer.
Gay beggars, lame and lyart-headed,
Who long for charity had pleaded
With success good and bad by turns,
Came limping o'er the dykes and burns.
Pipers, who in his early tours
Had spent with him delightful hours
In barn, and byre, and stable-loft,
Where they had nestled warm and soft,
In solemn droves, were seen to saunter,
With ribbands at each drone and chanter.
Fiddlers of all degrees and stations,
Of various languages and nations,
Hibernian, English, Welsh, and Scottish;
Some young and gay, some old and sottish;
From the street bowman blind and lame,
To minstrel of reputed fame,—
Some richly dressed, some scuffed and bare,
A motley crew were gathering there.
The gentle violiners, whose faces
Seemed formed for manners, smiles, and graces,
Were graced and paged by orphan boys,
Who bore their instruments of noise,

Which churls of ruder garb and mien
Flung o'er their backs in bags of green,
And bounced along with boast and bluster
To mingle in the general muster.

* * * *

'And when the day again was done
The sport seem'd only but begun;
And Morning from her misty cloud
Looked on an undiminished crowd,
For gentle strangers came and went,
Like pilgrims to a prophet's tent.

'Maggy like antelope or izard,
Or ape bedeck'd with mortal vizard,
Led up the dance with bounding feet,
Which hourly seem'd to grow more fleet;
While crazy Johnny sat and gazed,
And bit his lip and glibly praised,—
Till, overcome by love and transport,
He too gat up to try a dance for't,
With youthful air flung down his fiddle,
And seized his pike-staff by the middle,
Firmly resolved that all should see
His strength and his agility.

'His guests came round him in a ring,
As courtiers gather round their king,
Tho' not to rev'rence but to laugh
At the poor hero of the staff.
Johnny inflamed by love and pride
Stood stoutly to his bounding bride,
And bravely strove his feet to move—
But both denied the call of love.
Yet he had no prevailing notion
To stand while all around was motion;
Inspired by Maggy's peerless charms—
Maugre his feet, he waved his arms

Forgetful of the staff—Alas!
That such a doom should come to pass—
That motion of unbounded mirth
Brought Johnny headlong to the earth!
The falling staff with fearful blow
Shivered the chief musician's bow;
And there was worse and greater wreck,
For Johnny fairly broke his neck!—
And mirth, and dance, and music failing
The bridal shout was changed for wailing,
For sorrow poured from every quarter,
On the poor matrimonial martyr,
* * * *
Who left his Maggy but the dead
To fill her widowed bridal-bed.
   'Thus ends my tale. The crowd departed—
I will not say, half broken-hearted.—
But Johnny's death affords a moral
To every time-worn amorous carle,
Whose wanton eyes begin to rove,
When his stiff limbs refuse to move.'

No. III.

'THE SISTERS.'

The scene is laid on the margin of a lake or loch. The hero of the tale is the son of a considerable farmer, who relates the story in the first person. When a boy in his seventeenth year, he is sent by his father to tend cows by the side of the loch. In that capacity his love of natural scenery is indulged and fed. By and by he becomes acquainted with four daughters of a small farmer whose possession lies at the top of one of the glens which shoot out from the loch. These he met with frequently by the loch, to which they brought their washings; and he was invited by them to go up to their father's house and get a drink when he was thirsty, or warm himself when he was cold—invitations which soon he became anxious to take the full benefit of. It was in the month of August, the day after their great annual washing; and the four daughters of Andrew Marshall, Helen, Jane, Mary, and Ann had brought their clothes to bleach on the verge of the loch.—' The various articles had been spread out upon the grass, and *watered;* and my cows had sought shelter from the heat in the most cool and shady part of the Den, from which they seemed unwilling again to venture forth, so that I was almost at liberty to go where I pleased. We had sauntered for a while along the margin of the loch—sometimes picking up what we considered a beautiful pebble, and examining its colours; and sometimes gazing at the shoals of fishes, which, owing to the stillness and transparency of the water, we could see almost as distinctly as if they had been on dry land—when Mary's eye caught a water-lily which, by some accident, had been detached from its stem, floating within arm's length of the shore, a few yards beyond us; and, deeming it a treasure, she started off to secure it for herself. But Jane, whose eye had also fallen upon the aquatic beauty, started at the same moment, and, outstripping her, snatched the flower and held it up in triumph. At this the other seemed to feel both ashamed and disappointed —ashamed, as I fancied, at being outdone in the race; but for her disappointment I could not then account, though I have since learned the cause of it. Trifling as was the loss she had sustained, her gaiety for the time was gone; her feelings seemed to communicate themselves to me by some mysterious agency; and to comfort her and myself, and restore cheerfulness to the company, I promised to swim to the place where they grew, and bring her at least a dozen of water-lilies, the first time I bathed in the loch.' A boat was upon the loch: some suggested that they should take it and have a sail in order that they might more easily obtain a collection of the water-lilies.—' Each had selected what she deemed a sufficient quantity; and I was beginning to pull toward the shore, when Mary descried one with a particularly large chalice, and eager, as it appeared, to outdo her sisters in the selection, she requested me to pull up to it. I endeavoured to comply, and she took her place a-head to be ready to snatch it up in passing; but, when we were within a few yards of it, Jane, from a wish to make sport, laid hold of one of the oars, and, dipping it in the water, continued to laugh and to hold it there in spite of my efforts to the contrary. This gave an unexpected turn to our little vessel; a fresh breeze had also sprung up from the south-west; and from these causes operating together, the boat fell to leeward of the object upon which I had been directing it.

' " Jane! Jane!" cried Mary, in a half-humourous, half expostulating tone, " what are you doin'? But, nae, matter; I'll get it yet." With these words she bent over the boat's side to snatch the flower; but it was more distant than in her eager haste she had anticipated, and, losing her balance in her endeavour to reach it, she plunged in, and, with a bubbling cry, disappeared. All was now terror and confusion. Shrill screams and convulsive sobs, mingling with frantic cries for help, formed a scene which I cannot describe. But these cries were vain: no one was within hearing. Poor Jane wrung her her hands, and *literally* tore her hair, and would have leapt into the water after her sister, had not Helen prevented her. Guided by a sort of instinct, and almost unconscious of what I did, I dropped the anchor to prevent the boat from drifting away, threw off my coat and bonnet—my shoes were already off—and plunged in as near the place where she disappeared as I could guess.'

By desperate struggles and exertions he succeeded in bringing her to the shore.—' From that day, as often as circumstances would permit, I was a visiter at Robert Marshall's; and, though the whole of the sisters received me as a brother, they now seemed to understand that it was Mary who brought me there, and that she had a sort of exclusive right to my company. In eight or ten days, with the exception of a slight cough, she was almost well again; and if at any time she chanced to be out when I arrived, Jane was always the first to go and call her in.'

The amusements of harvest-home and the spells of Hallowe'en in which he and Mary had their share and of various omen, are then described at length. His visits to Robert Marshall's were, however, any thing but grateful to his father; and, on the latter evening, he continues, ' Katty Allan, accompanied by the *herd-laddie*, " to keep the bogles from her," as she said, came running in to tell me that my father had returned, and wished to see me immediately. With a thrilling sense of disappointment I bade the rest of the company good night. But, as I shook hands with Mary, my heart forboded something; and to her I felt as if I should have said *farewell;* but the words were choking in my throat, and, without uttering another syllable, I followed Katty to the door.

' When I got home, my father did not, as I had expected, upbraid me with my absence, and insist on knowing the cause of it: on the contrary, he seemed to take no notice of my confusion; but began to tell me, in calm, clear, distinct, tones, that he had been, for some time past, using all his influence with a friend in London to procure me a situation in the service of the East India Company—that he had, during his late journey, received a letter from his friend, informing him of the situation being now open, and that my utmost expedition would be necessary in making preparations for my departure, as I must go off on the day after to-morrow. To me his words were an earthquake which at once shook down all those castles I had been busy building in the air. But what could I do? Had I been a year or two older, perhaps I might have disputed his authority, and claimed the privilege of disposing of myself; but, hitherto, I had been accustomed to implicit obedience, and I knew not how to disobey.

'My little preparations were soon made; and on the evening of the following day, when it grew dark, I took my pocket bible, upon a blank leaf of which I had previously written the words, *Mary Marshall*, under my own name, and hastened to Denhead to take a long farewell of my friends there. I opened the door for myself, and walked in without any ceremony; but before I could salute them, Mrs. Marshall made a sign for me to be silent; then rising to receive me, she pointed to an empty chair—the one which Mary usually occupied—and I took possession of it without speaking. I was now told in whispers, that in less than an hour after I left them, Mary began to complain of noise in her ears and pain in her head. Symptoms of very severe cold were soon evident, and these were followed by fever, the common accompaniment of such cases. During the night, she had slept none; toward morning she had spoken rather incoherently, and she was now lying seriously ill in the other end of the house.

'"We heard this forenoon," continued her mother, that you are going off to India directly; but this we have kept a secret————————I fear it would break her heart, an' we might soon get her to bury. I can guess your errand," she added, after wiping away a tear, and looking me full in the face as she spoke; "I can guess your errand; but if ye hae ony regard for her faither an' her mither, or ony affection for hersel', I conjure you not to think of seeing her the nicht."

'I would have spoken, but my heart was too full to allow one word to escape. *   *   *   *   *

'"Ah, Davy, Davy," she continued, ". I fear she'll think on you lang, lang after ye've forgotten her. But if ye hae ony little keepsake that ye wad like to leave, or onything that ye wad like to say, ye may intrust it to me as ye wad do to your best friend."

'I drew the bible from my pocket—it was the only thing I had on earth which I could offer—and, opening it at the place where our names were written, I held it out to her.

'"That's a guid lad, indeed," said she. "May neither her nor you ever lack the comfort contained in that book. And noo," she continued, her voice faltering with kind emotion, "though it may look ill in me, I maun e'en advise ye no to stay owre lang the nicht. Your comin' here is maybe the cause o' your gaun awa—at least the fo'k says sae—an' if ye were to offend your faither again, wha kens what micht be the consequences?"

'My heart acknowledged the justness of this observation. I rose, said something about never forgetting them, shook hands with the sisters, trying to articulate the words, *farewell, Helen—farewell, Jane—*and *farewell, Ann:* it was all I could say. Each shed a tear as she dropped my hand, and they all rose to follow me; but their mother made a sign for them to sit down again, while she herself accompanied me out. When we were beyond hearing—

' " Davy," said she, " ye're gaun far, far frae hame, and God alone kens what may happen afore ye come back, or what ye may hae to encounter; but mind what the guidman said to you on the *maiden nicht*, an' *never despair*. Though I'm auld noo, I was aince young—I ken the trials that young fo'k meet wi'; an' I ken too that young fo'k's minds are subject to a hantle changes, an' that Mary, puir thing, is nae match for you. But for a' that, ye may maybe come back an' marry her, an' maybe no; but in this, as in every ither thing, I maun just say, *the Lord's will be done*. He only kens if ever I may see you again, an' that gars me speak mair freely. Ye may forget baith her an' me; but if I'm no far mista'en, she'll no soon forget you. And noo there's my hand in token, that whaurever your lot be cast, ye'll never want a warm friend in Jennet Marshall, as lang as she lives."

' I endeavoured to thank the kind matron for her advice and care over me; but must have failed, I suppose, for she pressing my hand, said " she knew what I would say if I could speak," gave me an encouraging clap upon the shoulder, and, " wishing that God might be my guide," bade me " farewell."

' I did not, however, immediately return home. A thought had struck me while in the house. I could not leave the place without seeing Mary once more. The apartment where she lay was lighted from a back window, where I was not likely to be discovered; and there I took my stand, to wait till some one should enter the room with a light. Her mother soon came to inquire " how she was?" and then I saw her raise herself upon her elbow, and pass her hand across her brow. I saw the flush of fever on her cheek, and its fire in her eye. I heard her try her voice; but it was not till the second or third attempt that she could articulate; and then, instead of answering her mother's question—

' " Has Davy been here the nicht ?" said she.

' " What gars ye speer that, lassie?" again inquired the other, evidently wishing to avoid an explanation.

' " I thought I heard his foot gang past the end of the house!" was her reply; " an' I'm maist sure he's been here, whether he cam' in or no."

' " Ye've surely been dreamin', lassie," said her mother; " what difference can there be between *his* foot and ony ither body's?"

' " There's juist that difference," rejoined she, " that I would ken *it* among a hunder."

' I could hear no more. These words had melted my heart; and, stepping back a little, I shed a flood of tears —the first I had shed since I was a mere boy; and with one exception, which yet remains to be mentioned, they were the last. For hours after the light was gone, I stood there on a dark, stormy, winter night, listening to try if I could hear her oppressed breathing—a vain effort amidst the howling of the wind, and the rattling of the rain. How I left the place, or how I got home, I cannot tell, but next morning I was on my way to the coast.'

www.ingramcontent.com/pod-product-compliance
Lightning Source LLC
Chambersburg PA
CBHW080050190426
43201CB00035B/2157